Daniel's Divulgement
THOSE WHO ARE WISE SHALL UNDERSTAND
— Marc Wheway Ph.D —

Ark House Press
arkhousepress.com

© 2021 Marc Wheway Ph.D

All rights reserved. Apart from any fair dealing for the purpose of study, research, criticism, or review, as permitted under the Copyright Act, no part may be reproduced by any process without written permission.

Unless otherwise stated, all Scriptures are taken from the New International Translation (Holy Bible. Copyright© 1996, 2004, 2007, 2013 by Tyndale House Foundation. Used by permission of Tyndale House Publishers Inc., Carol Stream, Illinois 60188. All rights reserved.)

Some names and identifying details have been changed to protect the privacy of individuals.

Cataloguing in Publication Data:
Title: Daniel's Divulgement
ISBN: 978-0-6452569-5-6 (pbk)
Subjects: Biblical Resource; Bible Study;
Other Authors/Contributors: Wheway, Marc Ph.D

Design by initiateagency.com

ABSTRACT

Like the book of Revelation, the book of Daniel, particularly chapters seven to twelve are often neglected due to controversy and confusion. The purpose of this work is to bring understanding by characterizing these chapters with consideration of the prophecy revealed through the book of Revelation.

Like the author's first two books, 'The Revelation The Revival', and The Revelation, Proclaimed and Explained', Daniel's Divulgement is presented positively. Although chapter seven gives two accounts of Daniel's distress caused by the vision (vv. 15, 28) and subsequent revelations closely related (8:17, 27; 9:20-21; 10:2-3, 7-10, 17; 12:8), the reader must remember, amidst judgment God is always present, forgiving and merciful to sinners (9:9). Comparable to the theme of 'The Revelation The Revival' (more hope than horror) a continuation of the same is presented in this work.

Albeit the aforementioned does not shy away from the intended disturbance of Daniel's dreams, visions, and angelic visitations. However, the aim of the 'secrete things of God' are not designed to terminally trouble (2:18; 4:9) but rather warn for the purpose of turning, thus avoid the judgment foretold: "Break off your sins by being righteous and your iniquities by showing mercy to the poor" (4:27). In the same way, the intended purpose of the great tribulation is to break people away from their sins, thereby turn them back to God through repentance. Sadly, however, the majority of mankind will not, (Rev. 6:16-17; 9:20-21; 16:9, 11) mirroring the original response of Nebuchadnezzar (4:29) and Belshazzar (5:22).

Regardless of the outcome, the opportunity to respond to God's goodness is still available to all, whether pre-tribulation or within the time of trouble to come (7:7-8, 19-26, 9:24-27, 11:36-45. 12:1-13, Rev. 6-19).

The watchman's call today, as it will be during the great tribulation, is to, 'Come out of the world (Babylonian) system' (Jn. 15:19; Rev. 18:4b). Yet again, few have responded, and fewer again will remain faithful this side of the time of trouble; however, countless multitudes will come to Christ during the tribulation; more than any other time before (11:33, Rev. 7:9; 14:4).

The common theme of Daniel's and John's revelation is 'Humility sandwiched in suffering.' Most will not come to the place of repentance before brokenness comes first.

Contents

Abstract iii
Introduction ix

Chapter One 1
   Part One: A Plan to Change God's People 1
   Lamentations: Water closed over my head; I said, I am lost! 8
   Part Two: Stand Up and Stand Out 11

Chapter Two 17
   Part One: The Latter Time 17
   Part Two: The Future Kingdom 22

Chapter Three 30
   Part One: Fall Down and Worship the (my) Image 30
   Part Two: If You Just Bow Down and Worship Me 36
   Part Three: Who Will Deliver You from My Hand? 45

Chapter Four 51
    Part One: That the Living May Know that the
    Most High Rules 51
    Part Two: That the Living May Know that the
    Most High Rules 58
    Part Three: Humiliation and Restoration 63

Chapter Seven 68
    Part One: The Little Horn 68
    Part Two: The Books were Opened 79
    Part Three: Dominionism 86
    Part Four: Anxious and Alarmed 93

Chapter Eight 102
    Part One: The Four Winds 102
    Part Two: The Appointed Time of the End 108

Chapter Five 114
    Part One: The Enemy is at the Gate 114
    Part Two: The Writing on the Wall 122

Chapter Six 128
    Part One: Daniel Prospered 128
    Part Two: All People are to Tremble and Fear Before God 136

Chapter Nine 142
    Part One: We Have Sinned 142
    Part Two: One Micro Minute to Midnight 150

Chapter Ten 159
    'Understanding Things Unseen, and Things to be Seen' 159

Chapter Eleven 167
   Part One: The Book of Truth 167
   Part Two: The People Who Know Their God
   Shall Stand Firm and Take Action 174
   Part Three: The Stage is Set 181
   Part Four: And they will know that I Am God 189

Chapter Twelve 198
   Part One: A Time of Trouble 198
   Part Two: Blessed is He Who Waits and Arrives at
   the 1,335 Days 206
Appendix 215

Introduction

The title of this book, 'Daniel's Divulgement', stems from chapter two, verse eighteen: "Seek mercy from God of heaven concerning this mystery so that you might not be destroyed." The mystery pertains to the end times, where Daniel was given an understanding of Nebuchadnezzar's dream.

The context: Unless Daniel could interpret Nebuchadnezzar's dream, he and his companions would be killed. Again, the dream referred to the "latter days" (v. 28) and served as a direct reference to Jesus' prediction of the great tribulation (Lu. 21:24), otherwise known as the Olivet Discourse. The Olivet Discourse discusses the signs leading to the end times, later recorded in Revelation, chapters six to nineteen.

By studying the book of Daniel, alongside the book of Revelation, two central truths are made clear: 1). God and His plans and purposes are made known through His word, through His prophets, dreams, and visions (2:47) and 2). God is merciful (2:18, 9:9), righteous (9:7, 14, 16), and just (4:24), warning of pending disaster to seek to save the lost through repentance (9:18-19).

Throughout scripture, references to God's mercy and forgiveness are seen many times. Bible prophecies of the end times contained both in the book of Daniel and the book of Revelation hold fast to this central theme. While God is both kind and severe (Rom. 11:22), He is always seeking to save the lost (Lu. 19:10). Thus, salvation secured through suffering is the focus of this book.

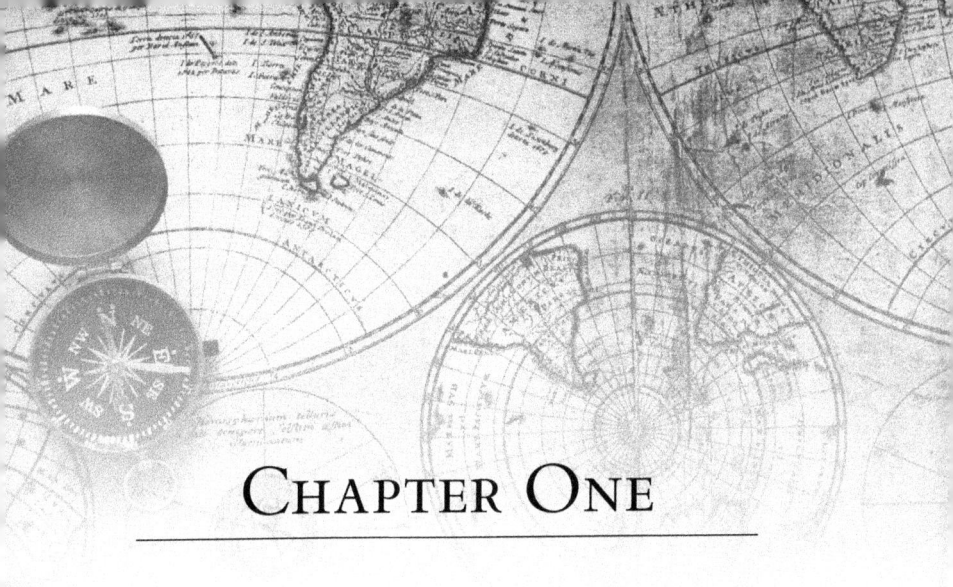

Chapter One

Part One

'A Plan to Change God's People'
(vv. 1-7)

The opening chapter of the book of Daniel introduces the Babylonian King, Nebuchadnezzar, also stating the year of captivity (cf. Jer. 25:1). After twenty-three years of warnings from the prophet Jeremiah, falling on Judah's deaf ears, deceived by her false prophets, that declared disaster would not come (Jer. 5:12, 23:17), falsely promising peace, peace (Jer. 6:14, 8:11), disaster did come, fulfilling the prophecy. And the Jewish people were taken into captivity. The Babylonian's invasion of Israel's land in 605 B.C. is also known as the beginning of the Gentiles' time (the time of the Gentiles), which will conclude when Jesus returns (Lu. 21:24).

With this invasion by Nebuchadnezzar, Walvoord (1985) states a significant prophetic period—the times of the Gentiles (Luke 21:24)—began. The Gentiles' times are that extended period in which the land given in covenant by God to Abraham and his descendants is occupied by Gentile powers. The Davidic throne is empty of any rightful heir in the Davidic line. The Gentiles' times, begin with Nebuchadnezzar's invasion of Jerusalem in 605 B.C. and will continue till the Messiah returns. Then Christ will subdue nations, deliver Israel's land from its Gentile occupants, and bring the nation Israel into her covenanted blessings in the millennial kingdom.

Regarding the invasion, the warnings from Jeremiah to Judah were many, supported and strengthened with illustrations of judgement (Jer. 13:1-11, 19:1-15, 24:1-10, 27:1-2, 28:12-14), yet, no one listened, not even one (Jer. 5:1). While there was plenty of religious folks quoting "As the Lord lives" (5:2), therefore so would they; none were interested in listening to the living God by seeking truth (v. 3). Sound familiar?

Like today, Jeremiah lived among seeker-sensitive people who sought a 'pleasing' word, tickling the ear, moreover what they needed to hear. But, instead of having ears to listen to what God was saying, they were drawn to a sugar-coated 'gospel' peddled by self-serving prophets and false teachers, driven by greedy gain. So, the people of God exchanged the knowledge of God for idolatry, and yet they still expected to be blessed, and that all would remain well with their soul, "As the Lord lives..." But that was not to be!

Israel rejected God, and now God will reject them also for breaking His covenant that was established while in Moab (Deut. 28–30) just before they entered the Promised Land (Deut. 29:1). The covenant established in Moab was a decree given by God declaring how He would deal with His people. Obedience would result in abundance (Deut. 28:1–14); disobedience would result in discipline (Deut. 28:15–68). Judah received the latter for her sins that included ignoring God's covenant, neglecting the Sabbath Day and the sabbatical year (Jer. 34:12–22), and idolatry (Jer. 7:30–31). As foretold by the prophet Jeremiah,

God's chosen instrument for disciplining His people was Nebuchadnezzar (cf. Jer. 27:6; Hab. 1:6).

Jeremiah, chapter twenty-nine reveals what God's judgement looked like (vv. 15-23), fulfilling the warnings over the past twenty-eight chapters - with a further warning, not to listen to false prophets (vv. 8-9). Because Judah would not listen to the word of the Lord, favouring a false promise of prosperity, judgement finally fell. The Babylonians swooped down and attacked Jerusalem, taking Judah into captivity. Within Jeremiah, chapter twenty-nine, the well-known and most often misquoted verse is found, "For I know the plans I have for you, declares the Lord, plans for wholeness and not for evil, to give you a future and a hope" (v. 29). Although the verse is a favourite amongst biblically illiterate charismatics, the context provides a very different application from that often used. The context states that Judah is in utter disappear, taken into captivity, thought to be abandoned by God for continual disobedience, by ignoring the voice of the true prophet, Jeremiah. All hope was now lost! Instead of heeding the warnings from God, they chose to listen to false prophets, peddling a false message of peace and security. Due to their continual disobedience, God brought them to a place where they would, once more, have an opportunity to repent and be restored, but not before everything that distracted them from God was removed, and replaced with tribulation.

Daniel, chapter one, verses two and three reveal that Jerusalem was lost to the Babylonian king, Nebuchadnezzar. The land was lost, as well as the sacred temple items. The vessels from the house of God and the people from the land of God have now been taken to Babylon (a city devoted to materialism and sensual pleasure (cf. Rev. 18). The people of God had corrupted everything holy, and now everything sacred was given over to the people of sin in Babylon. After invading Israel, when Nebuchadnezzar returned to Babylon, he placed the vessels of the house of God in the temple of his god (cf. 2 Chron. 36:7). "His god" (Dan.

1:2) was Bel, also called Marduk, the Babylonians' chief god. The act would demonstrate and openly display the defeat of the God of Judah by the Babylonian deities.

Everything Judah placed their confidence in was now lost - the land (Jerusalem), the temple, the temple artifacts, and the Torah. Stephen addressed the same to the religious leaders of his day (Acts 7). Israel had, again, put their trust in the land (7:3), the law (7:38), and the temple (7:44, 47), all the while, resisting the Holy Spirit (7:51).

The same is true today - the power of the Holy Spirit has been replaced with prosperity, seen in church buildings, professional musicians, state-of-the-art media, and celebrity preachers. The glory of God has been exchanged for cheap gold, fool's gold (cf. Rev. 3:16-17). It has always been that way, right from the beginning (Gen. 3:5-6), history keeps on repeating itself. And, as long as it does, God will keep on separating us from the very thing that distracts and keeps us from Him.

If losing the very things Israel/Judah depended on for confidence and salvation was not enough, on top of that, the people of God even had their names changed. The significance of this is that the covenant of God directly connected their name's meaning. Daniel, Hananiah, Mishael, and Azariah were all named in honour of the God of Israel, and consequently, their names were changed by their Babylonian imprisoners. Daniel means 'God has judged' (or God is my Judge) and was changed to Belteshazzar (Bēlet-šar-uṣur in Akk.), which means 'Lady, protect the king.' Hananiah, meaning, 'Yahweh has been gracious,' was changed to Shadrach, meaning 'I am fearful' (of a god). Mishael, meaning, 'Who is what God is?', was changed to Meshach, which means, 'I am despised, contemptible, humbled' (before my God). Azariah, meaning, 'Yahweh has helped,' was changed to Abednego, meaning 'Servant of Nebo' (Nego being a Heb. variation of the Babylonian name of the god Nebo). Nebo (cf. Isa. 46:1), son of Bel, was the Babylonian god of writing and vegetation. Thus, the chief court official (Ashpenaz, v. 3) set about to change the people of God by removing any testimony to their God. By renaming the four men (Daniel, Hananiah, Mishael, and Azariah) the significance was that they were now subject to Babylon's gods, to be re-educated, converted, and cultured in the Babylonian system. In doing so, God was to be eradicated.

To gain a complete understanding of the situation, to see it through Judah's eyes, we need to read the book of Lamentations. The book of Lamentations describes what God's judgement looked like when it fell and how Judah responded. Again, the problem then, like today, is that Judah thought God would not judge them for their sins (Jer. 12:4, Ezek. 8:12, 9:9), even though they were repeatedly told that He would. Still, they did not listen to God's voice (Jer. 11:8, 10, 13:10, 11); in fact, they turned their backs on God instead of their faces towards Him (Jer. 32:33). Moreover, they plotted against those speaking on behalf of God (Jer. 18:18, 23), forbidding true prophecy in His name (Jer. 11:21). Still, Jeremiah refused to be silenced, pleading with them to 'turn away from God's wrath' (Jer. 18:20, 25:5, 26:3, 13). Again, Jeremiah did this for twenty-three years (Jer. 25:2-3), preaching what they needed to hear, not what they wanted to hear (cf. 2 Tim. 4:2-4).

At this point, it is essential to note that the book of Jeremiah primarily addresses Judah in a time of pre-judgement. In contrast, the book of Lamentations looks at Judah amidst judgement. Due to its relevance, a brief commentary on the book of Lamentations has been provided, following this section. The judgement of Judah is something they never saw coming, although repeatedly warned that it would and that it was close (Lam. 1:21, 2:16-17, 4:18). They did not believe it would come due to being deceived (Jer. 6:14, Ezek. 13:10, Lam. 2:14). They were betrayed by stupid shepherds (Jer. 10:21) and lying prophets (Jer. 14:14, 15), those who were without knowledge (Jer. 10:14; 14:18). God's people were led astray (Jer. 50:6) by trusting in vanity (Lam. 4:17) and lies (Jer. 28:15, 29:32). The false prophets had convinced the congregation they would be delivered (v. 10) instead of warning them of the danger ahead. In short, Judah's leaders had failed the assembly by distracting them with friendly yet fatal words (Jer. 12:6, 19:6), just like today.

Following the false prophets, instead of the true prophet, Judah now finds herself in 'tribulation' (Lam. 3:5). Despite the false claims that God was pleased and would prosper them (Jer. 6:14, Ezek. 13:10), their unexpected' end had come' (Lam. 4:18). Now in the tribulation, they remember what they have lost (Lam. 1:1-5a) and why (Lam. 1:3, 5b-22, 3:37-42). They also recognize the false prophets (Lam. 4:15-16), and they remembered God (Lam. 3:20, 31-33). In doing so, they wanted God to remember them, too (Lam. 3:19-33, 5:1). Now, while in tribulation, they acknowledge their sins (Lam. 1:8, 18, 20, 22, 3:42) and admit, 'they are lost' (Lam. 3:54). Admitting you are lost is the starting point to being restored (Lam. 5:21), as illustrated with the parodical son (Luke 15:18, 21, 24). But, for Judah, could it be a case of 'too little, too late?' Although they remember the faithfulness of God (Lam. 3:21-33), they had been faithless (Lam. 1:8, 18, 20, 22, 3:42, cf. Deut. 7:9, cf. 2 Tim. 2:13). There is now no guarantee God was going to remember them (Lam. 5:20, 22), hence the saying, "Water closed over my head; I said, I am lost!" (Lam. 3:54). The sense of loss and hopelessness caused Judah great distress (Lam. 1:2, 3, 9, 16, 17, 20, 21, 2:13).

Instead of God remembering the love He had for Judah (Deu. 7:9), now, God pours out His wrath in her time of tribulation (Lam. 2:4, 4:11). The wrath of God is seen through the sword (Lam. 5:9), famine (Lam. 5:10), and sickness (Lam. 5:17). With such, there is a fascinating parallel with the book of Revelation, chapter six. In the coming tribulation, following deception (Rev. 6:2, cf. Lam. 2:14), represented by the rider of the white horse, the antichrist, is the red horse (war), then the black (famine), followed by the pale horse (sickness). And no one escapes or survives (Lam. 2:22, 3:7, Rev. 6:17, 19:17-20). The similarities between Judah (Lam. 5) and what is just ahead of us (Rev. 6) are striking! Judah's experience will be shared by those thrown into the coming tribulation from the church (Rev. 2:22) for the same reasons. Those thrown into the coming tribulation will be members of the loveless, compromised, corrupt, dying, and lukewarm church who failed to listen, therefore failed to repent (Rev. 2-3), even though they had many, many chances to do so, just - like - Judah!

Through deception, confessing Christians forsake God (Jer. 2:13; 5:7, 19; 9:13; 16:11, 17:13; 19:3b; 22:9), forget God (Jer. 13:25, 18:15) and replace God (materialism). These categories are the same listed in five of the seven churches in the book of Revelation (Rev. 2-3).

Like Judah, those guilty will soon find themselves thrown into the great tribulation (Rev. 6-19); from there, they will remember what they have lost and who they have lost (Jesus). They will remember why they have suffered the loss (by following false preachers). Hopefully, they will also remember what they now need to do: Confess their sin and return to God, which is the entire point and purpose of tribulation, then, and the one to come (Lam. 3:40, Rev. 9:20-21, 19:8, 11).

The plan to change God's people is both Satan's top priority and God's. While Satan desires to completely eradicate the testimony of God from the lukewarm church, in the same way the Babylonians did with Judah, God has purposed and will use the coming tribulation, and the antichrist as an instrument to restore His people, through shock and awe, leading to repentance.

LAMENTATIONS

'Water closed over my head; I said, I am lost!'

Due to the relevance of Daniel, chapter one, a brief commentary on Jeremiah's book, Lamentations, has been included here.

For decades leading to captivity, just like today, Judah thought God would not judge them for their sins (Jer. 12:4, Ezek. 8:12, 9:9), even though they were repeatedly told He would. Despite the many warnings, they did not listen to God's voice (Jer. 11:8, 10, 13:10, 11); in fact, they turned their backs on God instead of their faces towards Him (Jer. 32:33). Moreover, they plotted against those speaking on behalf of God (Jer. 18:18, 23), forbidding true prophecy in His name (Jer. 11:21). Still, Jeremiah refused to be silenced, pleading with Judah to 'turn away from God's wrath (Jer. 18:20, 25:5, 26:3, 13). Jeremiah did this for twenty-three years (Jer. 25:2-3), preaching what they needed to hear, not what they wanted to hear (cf. 2 Tim. 4:2-4).

At this point, it is important to note that the book of Jeremiah primarily addresses Judah in a time of pre-judgement. In contrast, the book of Lamentations looks at Judah amid judgement. The judgement of God is something Judah never saw coming, despite being repeatedly warned that it would and that it was close (Lam. 1:21, 2:16-17, 4:18).

Judah did not believe judgement would come due to being deceived (Jer. 6:14, Ezek. 13:10, Lam. 2:14). Like today, God's people were betrayed by stupid shepherds (Jer. 10:21) and lying prophets (Jer. 14:14, 15), those who were without knowledge (Jer. 10:14; 14:18). God's people had been led astray (Jer. 50:6) by trusting in vanity (Lam. 4:17) and lies (Jer. 28:15, 29:32). The false prophets had convinced the congregation they would be delivered from their enemies (v. 10) instead of warning them of the danger ahead. In short, Judah's leaders had failed the congregation by distracting them with a disguise of friendly discourse that camouflaged fiendish, fatal words (Jer. 12:6, 19:6).

As a result of following the false prophets instead of the true prophet, Judah now finds herself in 'tribulation' (Lam. 3:5). Despite the false claims that God was pleased and would prosper them (Jer. 6:14, Ezek. 13:10), their unexpected 'end had come' (Lam. 4:18). In the tribulation, they remember what they had lost (Lam. 1:1-5a) and why (Lam. 1:3, 5b-22, 3:37-42). They also recognise the false prophets (Lam. 4:15-16) and remember God (Lam. 3:20, 31-33). In doing so, they wanted God to remember them, too (Lam. 3:19-33, 5:1).

While in tribulation, they acknowledge their sins (Lam. 1:8, 18, 20, 22, 3:42) and admit, 'they are lost' (Lam. 3:54). Admitting you are lost is the restoration's starting point (Lam. 5:21), as illustrated with the parodical son (Luke 15:18, 21, 24). But, for Judah, could it be a case of 'too little, too late?' Although they remember the faithfulness of God (Lam. 3:21-33), they had been faithless (Lam. 1:8, 18, 20, 22, 3:42, cf. Deut. 7:9, cf. 2 Tim. 2:13). There is now no guarantee God was going to remember them (Lam. 5:20, 22), hence the saying, "Water closed over my head; I said, I am lost!" (Lam. 3:54). This sense of loss and hopelessness caused Judah's greatest destress (Lam. 1:2, 3, 9, 16, 17, 20, 21, 2:13).

Instead of God remembering the love He had for Judah (Deut. 7:9), now in her time of tribulation, God pours out His pre-warned wrath (Lam. 2:4, 4:11). The wrath of God is seen through the sword (Lam. 5:9), famine (Lam. 5:10), and sickness (Lam. 5:17). With such, there is a fascinating parallel with the book of Revelation, chapter six.

In the coming tribulation, following deception (Rev. 6:2, cf. Lam. 2:14), represented by the rider of the white horse, who is the antichrist, comes the red horse (war), then the black (famine), followed by the pale horse (sickness). When God's judgement is poured out, no one escapes or survives (Lam. 2:22, 3:7, Rev. 6:17, 19:17-20).

The similarities between Judah (Lam. 5) and what is just ahead of us (Rev. 6) are striking! As it was for Judah, it will also be for the left behind, who are thrown into the coming tribulation. Due to unrepented corruption and compromise, many people holding church membership will not be excluded from the things to come (Rev. 2:22). Those thrown into the coming tribulation will be members of the loveless, compromised, corrupt, sleeping, dying, and lukewarm churches who failed to repent (Rev. 2-3), even though having had many, many chances to do so, just - like - Judah!

Part Two
'Stand Up and Stand Out'
(vv. 8-21)

As discussed in the previous section, Jeremiah stood seemingly alone when confronting Judah's people in their sins. For twenty-three years, Jeremiah warned of the dangers to come, yet none responded. For their failure to hear and heed the message, favouring the false prophets' claims, who said that disaster would not come, God sent His people into exile. Every man followed the false prophets, and then later bowed down to false gods (3:10) except for a faithful few who took a stand for God (1:8, 3:28, 6:10, 13); perhaps so few, they were even named, Daniel, Hananiah, Mishael and Azariah (3:12, 18).

In exile, the faithful remnant would be tested by the Babylonians and by their God. Three times the faithful youth were tested, and each time the test came down to worship, the very thing that brought about God's judgement against them in the first place. The youth would either remain faithful to God by honouring Him alone or not. The test was threefold; the first involving food (1:8-21), the second test involved a golden image (3:1-30), and the third test involved the law of God (6:1-28). Each time the test came with the threat of death.

The first test: To assimilate Daniel and his faithful friends, the Babylonians would not only relocate and re-educate but sought to convert and bring about cultural/social conformity. Daniel and his friends were to be assimilated into the Babylonian way of life both outwardly and inwardly. Now dressed in Babylonian attire, renamed, and re-educated, they were also introduced to Babylonian cuisine. Not just any diet, but the same from the king's table, forbidden by the Mosaic Law, which had been sacrificed to idols. Partaking of this food would have been an indirect act of worshipping the Babylonian deities.

First-century Christians faced a similar dilemma (cf. 1 Cor 10:25–28), albeit Jesus was more concerned about what came out of the mouth than what went into it (Matt. 15:11). All the same, Daniel's refusal to eat the king's food was based upon his deep religious convictions. His desire to please God was greater than his concern of pleasing man. For the reasons mentioned above, to partake of the king's table would bring Daniel and his friends defilement. The defilement would serve to remove them further from their God and their God further from them.

Gā'al ("defile") occurs eleven times in the Old Testament (e.g., Mal 1:7, 12; Ezra 2:62; Neh. 7:64; Isa 59:3) and refers to moral or ceremonial defilement. Even though Daniel was no longer in his own land and culture, he knew he must remain obedient to God, following religious convictions by practicing Mosaic dietary requirements. By trusting in God alone, Daniel was determined not to defile himself (1:8), looking only to God to deliver him through a time of testing (1:12).

Partaking of the king's table was a big deal for both Daniel and the chief eunuch, whereas denial would endanger both of their lives (v. 10). Even so, Daniel was able to persuade Ashpenaz, the chief eunuch (v. 3), and the steward (v. 11), who showed compassion (v. 9) by allowing him and his friends to be tested for ten days (v. 12, 14). God intervened on behalf of Daniel and his friends, giving him favour with his captors. After ten days of testing, Daniel and his friends were found to be in better shape and appearance than all the other youth who ate the king's food (v. 15), demonstrating that God blesses those who trust and obey. From that point onwards, the steward only gave the youth what they had requested: water and vegetables (v. 16).

This incident would have been a lesson for Judah, as it is for us also; God demands obedience, no matter the cost. Judah's punishment came because of disobedience, but God still protected and sustained those who obeyed and trusted Him even during a time of discipline.

It is important to note that while king Nebuchadnezzar was preparing the youth for his service, later to be tested through performance and conformance, God was also preparing them for His service through the same test and time of testing. The time of testing would serve to separate one from the other and also strengthen those who remained. Having passed the test, God gave Daniel and his friend superior knowledge and wisdom, even when seemingly disadvantaged. They also received favour (1:9) and promotion (2:26-49) despite going against the grain. Daniel did not conform to a worldly culture, and he was not reliant on material means to be sustained and gain, but instead, he trusted in God for his deliverance and reward. Daniel was superior in knowledge and wisdom and understanding in visions and dreams (v. 17).

Predicting the future was a part of the Babylonian culture, practiced by the magicians and enchanters (v. 20b). Daniel was trained to operate in the same, forbidden by the Mosaic Law (Deut. 18:9-13). The king's magicians and enchanters were nothing less than sorcerers, influenced and empowered by demons. The sorcerers were inhabited and possessed by demons due to their participation in rituals, including eating meat sacrificed to demons (idols).

However, Daniel's source and his friends' ability were not the same as the Babylonian magicians but instead came from God. And because the original was from God, no other was found equal to them in the kingdom; Daniel was said to be 'ten times' better (v. 20). Ten times is an idiom for many times (cf. Gen. 31:7, 41; Num. 14:22; Job 19:3). They were many times better than any other. Better than all the wise men within the Babylonian kingdom (2:12–14, 18, 24 [twice], 48; 4:6, 18; 5:7–8, 15). In other words, there was a significant, salient difference between Daniel and his friends to any other. They were different because they stood up, and because they were different, they stood out, which attracted both positive and negative attention.

In sum, Daniel chose to obey God even though he was in a kingdom of those who did not, including his fellow exiles. Daniel remained faithful, continuing to trust God when most did not, and God rewarded him. Daniel was not only promoted above his peers, but he was also God's spokesman, showing the way for all of Judah to follow, and us while sharing God's wisdom and revelation amongst the lost. Again, Daniel was tested for ten days, then after the time (v. 18) of three years (v. 5), he and his friends were found to be ten times better than all the magicians and enchanters that were in all the kingdom (v. 20).

The takeaway and lesson learned for us today from the first chapter of Daniel are apparent. Despite the circumstances, we must remain faithful to God, knowing that He is the rewarder of those that diligently seek Him (cf. Heb. 11:6). Daniel was tested for ten days and seventy years while in exile, which reflects a lifetime of obedience, enduring unto the end.

From chapter six, we know that Daniel survived at least a couple of years into Persia's administration after Cyrus conquered Babylon in 538 BC. We also know that Daniel was at least a teenager when he was taken to Babylon in 605 BC (1:1). Therefore, Daniel was around eighty-two years old when the events of chapter six occurred.

There is yet another example of being tested for ten days, this time as seen through the faithful, yet poor, church of Smyrna, found in the book of Revelation (2:8-11). Smyrna's church was one of two faithful churches among seven, representing a remnant of just thirty percent. While most churches (70%) trusted in themselves and worldly means to survive and even thrive, the churches of Smyrna and Philadelphia looked to God alone (Rev. 2-3). Like Daniel, Smyrna's church was also persecuted by the religious within for taking a stand of righteousness. To avoid tribulation, all they had to do was go with the flow. Daniel likewise could have gone with the flow, justifying himself in so many ways for partaking of the king's table, such as:

- We are no longer in Jerusalem and arguably outside of ceremonial requirements
- The culture is different here; we need to be relevant
- Everyone else is doing it...
- We needed to be what the Babylonians are that we might win some
- God knows our heart (therefore, He will overlook our sin)
- We are in covenant with God, secure in His love, and mercy (Lam. 3:22-25)
- The king's table was God's provision, blessing, and prosperity
- The wealth of the wicked has been laid up for the righteous

As lame and twisted as the excuses mentioned above are, you will often hear them in churches today, across the globe of all denominations, albeit mostly in Pentecostal and Charismatic types. Although the above-listed excuses are primarily seen in the church's theological lightweight division (neo-Pentecostalism), all are guilty, with only a few, just the remnant, remaining faithful by not defiling themselves. The defilement comes by mixing with the world, mostly seen in the megachurches where it is almost impossible to tell them apart from the world.

The church of Sardis is an excellent example of this, charged with defilement, having soiled their garments (Rev. 3:1-6). The church of Sardis would be likened to modern-day megachurches, having a reputation of being alive, but was dead. Most megachurches are of the Pentecostal denomination who were once known and named for operating in Pentecostal gifts, such as speaking in tongues, prophesying, giving words of wisdom and knowledge, as well as interpreting dreams, and visions, like Daniel (1:17, 217-45, 4:19-27, 5:13-30). However, these gifts are seldom seen today; in fact, the bigger the church is, the less likely you will see or even hear of these gifts. The gifts were lost due to replacing the glory of God with worldly gold (materialism). Such was the condition of the church of Laodicea (Rev. 3:14-22), who had plenty of gold but had no glory.

Likewise, the 21st-century Laodicean church has substituted God's glory (fire) for false fire, evident with manifestations of shaking and other uncontrollable behaviour void of repentance. The church of Laodicea is the opposite of Smyrna's church, which had no gold but had the glory. The church of Laodicea prophetically represents us, the lukewarm, and the last church before Jesus returns. Sadly today, most have gone the way of the Laodicean church, just as Jesus predicted (Matt. 7:21-23), and Paul (2 Thess. 2:3), fulfilling end times prophecy. In the same way of Danial's day, few dare to stand, prepared to trust God enough to go against the flow. Instead, most are easily assimilated into the current culture, defiling themselves with worldly idolatrous practices. Jesus warned the churches addressed in the book of Revelation of the same, perhaps none more so than the church of Thyatira. They were specifically warned of practicing idolatry (Rev. 2:20) and were in danger of being thrown into the great tribulation (v. 22).

As it was for Judah, so it is for us. The question is - while most go with the flow, who will dare to be a Daniel, daring to stand up, and therefore stand out?

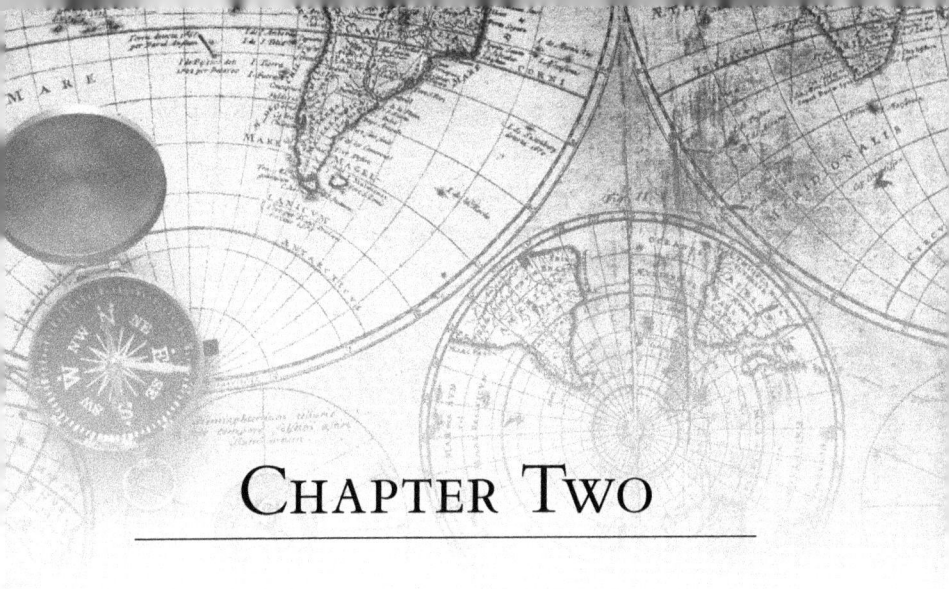

Chapter Two

Part One
'The Latter Time'
(vv. 1-30)

To recap - Nebuchadnezzar was king over Babylon, the then greatest ancient empire and cultural region occupying southeastern Mesopotamia between the Tigris and Euphrates rivers (modern southern Iraq from around Baghdad to the Persian Gulf). In 606 B.C, Nebuchadnezzar besieged Judah. As a result, the Babylonians captured Daniel renaming him Belteshazzar (meaning: Lady, protect the king). Subsequently, Daniel/Belteshazzar was God's mouthpiece due to interpreting Nebuchadnezzar's dream.

In the previous section, we saw that Daniel had an understanding in all visions and dreams (1:17). At the end of three years (1:5), Daniel and his friends were ten times better than others within the kingdom regarding wisdom and understanding (1:20). Daniel was often better than the other magicians and enchanters (sorcerers), which suggests that he was better at interpreting natural matters and supernatural matters. The fact that Daniel was better than all the other sorcerers is supported in chapter two of Daniel's book, where he alone could interpret the king's dream (vv. 29-45). No other wise man could do what the king demanded, and they stated, gods alone can do this (2:11). Daniel concurred, with a difference, saying only God (not gods) can interpret dreams (2:27-28).

Another disclaimer is that the sorcerers were not saying that only the gods can interpret dreams, but only the gods can know a man's mind (2:30). The statement is true, and with it, the king was testing the sorcerers, demanding that they first tell him the dream and then give the interpretation since they made such boastful claims. The king knew that unless they could first reveal the dream, they would attempt to deceive him with the interpretation (2:8, 9). The demand was so firm (2:8), and it came with the threat of death (2:5, 8, 9, 12, 13, 14, 18, 24). The threat of death was not just for the sorcerers, but also for Daniel and his friends (2:12, 13 14, 18, 24).

Interestingly, what the king was threatening to do with these sorcerers is what God demanded for false prophets within Israel's nation; they were to be removed from the nation, even put to death (Deut. 18:20-22). If Israel had have responded to the false prophets according to God's word, they would not have found themselves in the condition they did. The same is true today; we have been instructed to test prophecy (1 Cor. 14:29, 1 Thess. 5:20-21) and then separate the true from the false. False prophets were disqualified due to failing to teach correctly by mishandling the word of God.

Paul's letter to Titus teaches us how to respond to false teachers (1:10-13) - first recognise them, then sharply rebuke them (vv. 13-14), and then resist them (vv. 15-16). Because we fail to do as instructed, failing to test prophets and prophecy, as Israel did, the church has been plagued with false prophets and false prophecy, now having free reign from the pulpit the world over. In doing so, they are fulfilling biblical prophecy (Matt. 24:11. 1 Tim. 4:1-2, 2 Pet. 2:1-3, Jude 4).

Interestingly, Paul's instruction to the Thessalonians, to test prophecy, is in the context of the coming day of the Lord (1 Thess. 4:13-18, 5:1-10), as was Nebuchadnezzar's dream (Dan. 2:34-35, 44-45).

Regarding the king's request to reveal the dream first before interpreting it, some say that he had forgotten the dream, therefore, needed the sorcerers to first 'remind' him of it. That is unlikely, for the king was thinking about the dream (2:30) that was troubling him (2:1, 3). If the king had forgotten the dream, the sorcerers could have made something up and then given an interpretation, which would have saved them from the penalty of death. They knew that the king was testing them, as we should do the same with all prophets and prophecy.

Due to the sorcerer's failure to meet the king's demands, he was both angry and very furious (2:12), which seemed to be characteristic (3:13, 19) of this successor to the throne (2:1). The new king did not suffer fools gladly; nor should we (2 Cor. 11:19). The king inherited the wise men from his father; however, he was not as accommodating as his father was. Again, suspicious of their claims, he tested them, and his thoughts were confirmed when they said, only the gods, whose dwelling is not with flesh (2:11), can do what the king asks. With this statement, the sorcerers contradict themselves, whereas they have previously claimed supernatural ability (2:4, 7).

Now that their deception had been exposed, Daniel and his friends were also under the same penalty of death (2:13), even though Daniel was not with the wise men when first summoned to the king's chambers. An explanation for this is that perhaps he was distancing himself from the fools who thought themselves wise. Even so, Daniel was tarred with the same brush when the decree was made, and judgement fell. There is a lesson in this for the church also. Do not associate with false prophets, for when judgement falls, we will need to be distinct and separated from them.

In response to the king's decree, like in chapter one, Daniel respectfully and tactfully addressed the guards' captain (2:14) and the king (2:16). Unlike the foolish 'wise men,' Daniel did not make boastful claims, stating he could make known mysteries, but instead, he went to his friends, Hananiah, Mishael, and Azariah, who then went to God concerning the mystery (2:17, 18). The king trusted Daniel more than the other wise men, having granted him time (2:16) to interpret the dream. The sorcerer's request had previously been denied for more time to make the dream known (2:8, 9).

Once again, Daniel found himself in a time of testing (2:17-19). Daniel had to wait on God for the answer to the king's demand, which he received in a vision (cf. 1:17) and acknowledged and confirmed that only God could reveal deep and hidden things (2:22) and that He has made known to Daniel what he had asked (2:23).

Once Daniel knew the mystery dream and received the interpretation, he approached Arioch, the king's chief executioner (2:24), who had previously sought to kill Daniel (2:14). Daniel requested, of Arioch, that the wise men's slaughter be delayed a little longer (2:24), that he knew the interpretation, and requested a meeting with the king. Knowing there was no time to waste, in haste, Arioch did as Daniel asked (2:25). Daniel found favour with Arioch, like with Ashpenaz (1:8), who did not want to carry out the king's decree and kill Daniel. However, like the sorcerers, Arioch promoted himself before the king, having falsely claimed he found the one who can meet the king's demand (2:25). Arioch did not find Daniel, but rather Daniel found Arioch. Unlike the sorcerers and Arioch, Daniel did not take any credit for what he claimed to be able to do but instead gave God full credit (2:27, 28, 30). In doing so, Daniel refers to 'the God in heaven' (2:28), who is able to do what the king demands. Four times Daniel acknowledges the God in heaven

(2:19, 28, 44, 5:23), who is distinct from the false gods the sorcerers were consulting, and the Babylonians were worshipping. Only this God can reveal mysteries (2:28), which was later acknowledged, and admitted to by the king (2:45, 47).

After acknowledging the source of making the mystery known and before interpreting the dream, Daniel starts by telling the king that the dream refers to the latter days (2:28), the things that will take place after this, and what is to be (2:29). The dream relates to events leading to and fulfilling the end times, which are again revealed in greater detail in the book of Revelation.

Daniel's book found the words 'after this' five times (Dan. 2:29, 45, 7:6, 7, 24). On each occasion, Daniel referred to the same events recorded by John in the book of Revelation, starting with Revelation, chapter four, verse one. John, however, goes further and more profound than Daniel, writing in greater detail what takes place during the tribulation (7:1, 7, 15:5, 18:1, 19:1). Like John, Daniel 'saw' the things to come, progressing from one event to the next. John shared supernatural insight with Daniel, seeing into the future, revealed in the book of Daniel and the book of Revelation.

In sum, Daniel, chapter two deals with the subject of the latter days, the things that must take place, and in doing so, separates the true from the false. Through a time of testing, it was revealed Daniel was to be truly of God, and the rest were exposed to be deceivers. Throughout the time of testing, the king was shown to be wiser than the supposed wise men, setting a test to determine who could be trusted. The test would serve not only the king but also God. Through the test, Daniel was positioned through promotion, and as a result, the king came to know that the God Daniel served was indeed 'A great God' (2:45), the God of gods, and Lord of kings (2:47). In other words, Daniel's God is greater than all the other gods in Babylon and anywhere else for that matter.

Part Two
'The Future Kingdom'
(vv. 31-49)

Following Daniel's acknowledgment of God (2:27-28), he tells the king what he saw in a dream - a great image (2:31-33). Although the image was great, it was not infinite and would be struck down by a stone, not made with human hands (2:34). Like everything else in this world, the image would be reduced to chaff and then blown away by the wind (2:35a). The stone (Jesus) that struck the image (representing Gentile kingdoms) replaced it, and became a great mountain, and filled the whole earth (2:35b). Unlike the Gentile kingdoms, the stone represented an eternal kingdom, starting with the millennial, or Messianic reign.

While the dream in itself was pretty basic, the meaning troubled the king (2:2, 3, 30). The image frightened the king (2:31), which further supports, the king did not forget the dream but instead withheld it from the sorcerers to test them. Although the KJV translates verse five as "the thing is 'gone' from me." The ESV, NASB, and NIV translations replace the word 'gone' with 'firm' or 'certain.' Even the NKJV agrees with the ESV, NASB, and NIV. Most scholars (e.g., Montgomery, Archer) agree with the modern translations, which are supported contextual (2:1, 3, 5, 8). Therefore, the dream was not gone, as forgotten, but rather the king's words were firm, and they were certain (2:5b, 12-13).

After Daniel revealed the dream, he then gave the interpretation of the dream. Again, the dream referred to the Gentile kingdoms, which would trample the Holy Land until Jesus returns to rule and reign (cf. Lu. 21:24), just as Nebuchadnezzar had done. And, although, at the time, king Nebuchadnezzar was great and powerful, ruling the then known world (3:4-6), Babylon would be succeeded by another temporal kingdom, the Medes and Persians (cf. 5:28; 6:8; also cf. 5:31). The Medes and Persians would also be succeeded by another again, the Grecian Empire (cf. 8:20–21), that was defeated by the Romans, being the fourth empire. The Romans were the last ruling empire - there have been no other hegemonic powers since Rome.

The closest we have seen to represent a hegemonic power is the United States, albeit the US is a regional power, not a global power. The next hegemonic power will attempt to be a global power, forming a New World Order (NWO), otherwise known as the 'revived Roman Empire.' Soon, Rome will reappear under the antichrist's rule (Dan. 7:7, 8, 19-24, cf. 2:41-43, Rev. 13:1). The revived Roman Empire will consist of 'ten toes' (2:42), which are the 'ten horns' (Dan. 7:24) which Jesus, the Rock (stone) will smash (Dan. 2:34-35). The revived Roman Empire will consist of ten-nations and be the last and shortest-lived empire, succeeded by the eternal kingdom, to come (cf. Matt. 6:10).

The last and eternal kingdom shall never be destroyed (Dan. 2:34-35, 44-45). When the last and everlasting kingdom is established, everyone will know that the God Daniel served is the God of gods, and Lord of kings (2:47). Up until that time, God will give each of the Gentile kingdoms a time and a season before removing and replacing them with a successor (2:21). Again, the last of which will be that of the antichrist (Rev. 17:11).

To summarise: Daniel, chapter two, is the first within the book to reference the future kingdoms, divulged to Nebuchadnezzar in a dream (2:3, 30). Aforementioned, the king's dream revealed what takes place after Nebuchadnezzar's reign, right up until the return of Jesus where: "God will set up a kingdom that shall never be destroyed, nor shall the kingdom be left to another people" (v. 44a), and: "It shall stand forever" (v. 44b). Paralleled with chapter seven and Revelation chapter seventeen, these chapters collectively serve humanity, covering a period of three millenniums with critical and compelling information about future world rulers and empires. The information provides a timeline indicating where we are in the biblical calendar in relation to Jesus Christ's return. Evidently we are right at the end, even in the last hour (cf. 1 Jn. 2:18).

History supports the prophetic accuracy of the dreams up until that of the coming final world ruler, the antichrist (Dan. 7:7, 20; Rev. 17:9-13). However, the mathematical probability of the antichrist fulfilling the yet to be fulfilled prediction both literally and historically, going by the prophetic accuracy of the previous, is veridical evidence. The probability of just eight Old Testament prophesies being fulfilled is 100,000,000,000,000,000. The odds of winning the lottery are 1 in 259,000,000, which goes 259 times into the above figure.

Daniel chapters two and seven, alongside Revelation chapter seventeen, provide exactly eight accounts predicted ahead of time. Six of these have been fulfilled to pinpoint literal and historic accuracy suggesting the remaining two (the destruction of the next Gentile kingdom (NWO) and the coming kingdom of the Antichrist) will be fulfilled in the same manner.

The following list provides eight biblical prophesies of then, or coming powers identified by Daniel (chapter 2 & 7) and John (Rev. 13; 17; 19; 20), that would/will be destroyed; some of which were not in existence, or even conceivable at the time of the prediction:

1. Isaiah predicted the destruction of Egypt as a world power (Is. 19, cf. Rev 17:9-13)
2. Nahum predicted the collapse of Assyria (Nah. 1:8-9; Rev. 17:9-13)
3. Daniel predicted the destruction of Babylon (Dan. 2:27-38, 7:4-5)
4. Daniel - The Medes and Persians (Dan. 2:39; 7:5-6)
5. Daniel - Greece (Dan. 2:39-40; 7:6-7)

6. Daniel - Rome (Dan. 2:40; 7:20)
7. Daniel - The Gentiles (Dan. 2:34-35; 7:26-27)
8. Daniel and John - The antichrist (Dan. 12:8; Rev. 17:13; 19:20; 20:10)

When considering the odds of just eight prophecies coming to pass against the many thousands more contained within the scriptures, that is proof enough the Bible is true, trustworthy, and a reliable source, thereby providing evidence enough of God's existence. For example, there are some three hundred and fifty prophecies about Jesus' first coming, some dating back thousands of years before He arrived, and Jesus fulfilled every one of them with pinpoint accuracy. There are as many again predicting His second coming. It, therefore, stands to reason if the first group was fulfilled historically and literally, then the second group will be likewise in the same literal manner.

While many pastors and Christian leaders today dismiss or ignore Bible prophecy, they overlook that the Bible is thirty percent prophetic or predictive. Those who ignore Bible prophecy risk misinterpreting the remaining seventy percent of scripture and subsequently fall into error. For example, being ignorant of Bible prophecy is the root cause of replacement theology. It is also the root cause of false 'kingdom now' 'seven mountains' teaching, also known as dominionism and reconstructionism. Prosperity teaching is also a result of mishandling scripture, whereas prosperity teachers twist verses dedicated to Israel and apply them to the church. An example of this is Deuteronomy (11:24), also seen in Joshua (1:3), "Every place where the sole of your foot treads will be yours." Needless to say, these verses, and many like them, have nothing to do with the church. The church is not inheriting lands and establishing earthly kingdoms here and now.

As outlined in the book of Daniel and supported by the book of Revelation, God's succession plan involves Gentile (worldy) kingdoms, ending with the seventh and eighth rule of the antichrist, albeit for just one hour (Rev. 17:12). The plan, therefore, leaves no room for the church to be ruling and reigning on earth this side of Jesus' return, unless the church was, in fact, a Gentile kingdom under the rule of the antichrist. Unfortunately, that is the case for so many, fulfilling scripture (2 Thess. 2), as the apostate church indicating the nearness of Jesus' returns for His bride.

Regarding Daniel's interpretation of kingdoms to come: The chart below provides a comparison of the dream/vision of each prediction progressively revealing a little more detail, covering eight predictions in all. Revelation chapter seventeen not only exceeds that of Daniel's account, but it also gives the reader additional understanding of the times we currently live in, providing both a historical, chronicle and future prophetic prediction. A time-map if you will.

Daniel, Chapter Two	Daniel, Chapter Seven	Revelation, Chapter Seventeen
Vv. 37-38 Babylon	Vs. 4 Babylon	Vv. 9-10 Egypt
Vs. 39 Medes & Persians	Vs. 5 Medo-Persia	Vv.9-10 Assyria
Vs. 39 Greece	Vs. 6 Greece	Vv. 9-10 Babylon
Vs. 40 Rome	Vs. 7 Four Kingdoms:	Vv. 9-10 Medo-Persia
Vs. 44 God	• Babylon	Vv. 9-10 Greece
	• Medo-Persia	Vv. 9-10 Rome
	• Greece	Vv. 9-10 Babylon (NWO)
	• Rome	Vv. 9-13 The Antichrist
	Vv. 7, 20 The Antichrist	

When taking into consideration chapter seven, alongside chapter two, Daniel's interpretation of the dream combined with historic accounts reveals the symbolism. The lion is Babylon (Dan. 7:4); and the bear represents the Medes and Persians (Dan. 7:5; 8:8, 21-22); the leopard as Greece (Dan. 7:6; 8:8, 21-22); and the kingdom of iron (Dan. 2:33, 40; 7:23-34) is Rome. The ten horns and ten toes (Dan. 2:41-43) represents the final Gentile power in the end times, and the little horn is the antichrist (Dan. 7:8, 20-22, 24-27; 8:23-26; 11:36; 2 Thess. 2:3-8; Rev. 13:5-6). The Babylonians, the Medes, and Persians, Greece, and Rome are otherwise known as the four Gentile world empires spanning from 626 BC to 1527 AD.

The chart below provides further insight into the times and prophecies of reigning Gentile kingdoms, sourced from: http://getbackontrack.org/cms/resources/bkt/bi/gentileKingdoms.pdf

A Chart Showing the Prophecies of Reign of Gentile Kingdoms

Dan.2 The IMAGE	Daniel 7 The FOUR BEASTS (State)	(Church)	Daniel 8 The RAM and GOAT	Revelation 13 The BEAST and IMAGE (State)	(Church)	Rev 17 BABYLON and BEAST	Explanation of Symbols	The EVENTS fulfilled in HISTORY
Head of GOLD v. 32, 38	1st BEAST like LION v. 4						1st HEAD of prophetic BABYLON	The CHALDEAN EMPIRE (Babylon) 625-539 B.C.
Breast and arms of SILVER v. 32, 39	2nd BEAST (BEAR) v. 5		RAM with 2 horns v. 3, 4, 20				2nd HEAD of prophetic BABYLON	The PERSIAN EMPIRE (Medo-Persia) 558-330 B.C.
Belly and thighs of BRASS v. 32, 39	3rd BEAST (LEOPARD) 4 heads v. 6		HE GOAT with great horn and 4 notable ones v. 5-8, 21, 22				3rd, 4th, 5th, 6th HEADS of prophetic BABYLON	GREECE, under Alexander the Great, and four divisions, began 333 B.C.
Legs as IRON v. 33, 40-43	4th BEAST strong like IRON with 10 HORNS v. 7, 23, 24			The BEAST with 7 HEADS and 10 HORNS v. 1, 2			7th HEAD of prophetic BABYLON, with ten HORNS	The ROMAN EMPIRE, 31 B.C.-A.D. 476, in 2 divisions, West and East
				The DEADLY WOUND v. 3				Fall of the ROMAN EMPIRE A.D. 476
		1st HORN (plucked by roots)		1st HORN			These three horns, destroyed at behest of Pope, fill the "Transition Age" (Myers)	The VANDALS A.D. 429-533
		2nd HORN (rooted up)		2nd HORN				The HERULI, Odoacer's government, A.D. 476-493
		3rd HORN (rooted up)		3rd HORN				The OSTROGOTHS A.D. 493-554
		LITTLE HORN among ten v. 8, 20-22, 24-27			2 horned "LAMB DRAGON" and "IMAGE" v. 11-18	SCARLET WOMAN who rode the BEAST v. 1, 2	Ruled the beast, so called BABYLON the GREAT	FALSE CHRISTIANITY and church government, or "image" of Roman Empire government
	4th HORN			1st of remaining 7 horns— DEADLY WOUND HEALED (to continue 1260 years) v. 5		1st HEAD of BEAST (healed) ridden by scarlet-clothed woman	Since the "Great Whore" never rode any of the 7 heads of the 1st 4 beasts, but did mount and ride the last 7 horns of Daniel's 4th beast it follows that the last 7 horns of Dan. 7 and Rev. 13 are the 7 HEADS of Rev. 17 (5 fallen at collapse of Napoleon).	"IMPERIAL RESTORATION" of empire by Justinian, A.D. 554. He recognized supremacy of this world's Christianity
	5th HORN			2nd of remaining 7 HORNS		2nd HEAD ridden by woman		FRANKISH KINGDOM Began 774. Charlemagne crowned A.D. 800
	6th HORN			3rd of remaining 7 HORNS		3rd HEAD ridden by woman		HOLY ROMAN EMPIRE (German head). Otto the Great crowned, 962.
	7th HORN			4th of remaining 7 HORNS		4th HEAD ridden by woman		HAPSBURG dynasty (Austrian head), Charles V crowned, 1520.
	8th HORN			5th of remaining 7 HORNS		5th HEAD ridden by woman		NAPOLEON'S KINGDOM (French head), crowned, 1805.
				554-1814 = 1260 Years Beast continued				
	In 1814, just 1260 years after "deadly wound" was healed, the "HOLY ROMAN EMPIRE" was dissolved. "So closed a government that dated from Augustus Caesar" (West, p. 377).							
	9th HORN			6th of remaining 7 HORNS		6th HEAD ridden by woman	(One IS) Rev. 17:10	ITALY, united by Garibaldi, 1870 to 1945
The TEN TOES	10th HORN			7th and last HORN	Beast ascends out of pit	7th head and ten HORNS	(One yet to come)	Revived ROMAN EMPIRE, by 10 rulers under one leader.

In sum, the point and purpose of Daniel chapters two and seven, alongside Revelation chapter seventeen, is to provide an outline of future kingdoms, providing the serious and studious follower of Jesus Christ detailed information leading to His second coming. The importance of this study is that the information reveals where we are within the biblical calendar, what we are dealing with currently, and what is next to come. Currently, we are in the time between the sixth kingdom and the seventh kingdom (Rev. 17:10).

At the time of John's writing, the current (6th) kingdom was Rome, "The one that is." The seventh will be the revived Roman Empire, the ten toes and ten horns (Rev. 17:12), which will give birth to an eighth, being the kingdom of the antichrist (Rev. 17:11). The antichrist kingdom will last only 'one hour' (seven years) before Jesus returns and destroys it (Rev. 17:14, cf. Dan. 2:34-35, 44-45). The seventh and eighth kingdoms will rise up during the tribulation, which means the bride of Christ will not be on earth when those kingdoms come into power.

The church is raptured (Dan. 12:1) before the tribulation (Rom. 5:9, 1 Thess. 1:8, 5:9, 2 Thess. 2:7, Rev. 3:10, 4:1). The rapture is the next event on the biblical calendar, triggered by the signing of the Middle East Peace Treaty. The antichrist is revealed as the one who successfully has the peace treaty signed (Isa. 28:15, 18, Dan. 9:24-27) yet cannot be revealed until the church is first removed (2 Thess. 2). The Middle East Peace Treaty will be addressed later in this study.

Chapter Three

Part One
"Fall Down and Worship the (my) Image" (vv. 1-7)

In the previous chapter, in King Nebuchadnezzar's second year of reign (2:1), he acknowledged that the God Daniel served was superior to any other god in Babylon: "Truly, your God is God of gods and Lord of kings, and a revealer of mysteries, for you have been able to reveal this mystery" (2:45).

Now in chapter three, in the king's eighteenth year of reign (3:1, cf. Septuagint), one year before the fall of Jerusalem (2 Kgs. 25:8), it seems that the king has forgotten Daniel's God by promoting himself as a god that the whole world must worship, or else die. Chapter four supports the above-made statement by providing further evidence; Nebuchadnezzar had indeed forgotten God (4:25b, 31-33), even after acknowledging Him twice before (2:47, 3:29, 4:1-3). Hence, the forgetful king was warned and given an opportunity to repent (4:27) before judgement fell. While the threat of judgement served to save, not destroy, the judgement in itself turned the king around (4:34-37), which will also be the point and purpose of the coming tribulation. Interestingly, both terms of the announced judgement (Nebuchadnezzar's and the tribulation) are seven years each (4:16, 23, 25, 32, compared with 7:25, 9:27, Rev. 11:2, 12:6, 13:5).

Before Nebuchadnezzar's time of trouble (tribulation) and through it, coming to the place of repentance, the king set up an image of himself as ruler over the nations (3:2-3), positioning himself as the one world ruler. Every official was summoned to Babylon to fall down and worship the golden image. The officials represented peoples, nations, and men of every language (cf. v. 7; 4:1; 5:19; 6:25; 7:14), including king Zedekiah. Zedekiah was Judah's last king, who was also summoned to Babylon for this occasion (Jer. 51:59). Zedekiah's participation in false worship is confirmed by II Kings (24:18-20a), II Chronicles (36:11-14) and Jeremiah (53:1-3a).

False worship was something that Israel/Judah was well accustomed to, wounding (breaking, grieving) God with their treachery (Ezek. 6:9); and for this reason, God made an example of them (Ezek. 5:9, 15). Alongside the king of Judah, all of the officials from every other nation were to fall down and worship the image, which implies both religious and political significance. The word 'worship' is referenced ten times in chapter three (vv. 5, 6, 7, 10, 11, 12, 14, 15, 18, 28), which supports that worship is the big idea of the passage. The people of God are being 'tested' by God as to who they will serve (cf. Deut. 13:3).

The image that king Nebuchadnezzar set up (3:1, 2, 3, 5, 7, 12, 14, 18, 28) was 90 feet high (about the height of a present-day eight-story building) and only 9 feet wide. The Hebrew word for 'image' (ṣelem) is a general term that allows the image to have been in a human form. As mentioned earlier, the human form that the image represented would have been that of Nebuchadnezzar himself, that is, his own image, probably replicating his dream (2:38).

Due to the requirement to fall down and worship the image, the image represented a god. Although the image represents a god, no Babylon god is mentioned, suggesting that Nebuchadnezzar was promoting himself to be a god and not just any old god, but as the god over all other Babylonian deities, and also those of the entire world. This statement's evidence is in verse four, where people of other nations and different languages were required to worship the image. The other nations had their own gods but were required to worship Nebuchadnezzar's image as the God of gods, which is the title he previously gave to Daniel's God (2:47).

An interesting side point is that the words, 'Babylon's god' in Jewish Gematria equals 666. Evidently, by setting up the image that was to be globally recognised and worshipped, Nebuchadnezzar stated that he was the new world ruler and god. In doing so, he was also establishing a new world religion within a new world order, and it was with God's blessing (Jer. 27:7).

Anyone from any nation or any language who refused to fall down and worship the image at the musical instruments' sound would be sentenced to death. Essentially, they would be sacrificed in the fire (3:6, 11). Scriptural silence on the threat carried out against any other, except for Shadrach, Meshach, and Abednego, and obviously Daniel, suggests that no other refused the king. Daniel, on this occasion, was not named. Shadrach, Meshach, and Abednego were the only ones named who faced the consequence of refusing to fall down and worship the false god, which was the golden image.

Before addressing Shadrach, Meshach, and Abednego, who refused to fall down and worship the image, it is worth reminding ourselves of the surrounding and supporting information of the previous chapter, Daniel chapter two, and later, Daniel chapter seven (2:42-44, 7:7, 20,

24) alongside the book of Revelation, chapter thirteen and chapter seventeen. Like Daniel, chapters two and seven, and the book of Revelation, chapters thirteen and seventeen reference the ten kingdoms, which is essential to consider alongside chapter three. The future ten kingdoms will make up the antichrist's alliance in the new world order (Rev. 12:3, 13:1, 17:3, 7, 12, 16). Daniel is the first to mention the ten kingdoms, which is the end-time coalition (Dan. 7:7, 20, 24). In Daniel chapter three, the significance of the united kingdoms is that Nebuchadnezzar is also uniting the known kingdoms (3:2-3) and is setting himself up as the new, and one world ruler (3:4-7) as God's servant (Jer. 27:6) having God's blessing (Jer. 27:7). The coming antichrist will do likewise during the tribulation (Rev. 17:10-13) and be sent by God (2 Thess. 2:11). The topic of the antichrist will be adequately addressed in chapter seven of this study, but for now, it is worth noting the similarity, the type, and shadows of the things to come even from Daniel chapter three.

The most striking similarity is that both king Nebuchadnezzar and the antichrist will assume global political and religious power, setting up an image in their own likeness to be worshipped. Those who refuse are sentenced to death. The book of Daniel references the word 'image' fifteen times, four times in chapter two (vv. 31, 32, 34, 35) and ten times in chapter three (vv. 1, 2, 3, 5, 7, 10, 12, 14, 15, 18), and once more, in chapter eleven (v. 8). As mentioned earlier, the references from chapters two and three are linked. The image Nebuchadnezzar set up was of himself, as seen in the dream (chapter two), depicting himself as a god. As stated earlier, Nebuchadnezzar was not likening himself to another Babylonian god, but a new god above any other, being himself 'the' god of Babylon, and even the known world, like Pharaoh, did.

Although Egypt also had many gods, Pharaoh was number one, a supposed god dwelling in the flesh. The antichrist will do the same thing by making the same proclamation (2 Thess. 2:4). The antichrist's sidekick, the false prophet, will also set up an image of the antichrist, which is to be worshipped (Rev. 13:14). Again, any refusing to worship the image would be slain (v. 15). Total submission to the antichrist will also require receiving his mark (666) on the right hand or forehead (v. 16). Anyone refusing to accept the mark will not be able to buy and sell (v. 17), which means they will not function within society. Commercial trade and travel will be off-limits to any rejecting the antichrist by refusing to worship him and accept his mark.

To recap: in the same way, the antichrist will set up his image to be worshipped (Dan. 11:31. 12:11), as Nebuchadnezzar did (3:1, 2, 3, 5, 7, 12, 14, 18, 28). Similarly, the words 'Babylon's gods' equal 666 in Jewish Gematria, and the antichrist's name will also represent 666 (Rev. 13:18). Again, the same Nebuchadnezzar who previously acknowledged God (2:47) set himself up as God (not a god), which is a shadow of what the antichrist will do during the tribulation (2 Thess. 2:4). In the same way, Nebuchadnezzar once acknowledged God and proclaimed to be God - the antichrist will do, even coming out of the church (1 Jn. 2:18-19). Again, the consequence of failing to worship the image that either Nebuchadnezzar or the antichrist sets up is death (Dan. 3:6, 11, 15, Rev. 13:15, 15:2). However, the consequence of worshipping the image (a false god) is also death (Deut. 13, 1 Cor. 10:1-22, Rev. 14:9-11, 16:2, 19:20, 20:4).

The same choice presented before Shadrach, Meshach, and Abednego, will be represented to the 'left behind' to endure the coming tribulation. As for Shadrach, Meshach, and Abednego, the choice for those left behind will also come down to 1). Trade temporal life for eternal life, or 2). Trade eternal life for temporal life. In business terms, this is called 'opportunity cost,' which means one opportunity will cost you the other – you cannot have both.

The same choices are presented before us today (cf. Matt. 16:24-25) and were also evident within the letters to the seven churches (Rev. 2-3). In fact, Polycarp of the first century met his end due to refusing to participate in false worship by placing a pinch of incense in a brazier burning before a statue of Caesar. Polycarp replied, "Eighty and six years have I served Christ, and he never did me any injury: how then can I blaspheme my King and my Savior?" Polycarp was tortured and then burned to death, for his refusal, on public display for all to see.

When faced with the difficulty of choosing between worshipping God, alone, or death, we are reminded of Polycarp, and also the words of Shadrach, Meshach, and Abednego word's, who said when asked to give an account of themselves, "O Nebuchadnezzar, we have no need to answer you in this matter. If this be so, our God whom we serve is able to deliver us from the burning fiery furnace, and He will deliver us out of your hand, O king. But if not, be it known to you, O king, that we will not serve your gods or worship the golden image that you have set up. Like Polycarp, despite the imminent threat of death, Shadrach, Meshach, and Abednego refused to fall down and worship the false god that Nebuchadnezzar had set up. The same should be said of us, perhaps further motivated by the words of Jesus: "Do not be afraid of those who kill the body but cannot kill the soul. Instead, fear the One who can destroy both soul and body in hell" (Matt. 10:28).

Part Two
'If You Just Bow Down and Worship Me' (vv. 8-18)

In the previous section, we looked at the similarity of the image Nebuchadnezzar set up to be worshipped and the one that the coming antichrist will set up, also to be worshipped. Both images show that they represent the person setting them up, who proclaims to be God (not a god, but God). Both types have a numeric value of 666, and the consequences of refusing to fall down and worship the images are death.

Interestingly, there is another similarity, where on both accounts, the sorcerers were promoting and enforcing the worship of these false gods (images). In Daniel's report, the Chaldeans who were the ancient people living in Chaldea in 800 BC and ruled Babylonia 625–539 BC. The Chaldeans were renowned as astronomers and astrologers, which is why they were considered 'wise men' and were in the company of magicians, enchanters, and sorcerers (2:2). The Chaldeans were sorcerers, practicing magic and consulting with demons; therefore, they were demon worshipping priests and prophets (similar to modern-day 'Christian' clairvoyants).

Another direct link between Nebuchadnezzar's image and the future image to be set up is that the coming false prophet will also enforce worship of the antichrist's image (Rev. 13). There is no doubt that the false prophet is already conditioning and preparing deceived religious people through false worship, in preparation to worship the antichrist's image and receive his mark (666). The false prophet will come out of the church, like the antichrist, and is also a sorcerer (Rev. 13:13). Like the Chaldeans were, the false prophet will be deeply religious.

Revelation, chapter seventeen provides further information about the false prophet, who rides the beast (the antichrist), and is "dressed in purple and scarlet and adorned with gold and jewels, and peers, holding in her (false prophet's) hand a golden cup full of abominations" (Rev. 17:4). The description of the false prophet resembles that of a religious priest, particularly Catholic cardinals and the Pope. Some claim that the Pope is the false prophet finding further support with verse nine concerning the 'seven mountains' on which the woman (false prophet, and second beast) is seated, by connecting the seven mountains to Rome, being the city of the seven hills. However, the context supports that the false prophet is the 'ruler' of the seven heads (v. 9), which are the seven kings (v. 10). The seven mountains are seven rulers, like the Chaldeans were, ruling over Babylon. Like the Chaldeans, the false prophet will also rule over Babylon (Rev. 17:5) and be drunk with the saints' blood (v. 6). Babylon (cf. Rev. 17, 18) is symbolic of the world (and religious) system under Satan. The future ruling false prophet will be drunk with the saints' blood due to slaying them for refusing to bow down and worship the image of the antichrist (Rev. 13:15). The Chaldeans did the same, seeing to the execution of any who do not fall down and worship the image that Nebuchadnezzar set up.

On the instruments' sound, all the officials gathered in the courtyard to fall down and worship the image that Nebuchadnezzar had set up, which included Shadrach, Meshach, and Abednego (3:12; cf. 2:49). Although the gathering would have been quite large, Shadrach, Meshach, and Abednego's absence was quickly noticed and was reported to the king by the Chaldeans. Previously, Daniel saved his fellow wise men (2:18, 24), but now the same wise men he saved from death seek to destroy Shadrach, Meshach, and Abednego, perhaps driven by jealousy (1:20). Another reason would be religious conflict in the same way the false prophet will persecute believers during the tribulation. Either way, the sorcerers were on the lookout for the three Jews, knowing that they would not fall down and worship the false image.

The same is true of Daniel; however, he is not named, some say because of his high position as ruler over the whole province of Babylon and chief prefect over all the wise men in Babylon (2:48). For this reason, it is argued that the sorcerers would not dare to go up against Daniel. However, the presidents and the satraps (a provincial governor in the ancient Persian empire) later did (5:3-15), even though the satraps were under Daniel, and directly accountable to him (5:2).

Although the motivation behind the Chaldeans' accusation of Shadrach, Meshach, and Abednego is speculative, the word 'maliciously' (Dan. 3:8) provides intent. The Chaldeans had malice or ill will towards their Jewish peers and intended to do them harm by having them thrown into the fiery furnace (3:11). The accusation is seen in verse twelve, "There are certain Jews whom you have appointed over the affairs of the province of Babylon: Shadrach, Meshach, and Abednego. These men, O king, pay no attention to you; they do not serve your gods or worship the golden image that you have set up." *Note the distinction between the Babylonian gods and the image that Nebuchadnezzar had set up.

On hearing the Chaldeans report, the quick-tempered king (cf. 2:12) became furious with rage (3:13, 19). Although the Jewish wise men were better than any other (1:19) regarding their ability and performance, they were non-conforming. Performance and conformance are equally important. In business terms, the most dangerous person within the company is the high-performer, non-conformer. This is because the high performer will lead others, and when non-conforming they will lead and influence them counterculturally.

Culture is the most crucial consideration within any business; for this reason, it is said, culture is not a part of the game; it is the game. When an organisation has the right people, it can develop and maintain the right culture and achieve the desired goals and objectives. Where there are people resisting culture, being non-conforming, business will struggle, particularly in the area of continuous improvement (kaizen), resulting in competitive advantage, which involves change management.

Due to countercultural behaviour, the king was furious when hearing the Chaldeans' report regarding Shadrach, Meshach, and Abednego. The Jewish wise men's non-conformance could lead and influence others within the kingdom counterculturally.

Remember, when the Babylonians brought the Jews into captivity, they intended to change them in every way. The intention was to remove their God from them and them from their God, including changing their names. In other words, they were re-cultured into Babylonian culture, which required worshipping Babylonian gods. As discussed in the previous section, for most Jews, there was no problem worshipping false gods (Jer. 7:3-11), which broke God's heart (Ezek. 6:9).

Despite being furious with rage, Nebuchadnezzar still took the time to inquire about the incident before executing judgment (3:13), allowing Shadrach, Meshach, and Abednego the opportunity to respond by falling down and worshipping the image (3:15). Instead, the three Jews rejected the king's offer, placing themselves entirely in the hands of their God (vv. 16-18). Should they have had done as the king requested, they would have been spared the sentence of death and may have even been further rewarded (3:30).

So confident of himself, Nebuchadnezzar asked the Jewish wise men, "Who is the god who will deliver you out of my hand?" (3:15). The statement confirms that Nebuchadnezzar had put himself above God, suggesting that not even He could save His people from the king's hand. Again, the forgetful king had forgotten Daniel's God, who he previously acknowledged as the "God of gods and the Lord of kings" (2:27). The later part 'Lord of kings' supports Nebuchadnezzar once recognised God as his Lord, as a king under Him. But again, the king had forgotten God, arguably due to surrounding himself with mixed counsel (wise men), and thereby replaced Him with another – which was himself. And the same is true today.

Today we forget God when we surround ourselves with mixed counsel, and for some, they even become god (in their own mind). Eve desired this (Gen. 3), and so did the church of Laodicea by elevating themselves, and by replacing God with materialism. The church of Laodicea boasted to have everything and no need for anything (Rev. 3:14-22). While they had everything worldly, they did not have Jesus, and neither did they have any need for Him. Remember, Jesus was standing on the outside of the church, knocking on the door, all the while the lukewarm church was on the inside, and apparently worshipping Him. It is more likely that they were worshipping 'another Jesus' (2 Cor. 11:4) as many are today.

Laodicea means, 'People ruling,' which reflects the problem at hand. The people were ruling in replacement of God. This lukewarm church is also identified as one deceived by the prosperity gospel, filled with everything materialistic yet empty of God. The first NT reference to the prosperity gospel is where Satan tempted Jesus in the desert (Matt. 4:1-11). It could also be argued that Jesus was tempted again in the garden (Lu. 22:44). Jesus was first tempted in the desert by Satan, where Satan promised Him everything if He just bowed down and worshipped Him (Matt. 4:9). The same in the garden; only on that occasion, Jesus' life could have been spared if He changed course by rejecting the cross. However, Jesus was triumphant over the devil on both accounts. On the other hand, Adam and Eve, who were the first to be tempted in the garden (Gen. 3), failed the test, resulting in every other problem since.

You could say that the Bible is a book of two gardens, the first involving Adam and Eve and the next, Jesus, the second Adam (Rom. 5:14, 1 Cor. 15:45). Interestingly, Babylon was also famous for its hanging gardens, known as one of the world's seventh wonders. Within the Babylonian gardens were shrines and temples dedicated to false gods, and quite possibly, the image of Nebuchadnezzar was also located there.

Therefore, Shadrach, Meshach, and Abednego represented a type and shadow of Jesus, rejecting and refusing false worship at the cost of materialism and even their natural lives.

The two biblical gardens are still very relevant today. We either repeat the first Adam's error, rejecting God by replacing Him with our elevated selves, or we imitate the example of the second Adam (Jesus) by living for God and dying to self. The first example (of failure) is more evident in the church in these last days, where most fulfil Bible prophecy as 'lovers of themselves' (2 Tim. 3:2). Loving self moreover God follows the immediate context of being a good soldier of Jesus Christ (2 Tim. 2:1-11). Most are not meeting their enlisted (covenant) requirements.

As a result of failing the test, most can no longer call Jesus Lord (Lu. 6:46, cf. Matt. 7:21-23), which is why they can no longer endure sound doctrine, but instead, have itching ears to hear whatever they want, being the things best suited to their passions (2 Tim. 4:3). For this reason, God will send them the strong delusion, who is the antichrist (2 Thess. 2:11), who is already operating within the church today (2 Jn. 2:18-19).

Out of the above-mentioned, antichrist deception has produced the false self-centred doctrine that we are 'little gods,' which is taught by several confused Charismatics today. The 'little (false) gods' theory teaches that we are gods, having the same DNA as God. Therefore, we can speak things that are not, as if they were, that they may be, just like God. To arrive at this conclusion (speak things that are not, as if they were, that they may be), Charismatics misuse Romans, chapter four (v. 17).

One of the leading proponents of this false teaching is famous for saying, 'Whenever I read, "I AM" in the Bible, I just smile and say, "I am too." The doctrine of little (false) gods is rooted in Mormonism, and Roman Catholicism, albeit more widely promoted through the Word of Faith movement today, originating from Genesis (1:27). The basis for the 'little gods' claim is found in two Scripture passages, Psalm (82:6), which reads, "I said, 'You are "gods"; you are all sons of the Most High.'"

Further supported by Jesus, who quotes this Psalm in (Jn. 10:34), "Is it not written in your law, 'I have said you are gods'?" However, both passages include explanations in the immediate context that do not indicate human divinity. Psalm (82:6) is followed by a warning that, "You will all die like mere men; you will fall like every other ruler" (verse 7). The reference is to mortal men representing God's authority in the world—kings, judges, and magistrates. Psalm (chapter. 82) is a warning to unjust leaders who consider themselves "gods" (Ps. 82:1) yet who "know nothing," who "walk about in darkness" (Ps. 82:5). Jesus used this passage in response to those who accused Him of blasphemy. Essentially, Jesus asked why, when human rulers were called gods, "The one whom the Father set apart as His very own and sent into the world" (Jn. 10:36) was blaspheming by claiming to be God's Son. In sum, anyone else but God (Jesus), claiming deity, is committing blasphemy.

Alongside the false teaching stating that believers are little gods, coming from the same group of confused Charismatics is reconstructionism or dominionism. Reconstructionism states believers are to take dominion over seven mountains culture-shaping influence, made up of:

1. Media,
2. Government,
3. Education,
4. Economy,
5. Family,
6. Religion, and
7. Celebration (arts and entertainment)

Essentially, reconstructionism is religious rubbish attempting to recreate and re-establish what was lost in the garden of Eden, instead of looking forward to what Jesus will recreate and re-establish in the future, during the millennial dispensation. Reconstructionism overlooks the fact that Satan is the prince (Eph. 2:2), ruler (Jn. 14:30, 16:11), and god of this world (2 Cor. 4:4), not and never Christians this side of Jesus' return. Reconstructionism goes hand-in-hand with the doctrine of 'little gods' due to having a focus on the god of 'self' by dominating instead of enduring in this world (cf. 1 Cor. 4:11-13, 1 Cor. 10:13, 2 Tim. 2:11-13, 1 Pet. 2:20). If you are attempting to dominate this world as reconstructionism teaches, then by default, you are following the ruler of this world; therefore, you are serving Satan, not God.

Reiterated, if you have been deceived by dominionism, you have come under, and are submitted to, false antichrist teaching. The promise for believers is that in this world, we will have trouble (Jn. 16:33), which runs in the opposite direction to the teaching of dominionism. Having trouble in this world was the expectation, and the experience for Shadrach, Meshach, and Abednego, as it was with the disciples of Jesus Christ.

In conclusion, in the same way Nebuchadnezzar has set himself up as God (not a god), the antichrist will do likewise. King Nebuchadnezzar's failings repeat those of Adam and Eve in the garden but were not repeated by Jesus. Like Jesus, Shadrach, Meshach, and Abednego refused to fall down and worship a false god, as is the requirement of every believer today. Today, false gods can include 'self' and are very much at the centre of the false 'little god's' doctrine, promoted by the prosperity-driven Word of Faith movement. The (false) god's doctrine can be summed up as a doctrine of demons (1 Tim. 4:1).

The Laodicean church is an excellent example of a prosperity-driven church, representing the lukewarm church today within the prophetic calendar as the last church before Jesus returns. Likewise, the Laodiceans put themselves on the same level as God, ruling in replacement of God and substituting God's glory with gold. The Laodicean church failed where Jesus was triumphant (Matt. 4:1-11). Due to bowing down to the god of materialism, this lukewarm church had everything, and no need for anything, including Jesus, following in the footsteps of Israel. Due to Idolatry, Israel broke God's heart (Ezek. 6:9), in the same way the church does today (Ja. 4:4-5), which will result in judgement (cf. Ezek. 7:1-13, Rev. 2-3, 6-19). Here lies the danger of false worship - false worship causes you to forsake, God, forget God, and then replace Him, even with yourself, as a (false) god.

Part Three
'Who Will Deliver You from My Hand?' (vv. 19-30)

Picking up from the previous section, King Nebuchadnezzar challenged the God of Shadrach, Meshach, and Abednego by stating, moreover asking, "Who will deliver you from my hand" (3:15). By doing so, Nebuchadnezzar was positioning himself as God above every other. The evidence shows that the king had established himself apart from the other Babylonian gods as the primary deity to be worshipped (3:12). Further supporting evidence is found in the king's statement where he said, "Blessed be the God of Shadrach, Meshach, and Abednego, who has sent his angel and delivered his servants, who trusted in him, and set aside the king's command, and yielded up their bodies rather than serve and worship any god except their own God" (3:28). In this case, the reference to 'any other god' was the golden image that Nebuchadnezzar had set up of himself (3:1-7).

Nebuchadnezzar's claim of deity and the pompous statement was quickly countered by Shadrach, Meshach, and Abednego, frustrating the challenge by acknowledging the one true God, 'the God of gods' (2:47), and His ability, alone to deliver (3:17).

Shadrach, Meshach, and Abednego's response not only frustrated the king but infuriated him (3:19), further supporting his claim to be God (not another god). The king was so filled with fury, in the heat of the moment (3:22), he ordered that the three Jews be thrown into the fiery furnace, but not before ordering the furnace to be heated seven times more (3:19). As a result, the furnace temperature rose quickly, and the three Jews were thrown in. Usually, before being thrown into the furnace, the victims would have first been stripped of their clothing, but due to the king's haste, the three Jews remained fully clothed (3:21, 27), even bound (tied) with their clothes (3:20, 23, 24, 25). The sudden and significant temperature increase caused the furnace to overheat, killing the king's soldiers as they threw Shadrach, Meshach, and Abednego into the fire (3:22).

As fast as the king had Shadrach, Meshach, and Abednego thrown into the fire, he was just as quick to rise and declare that there was another in the furnace, alongside the three Jews (3:24). Although Nebuchadnezzar did not recognize the fourth person, he did discern that He was supernatural (3:25, 28). Interestingly, the king's choice of words is significant of Jesus, 'Like a son of the gods.'

Previously, Nebuchadnezzar acknowledged God (2:47), and now he references Jesus Christ, unbeknownst to him. The fourth person in the furnace was arguably Jesus Christ pre-incarnate. Further evidence of the king's recognition of the fourth person deity is in his declaration, "Shadrach, Meshach, and Abednego, servants of the Most High God, come out, and come here!" (3:26). Remember, up until this point, Nebuchadnezzar, the forgetful, had positioned himself as the God of gods, assuming none other could deliver from his hand (3:15). However, the God of the faithful Jews, as previously proclaimed (3:17), did deliver them from the fire and in doing so, also revealed Himself to the king (3:25).

The king's challenge (who will deliver you from my hand?) was met and overcome. As a result, Nebuchadnezzar acknowledged the God of Israel apart from any other by saying, "There is no other god who is able to rescue in this way." (3:29). The statement not only included every Babylonian god but also himself. Although the king had the power to throw someone into the fire (3:15), he could not deliver them. Only the Most High God could deliver someone from the fiery furnace.

The term "the Most High (lit., the Highest) God" or "the Most High" occurs thirteen times in Daniel, more than in any other book except Psalms. Of those thirteen occurrences, seven pertain to Nebuchadnezzar (3:26; 4:2, 17, 24–25, 32, 34) and two to Daniel/Belshazzar (5:18, 21). The other four are in chapter seven (7:18, 22, 25, 27).

Again, only the Most High God could deliver someone from the fire. In fact, only God can deliver and save any of us, period! (Isa. 43:11-13, 25, 44:6b, 8b, 22, 45:5, 6, 14c, 18c, 21c, 22, 46:9, 47:8b, 10c, 48:12 cf. Jn. 14:6, Acts 4:12).

The acknowledgment of God's sovereignty and superiority is a repeat of chapter two (2:47), where Nebuchadnezzar placed the God of Israel over and above every other God. In chapter one, the king had submitted the Most High to the Babylonian deities by placing the Jewish temple artifacts in the Babylonian temple (1:3). The purpose of doing so was to make a statement; the Babylonian deities have defeated Israel's God. In chapter two, the king later submitted to the God of Israel by stating He was the Lord of kings (2:47); therefore, God was king Nebuchadnezzar's Lord also, but for a time.

Previously stated, the king of Babylon was forgetful, as was Judah. The people of God had also forgotten their God - they had forsaken Him, and had even replaced him with others (Jer. 44:8, Ezek. 14:1-11, etc.). However, Shadrach, Meshach, and Abednego went against the flow by remaining faithful. Although they had no power over where and how they lived, they did have power and control over who and how they worshipped (3:12, 14, 18, 28), even if it meant going into the fire.

Fire tests faith, refining and purifying it (1 Pet. 1:7) yet also through it, suffer loss (1 Cor. 3:13, 15). Loss in the fire this side of glory is purposed to produce repentance (Ezek. 22:17-22). True and uncompromised worship comes at a cost (cf. Lu. 14:25-33), which involves fire (1 Pet. 1:7). Yet, compromise also comes at a price, as seen with five of the seven churches addressed in the book of Revelation (Rev. 2-3). A cost leading up to the tribulation is an exchange of pursuing your 'best life now,' for 'a better one to come' (Heb. 11:6b, 13:14). During the tribulation, the price will require your obedience unto death (Rev. 13-14).

Physical life was also at stake for the three Jews who were, at the time, in a position of privilege. They had a good life (3:49), and they could have maintained it (3:15), possibly even improved their lives (3:30). Nevertheless, they did not count their lives, or the treasures of this world comparable to the treasures of the following, which is analogous to Abraham, Moses, and many more, including Daniel (Heb. 11).

The writer of Hebrews, chapter eleven, makes the point clear; none of the listed heroes of the faith considered their lives when put to the test. None counted their life as anything, never mind their quality of life this side of heaven. Earth was not their 'best life now' (Heb. 11:26). Instead, they sought another, better existence (Heb. 11:14-16, 40, 13:14), which runs in the opposite direction to kingdom now 'theology.' Theology means the study and the knowledge of the nature of God; therefore, kingdom now 'ideology' fails to qualify as theology.

Hebrews chapter eleven, like many others, makes short work of kingdom now ideology. Kingdom now ideology is otherwise known as reconstructionism or dominionism, which focuses on the seven mountains of worldly influence. Enough has already been said about reconstructionism. Therefore, I will not repeat it here, other than to say this: reconstructionism/dominionism (ruling and reigning here and now – kingdom now ideology) was the furthermost thing from any of the faith heroes' thinking, such as the minds of Shadrach, Meshach, and Abednego. The same is true of Jesus, and His disciples, which include anyone else, alongside the twelve, calling themselves Christian. Simply put: this world is not your home; but if it is, then the God of heaven is not your God! (Heb. 11:14, Ja. 4:4, 1 Jn. 2:15-17).

Shadrach, Meshach, and Abednego had no regard for this world and neither their lives in it, yet God delivered them to proclaim His name.

God's name is revealed all the more where not a hair on their heads is harmed, and not even the clothes on three Jews' backs were singed, and neither did they smell of smoke (Dan. 3:27). This incident is not an example to support the false teaching that God will deliver everyone from harm (cf. Is 43:2, Heb. 11:34); clearly, He does not (cf. Heb 11:35b-39). The incident is, however, a model for remaining faithful when tested, which is also the point and purpose of Hebrews, chapter eleven.

When faith comes under fire, our testimonies are on open display, and our Christian witness can make the difference between life and death for us and for others. In the case of Shadrach, Meshach, and Abednego, by holding fast and remaining faithful (cf. Rev. 2:10, 3:11) Nebuchadnezzar (also representing the religious and the world) once again had an opportunity to acknowledge God. So convinced of the Most High, the king threatened anyone within the kingdom with death if they even spoke against the God of Israel (3:29).

For Shadrach, Meshach, and Abednego's faithfulness and courage, the king promoted them again (3:30), which is not the point and purpose of the story, as some within the Word of Faith movement have falsely claimed. Again, the big idea of the chapter is faithfulness; our faithfulness towards God, and His faithfulness towards us (3:17, cf. 2 Tim. 2:11-13). In a time when Israel was faithless, just a remnant of the Jews remained faithful. The same is true today within the church.

Looking forward: The incident of Daniel chapter three, involving Shadrach, Meshach, and Abednego has prophetic significance for us as well, yet more so for those 'left behind.' In the coming tribulation, a Gentile ruler (Dan. 7:8) will set up an image and demand worship as God (2 Thess. 2:4; Rev. 13:8). Anyone who refuses to acknowledge and worship him will be put to death (Rev. 13:15). In the same way, Nebuchadnezzar did, the coming ruler will assume political and religious power, and will target and oppress Israel (Rev. 13:7). During the tribulation, most, including many in Israel, will submit to and worship the Gentile ruler.

However, a remnant will refuse, like the three in Daniel's day. Those who refuse to worship the Gentile ruler, who is the antichrist, will be martyred for their faithfulness to Jesus Christ (Rev. 12:12, 13:10, 15, 14:13, 20:4). Just a few will be delivered from the persecutions of the Lord Jesus Christ's tribulation at His second coming. So bad will the tribulation be (Dan. 12:1, Joel 2:2, Matt. 24:21, Mk. 13:9), the blessed die early (Rev. 14:13).

However, during the tribulation, God will do again for the believing remnant what He did for Daniel's three companions. Shadrach, Meshach, and Abednego withstood the king's decree. Although they were not exempt from suffering and oppression, they were delivered out of it (which will be through death during the tribulation). Deliverance in the tribulation comes through repentance and death (Rev. 6:11, 7:9, 14, 14:13, 20:4, cf. Dan 12:10).

The story of Shadrach, Meshach, and Abednego serves any and all, leading up to, and going through tribulation, with comfort, consolation, and instruction. Moreover, it serves to warn, faithfulness is not optional; it is required (cf. Heb. 10:38, 11:6, Matt. 10:22, 13:21, 24:13, Rev. 13:10, 14:12).

Chapter Four

Part One

'That the Living May Know that the Most High Rules'
(vv. 1-18)

The Nebuchadnezzar of chapters one to four reigned for forty-three years (605–562 B.C.). We know from chapter one that he was in his second year of reign, and from chapter three, he was in his eighteenth year. Now in chapter four, several years more have passed from the events of chapter three. It is commonly thought that chapter four's announcement may have taken place in the thirty-fifth year of Nebuchadnezzar's rule, or about 570 B.C., which suggests upwards of around twenty years have passed between the incident of the fiery furnace and now. Some twenty years later, much has changed with, and in king Nebuchadnezzar, evident by the statement in verses one to three.

"All people, nations, and languages that dwell on the earth: Peace be multiplied to you!" (4:1). Much can be said about these opening verses of this chapter. For starters, this is not the Nebuchadnezzar we have seen in the previous chapters, who threatened to tear people limb from limb (2:5, 3:29), or throw those who did not worship him, into a fiery furnace (3:6, 8, 11, 15). Instead of threats, this king proclaims 'Peace!' Next, the same king who had previously set himself up to be worshipped, commanding all peoples, nations, and languages would fall down and worship him, are now invited to see the signs and wonders (that seem good to Nebuchadnezzar) that the Most High has done for Him. The opening statement is the king's testimony, linked to the concluding verses (vv. 34-37). The verses in-between are what 'seemed good to the king' (v. 2), which was his humbling by and before God, for the purpose of salvation.

Nebuchadnezzar's humbling came from his pride, which resulted in the third sign from God (v. 2). Before chapter four, the king already encountered two respective signs and wonders through 1). Daniel revealing and interpreting the dream (1:17-45) and through 2). the deliverance of Daniel's three companions from the fiery furnace (3:24-29). Through these two events, the king acknowledged Israel's God as the Most High (2:24, 3:29). Chapter four will provide the king with his third sign and revelation of God, which will, once again, cause him to acknowledge Him (4:34- 37), only this time through repentance (4:27).

From the opening statement in chapter four (vv. 1-3), linked with the closing statement (vv. 34-37), it is clear to see the king, through tribulation, did put his trust in the one true God. The verses in-between (vv. 4-33) show just how far off track he was before God humbled him.

From verse four, we see that once again, Nebuchadnezzar summoned Daniel to interpret (4:8, cf. 2:36). However, not before the wise men first attempted to interpret the dream (4:6-7). Before the king consulted with Daniel, the chief magician (4:9), consulted with the magicians, the enchanters, the Chaldeans, and the astrologers, who could not interpret dreams (2:27). Consulting with the wise men provides sufficient evidence (cf. 1 Cor, 15:33) that the king had not put his trust in the Most High, and, at the time, neither did he consider Daniel anything other than another, albeit more powerful magician. In sum, the king had surrounded himself with a mixed counsel of fools, which was the root cause of his ongoing deception.

Paul addressed the problem of tolerating mixed counsel by saying, "Bad company corrupts good character," which implies, false teachers will influence you negatively - therefore they should be avoided at all costs (cf. 2 Cor. 6:14–7:1). False teachers always claim great knowledge, as Nebuchadnezzar's magicians did, yet are ignorant of God (cf. 1 Cor. 8:2, 2 Pet. 2:17-18). Due to the deceptive nature, therefore the danger false teachers present, Paul instructs the church to have nothing to do with them. John agrees, saying, "Do not even let them enter your home" (2 Jn. 1:10), which also includes bringing their material into your home, or letting them enter in by watching them on 'Christian' T.V., and through the internet. Due to a continuation of the problem in the church of Corinth, in his second letter, Paul adds, "You gladly tolerate fools, since you are wise" (2 Cor. 11:19), which is where the saying, 'I/ you do not suffer fools gladly,' comes from.

Like the 'wise' Corinthians who were easily deceived (cf. 2 Cor. 11:3), Nebuchadnezzar was also, (before being humbled by God) still consulting with sorcerers and believing Daniel to be operating through his own god (4:9), perhaps Bel, alias Marduk, who he renamed after (4:8).

Daniel, the chef magician (soothsayer-priest) was thought to be not just operating through the king's god, but through many holy gods (cf. 4:9, 18; 5:11, 14). While it was said, the words 'holy gods' refers to God (Elohim), with 'gods' (plural) implying 'three times holy,' the Hebrew word 'holy' was translated 'angel,' and the word 'gods' (Heb. elah), refers to deity. The same word for gods was also used by Jeremiah (10:11), saying, "The gods who did not make the heavens and the earth shall perish from the earth and from under the heavens."

When considering the language of the text, it is unlikely the reference of 'holy gods' is positive, but rather suggests 'angel-gods' or demons (cf. 2 Cor. 11:14). The context also supports this conclusion, meaning the term 'holy gods' refers to demon-gods. Remember, Nebuchadnezzar does not know God, like the foolish teachers Paul addressed. Like the foolish Corinthians, Nebuchadnezzar was a fool led by fools! Nebuchadnezzar was both ignorant and polytheistic, although he had acknowledged God's sovereignty years before (2:47; 3:28–29).

However, while the king was not where he needed to be, there is still some evidence he was not where he used to be. In chapter four, the now twice failed (2:10, 4:7) magicians, the enchanters, the Chaldeans, and the astrologers were dismissed when coming up empty-handed. Previously they were sentenced to death (2:9, 12-13), and they would have been executed if Daniel/God did not come through, saving them (2:16, 18, 24). Twice (100%), the sorcerers failed, and twice (100%), Daniel was successful. On both occasions, Daniel's success came through his ability to interpret dreams, which is the theme of chapter four.

Once again, God revealed Himself to the king through a dream, which on both accounts, troubled (2:1, 3, 30) and terrified him (4:5), and for a good reason (4:19), yet not without cause (4:27, cf. Rev. 1:17). The first dream revealed the things to come, surpassing even our day, ending with the return of Jesus Christ. The second dream was much closer to home, involving none other than Nebuchadnezzar himself.

The language of the dream is symbolic, as with all recorded dreams in the Bible. There are over fifty dreams in the Bible, which are also in the form of a vision. Outside of Scripture, dreams and visions are a primary way God communicates with us, generally through the language of the heart, which is symbolic. Prophecy is often the same, using symbols to reveal and display a current and, or future event. Prophetic dreams are also known as words of knowledge (present) and words of wisdom (future). Nebuchadnezzar saw a vision in his head, which was a dream (4:9-10, 13) that combined both the revelation of a current condition (pride) and the future consequence (seven years of tribulation) unless repentance came first (4:27).

The dream used symbolic language connecting a recent trip to Lebanon and the eyewitness accounts with himself. While in Lebanon, the king saw the mighty trees, their size (v. 4:10), strength (4:11), and beauty, full of abundant fruit that supplied food and refuge for all (4:12). Following the tree's symbolic reference, Nebuchadnezzar saw a watcher, a holy one, come down from heaven (4:13). While the king understood the tree's literal application, he was also familiar with the following image, the watcher.

Some twenty years earlier, he witnessed an 'angel' deliver Daniel's three companions from his own hand (3:15) and the fiery furnace (3:28). The king unknowingly referenced Jesus, by likening the angel to a "son of the gods" (3:25). Again, we see the pluralistic reference of 'gods' demonstrating Nebuchadnezzar's inability to discern God and demons apart. Regardless, the angel (Jesus) who had previously delivered the faithful Jews is now warning of judgement, seven years of it (4:16, 23, 25, 32), unless repentance comes first (4:27). The reference 'seven periods of time' means seven years (cf. 7:25). For seven years, everything of the tree would be cut down and destroyed, causing panic and chaos, leaving only the shackled stump behind (4:14-16).

While the first part of the dream (4:10-12) would not have troubled (4:5) the king; however, the second part did (4:13-15a), the third part even more so (4:15b-16), especially if he had identified that the tree was symbolic of himself. However, the purpose of the dream was to save (4:27) rather than destroy. In order to save, the king had to first come to a saving knowledge of the Most High (4:17) through repentance (4:27), which required humbling himself before Almighty God (4:37).

To summarise: the passage, so far, could be summed up with the following:

- False worship (idolatry)
- Focus on self (pride)
- Consulting with sorcerers (a mixed counsel of fools)
- Warning of coming judgement
- Call for repentance
- Seven years of trouble (tribulation)
- That all would know that the Most High rules (not man)
- Everything destroyed, except the stump (saved remnant remaining)

The warning of judgement against king Nebuchadnezzar came as a result of false worship (4:7) lovelessness (4:27), and pride (4:30). While Nebuchadnezzar had previously had an encounter with God (twice), he did not yet know God, and consequently failed to place God in His rightful place (Most High, 4:17a) and himself in his proper place (lowliest, 4:17b). Sadly, many within the church today do the same. Although they proclaim a gospel, of sorts, they do not know God, evident by their self-promotion, resulting in false worship.

When comparing the 'gospel' of many today with Paul's gospel, it is clear, they are worlds apart. Paul writes his version of the gospel in his letter to the church of Corinth: "Now, brothers, I want to remind you of the gospel I preached to you, which you received, and in which you stand firm. By this gospel, you are saved if you hold firmly to the word I preached to you. Otherwise, you have believed in vain. For I delivered to you as of first importance what I also received: that Christ died for our sins in accordance with the Scriptures, that he was buried, that he was raised on the third day in accordance with the Scriptures" (1 Cor. 15:2-4). Note the centrality of the gospel, Jesus Christ, and the conditional IF! You are only saved IF you hold firmly to the word (Jesus) Paul preached, which is a far cry from what is often proclaimed today. Like the self-consumed, demon consulting Nebuchadnezzar!

Application: Nebuchadnezzar's treatment of God is repeated by many today, committing the same error by having a focus on self, resulting in false worship. By doing so we make little God and much of ourselves. The church of Laodicea did the same also, serving as a prophetic condition of the last church before Jesus returns. For the same reason Nebuchadnezzar was warned, the church has also been warned (Rev. 2-3) and will soon be judged in the same manner (4:28-33, Rev. 6-19) for failing to heed the warning through repentance.

The purpose of the prophetic dream was to reveal God's true nature to Nebuchadnezzar, which is also the purpose of scripture today. The book of Daniel, chapters two, seven to twelve, and the book of Revelation, in particular, serves this end. Despite most having a false perception of who God is and what true worship looks like, although they [falsely] proclaim His name, God will continue to attempt to turn them around, even in the coming tribulation, if necessary.

Part Two

'That the Living May Know that the Most High Rules' (vv. 19-27)

In the previous section, we considered Nebuchadnezzar's shared delusion with many today against the gospel of Christ, as proclaimed through Paul. When considering Paul's gospel against much of what is declared today, they are two very different gospels (cf. 2 Cor. 11:4). In the same way, Nebuchadnezzar thought he was saved (right with God), he was not, hence came the warning of judgement.

The same is true today, which was also the warning to the seven churches addressed in the book of Revelation (Rev. 2-3). They also thought they were 'right with God,' when, in fact, they were in danger of being cut down and cast into the great tribulation unless repentance came first.

Nebuchadnezzar's degree of error is evident where he sought understanding of the dream by summoning the wise men to interpret it, and then called Daniel when they could not. At first, Daniel was perhaps reluctant to translate the second dream, unlike with the first dream that exalted the king (2:38), as the head of gold.

The interpretation of the first dream lifted the king up, and the second prophesied that God was about to cut him down (4:14). However, before the bad news came, there was some good news (like the letters to the seven churches). Daniel stated that the king had become strong, reaching the heavens, visible to all in the whole world, that what he had established was beautiful, abounding in fruit that was food for the entire world. Nebuchadnezzar's kingdom had also provided shelter for all of humanity (4:20-21).

Going by the introduction of the dream alone, it would be easy to conclude this king was ticking all the right boxes. The same was true with the letter to the church of Ephesus (Rev. 2:1-7). However, both Nebuchadnezzar and the church of Ephesus were in danger of judgement unless repentance came first (4:27, Rev. 2:5). Like Ephesus's church, Nebuchadnezzar's report indicated he was stronger than any other around or before him, but now comes the bad news (4:23-25). This mighty king was about to lose what he had by being removed from his position, just like with the loveless church of Ephesus (Rev. 2:5b, cf. Dan. 4:27b). The command for the church of Ephesus was that, through repentance, they remember and return to God, or else (Rev. 2:4-5). The same was true for Nebuchadnezzar, who previously acknowledged the Most High (2:47, 3:29).

Note, through judgement, that the kingdom would not be destroyed but that Nebuchadnezzar would be removed for a time. The same for churches, and Christians, where some will be removed, and even lost, but the kingdom will remain forever. Like Nebuchadnezzar, who was under the threat of judgement by way of going through tribulation for seven years (4:16, 23, 25, 32), so are self-serving churches (7:25, 9:27, Rev. 2-3, 3:10, 11:42, 12:6, 14, 13:5).

Like with the churches (Rev. 2-3), Nebuchadnezzar's tribulation would be executed by Jesus (4:23), which was designed to humble the boastful king (4:25b, 30). Interestingly, a component of Nebuchadnezzar's judgement was that he would act like an animal. Within the last two decades, churches within the Charismatic movement have behaved similarly, barking like dogs, grunting like pigs, chipping, quaking, squawking, and flapping like birds. Others would roar like lions. Again, others would laugh and roll around on the ground uncontrollably, like a madman. These phenomena were said to be a move of the Spirit yet reduced man to the lowest level of creation, like with Nebuchadnezzar. This behaviour is like the mental illness known as zoanthropy (an illness observed in modern times), where a person thinks of himself as an animal and acts like one.

Not only would the king be reduced to the lowest of creation, adding to the humiliation, but he would also be shackled with iron and brass, like an animal owned (4:15, 23). The iron and brass would also prevent Nebuchadnezzar from growing, whereas before, he had become a great, strong, tall, beautiful, and fruitful tree. The band would also serve to secure him for future restoration.

The purpose of the condition is summed up in verse seventeen "The sentence is by the decree of the watchers, the decision by the word of the holy ones, to the end that the living may know that the Most High rules the kingdom of men and gives it to whom he will and sets over it the lowliest of men." Upon repentance and acknowledgement, the king would be restored (4:26b, 34-37).

Verses seventeen and twenty-five sum up the entire chapter and Bible - man, who thinks he rules and reigns, is to be humbled that he may know and submit to the true ruling and reigning King, Jesus Christ. As a result of pride, Nebuchadnezzar was given a suspended seven-year sentence hanging over his head; it could have been avoided if repentance came first but that was the not case. Nebuchadnezzar's experience will be shared by most living in this day, for the same reason.

Through the king's time of trouble, although he would be reduced to nothing, a stump would remain. Again the stump indicated that Nebuchadnezzar would be restored following repentance, which will be the exact condition and requirement within the great tribulation. Before restoration came, Nebuchadnezzar had to first acknowledge that God ruled the heavens, not man (4:26b, 34-35, 37).

Remember, before judgement fell, Daniel concluded by urging the king to renounce his sins (4:27). This points out the principle that any announced judgement may be averted if there is repentance (cf. the book of Jonah). Daniel urged Nebuchadnezzar to turn from his sinful pride and produce fruits of righteousness (doing what is right and being kind to the oppressed)—acts that stem from a submissive heart to God. Had Nebuchadnezzar done so, he would have averted seven years of tribulation. The same message was given to the seven churches in the book of Revelation (2-3), for the same reason: "That the living may know that the Most High rules the kingdom of men" (4:17, 25, cf. 37).

The problem facing Nebuchadnezzar is the shared problem for us today, pride (4:37). Pride blinded the king and brought about his fall (Prov. 16:18). God chopped Nebuchadnezzar down to humble him but then restored him following repentance (4:36). Humility is critical, bearing the fruit of repentance.

Contrary to Nebuchadnezzar's view of himself (high) and of God (low), the gospel of Paul points to Jesus who took the path of humility (Phil 2:8), and in return, bore much fruit (Jn. 12:24-26), resulting in an everlasting kingdom that greatly surpassed Nebuchadnezzar's (cf. Matt. 13:32, Mk. 4:32, Lu. 13:19). Of the everlasting kingdom, Jesus is the Vine, and we who follow Him (as long as we remain in Him, Jn. 15:6, 10, 14) are the branches that bear much fruit (Jn. 15:5, 16).

Contrary to prideful Nebuchadnezzar, Jesus humbled Himself (Phil 2:8), He died for our sin (Jn. 3:14-15, Rom. 5:6-8, 1 Cor. 5:14, 21, Gal 1:4, 3:13), but He rose again; He has Risen! (Matt. 26:8). Those who follow Christ by dying to self, are alive unto God, through Christ Jesus (Rom. 6:11, read the entire chapter). According to Paul (1 Cor. 15:1-11), THIS is THE GOSPEL, which is worlds apart from Nebuchadnezzar's previous view of God, revolving around self, due to being puffed up with pride.

Due to pride, God humbled Nebuchadnezzar, which was true also for Israel and Judah. Like Nebuchadnezzar, they too went well off track, resulting in their humiliation. However, while in 'tribulation' (Lam.

3:5), through God's love, mercy, and grace, following repentance (Lam. 3:18-41), they too received the promise of being restored (Ezek. 17:22-24), despite being temporarily (even to this day) blinded (Rom. 11). God's promise to Israel is that He will first prune her, that she will in time produce much fruit, that all will know that Jesus/God is the Lord (Ezek. 17:24).

Although Israel was temporarily set aside, God will bring her back into His redemptive plan after the Gentiles' full number have come in (Rom. 11:25). Once the total number of Gentiles (converted Christians) have come in (salvation), the church will be taken out of the way (raptured, 2 Thess. 2:7), and then, Israel's eyes will be opened (in the tribulation, Rev. 7), and then they too will be saved (Rom. 11:26-27).

However, in the meantime, the church is also warned not to follow in the footsteps of Israel, or else she too will share in the same humiliation (Rom. 11:22), which will be administered through the great tribulation to bring about repentance. The point and purpose of the great tribulation are to make God known. The churches addressed (representing all) in the book of Revelation (2-3) were warned that unless repentance comes first, they will be judged, just like Israel, Judah, and Nebuchadnezzar were. During the tribulation, the left behind (people ruling) church, alongside Israel, will then "Know that the Most High rules the kingdom of men."

Conclusion: The problem with Nebuchadnezzar is the shared problem today. Although many confess to have had an encounter and therefore knowledge of God, they do not know Him (cf. Matt. 7:21-23), evident by not obeying Him (Lu. 6:46). As a result, the same outcome will be shared, which will be seven years of tribulation (Rev. 6-19), that some will humble themselves through repentance and come to saving knowledge of God.

Part Three
'Humiliation and Restoration' (vv. 28-37)

Part two and three of chapter four considered the dream and its interpretation. The third section of this chapter will look again at the reason, the fulfilment and the reality of the prophecy (4:33). Remember, the root cause of the problem for Nebuchadnezzar is pride (4:37), resulting in false worship (self-righteousness) and lovelessness (4:27). You could also argue that Nebuchadnezzar was further blinded by prosperity (4:4, 30), which he could have kept if he had humbled himself through repentance (4:27). The evidence for the above statement is seen in verse thirty-six, where the king's prosperity was returned to him only after acknowledging God through repentance.

Important to note is that prosperity in itself is not the problem. Money is not the root of all evil - the love of money is (1 Tim. 6:10). Consider the context of Paul's reference to the love of money (1 Tim 6:3-10); here, Paul addresses the false prosperity teachers of his time. Like Nebuchadnezzar, false teachers fix their eyes on themselves and materialism, even imagining 'godliness is a means to gain' (1 Tim. 6:5). The desisre to be rich (1 Tim. 6:9), false teachers teach 'different doctrine' (1 Tim. 6:3), and 'another gospel' (2 Cor. 11:4), plunging people into ruin and destruction (1 Tim. 6:9).

Today is worse than when Paul wrote to Timothy in the church of Ephesus where people then, and more so now, are consumed with and in love with themselves (2 Tim. 3:2). The context of Paul's second letter to Timothy, referencing 'lovers of self' (2 Tim. 3:1-9) include the love of money, among other traits that were attributed to Nebuchadnezzar

(2 Tim. 3:2). Like with Paul's first reference (1 Tim. 6:10), his second (2 Tim. 3:2) was aimed at the religious who have an 'appearance of godliness,' yet nothing more (2 Tim. 3:5). These are those who cherry-pick verses out of context to 'work the word' in their favour. They merchandise God, and the people of God, for their own greedy gain. Seed-picking is what the false teachers accused Paul of in Acts (17:18).

On the contrary, it was not Paul who was the seed-picker, but his accusers, wanting to hear the latest teaching, picking and choosing what suited them, at the time. Nebuchadnezzar has a similar approach, cherry-picking what he liked while discarding the rest. Regarding Paul's comments, as mentioned above, the first reference (1 Tim. 6:10) speaks of the false teachers within his day, the second points to the false teachers in our day (2 Tim. 3:1), all caught up in pride and prosperity.

Nebuchadnezzar suffers the same deception, arguably contributed to by surrounding himself with sorcerers, 'wise men' claiming knowledge, yet were ignorant of God. False teachers always take the higher ground, claiming to be wise and at times know about God, but they do not know Him personally. The requirement of securing eternal life is to know God intimately (Jn. 17:3), not knowing about Him.

As for today's prosperity preachers, they are likened to Nebuchadnezzar's sorcerers, treating the Bible as a book of spells, working the word to meet and achieve their greedy desires to be rich (1 Tim. 6:9). Contrary to the false teaching of prosperity pimps, Paul says, "All who desire to live a godly life in Christ Jesus will be persecuted (not prosperous) (2 Tim. 3:12). Jesus said something similar, "In this life, you will have trouble" (Jn. 16:33). Paul's own testimony confirms that suffering is part of the package, causing us to rely on God and not on ourselves (2 Cor. 1:3-11). Later (2 Cor. 11:16-33), Paul boasts over his suffering and deliverance.

When comparing the gospels mentioned above (persecution and prosperity), it is clear that they are very different, and they have two very different outcomes. These two gospels are so far apart that you could never say one is like the other or even a different expression or understanding of the same thing. Simply put, if you believe one, you have to reject the other.

As mentioned earlier, Nebuchadnezzar cherry-picked what he liked and discarded the rest, like prosperity preachers, resulting in following 'another gospel' and was damned as a result, unless repentance came first. Nebuchadnezzar had been blinded, deceived, and seduced by pride. His pride led to a sense of entitlement and a false sense of peace and security. In the same way, God will humble today's prosperity-driven preachers; he humbled Nebuchadnezzar for salvation, resulting in restoration.

Despite the calling to repentance, twelve months later, while Nebuchadnezzar was gloating over his wealth and his accomplishments, in a single hour, it all came crumbling down (4:30). The same will be repeated for this generation during the great tribulation. In a single day (Rev. 18:8), and a single hour (Rev. 18:9, 10, 17, 19) the world system will be no more, no more, no more, no more, no more (Rev. 18:22-23).

Again, Nebuchadnezzar did first receive a time of grace (twelve months) before judgement fell. As with every dispensation, judgement always follows grace. The current age is known as the dispensation of grace (Eph. 3:2) yet will be followed by the worst judgement of all time (Jer. 30:6-7, Dan. 12:1, Matt. 24:21), taking most by surprise (Matt. 24:43, 1 Thess. 5:2, 2 Pet. 3:10, Rev. 3:3, 16:15).

Like so many today, Nebuchadnezzar, the forgetful, was so preoccupied with himself that he neglected to take heed of the warning. And, while the boastful king's words were still in his mouth, judgement fell swiftly. A voice from heaven announced what was previously prophesied and that it is now fulfilled (4:32). The same will be true of the tribulation, following the voice from heaven, saying, "Come up here" (1 Thess. 4:16, Rev. 4:1), triggering the rapture, the seven-year ordeal will then commence on earth sweeping up anyone who is not ready (Lu. 21:34-36, Rev. 6-19).

Like the above-mentioned, verse thirty-one also has a double reference, where God announced, "The kingdom has departed from you." Not 'will' depart, but 'has' departed! Instantaneous judgement was executed on the prideful, unrepentant king. The application for us today is the same. Many 'confessing' Christians believing they are secure within the kingdom will soon wake up realising that the kingdom has departed with the removal (rapture) of the church, leaving them behind to endure the seven-year tribulation.

Through and by the seven-year judgement of Nebuchadnezzar, God humbled him (4:32) for repentance, resulting in salvation and restoration (4:34-37). The king's repentant confession acknowledged God and His rule, His dominion, and His kingdom (4:34). Again, the same will be repeated during the coming tribulation (Rev. 11:15-18). Many confessing Christians ruling and reigning here and now (kingdom now theology = church of Laodicea) will receive a rude awakening through the tribulation. Realising their false perception of peace and prosperity has resulted in their humiliation by God and even their destruction (2 Thess. 2:9-12).

Following repentance, Nebuchadnezzar was restored, and his prosperity returned to him, similar to Job (Job 42); following repentance (Job 42:1-6), God restored Job (Job 42:10-16). God will do the same for Israel in the millennium (Ezek. 25-48), again, following repentance in the great tribulation (Rev. 6:9, 7:9-17, 11:13, 12:11, 14:13, 15:2-4, 20:4).

Remember, Nebuchadnezzar's same opportunity (grace) was also given to five of the seven churches addressed in the book of Revelation (2-3). Like Nebuchadnezzar, most quickly forget due to being preoccupied with themselves. Like so many people today (cf. 2 Pet. 3:1-13), Nebuchadnezzar probably thought judgement would never come (unlimited, unconditional grace), but it did, and it was swift. Like Nebuchadnezzar, many within the church will soon enter into seven years of tribulation, following a voice from heaven announcing the judgement.

In conclusion, as stated in previous sections, Nebuchadnezzar was blinded by pride due to following a false gospel that revolved around himself. The king was so self-consumed that he had lost sight of God, which is similar to the five churches addressed in the book of Revelation. The prideful prosperity-driven church of Laodicea was the worst, utterly void of God, yet 'worshipping' in His name. Here lies the danger in a self-centred gospel that focuses on meeting our desires moreover our needs.

Our need is for deliverance resulting in salvation through Christ Jesus, alone; that is 'the' gospel. Anything that distracts from Jesus is 'another gospel.' The desire to be rich and secure in this world is promoted by pride (self-worship), designed to distract and destroy. Nebuchadnezzar was only saved, thus eternally secured through tribulation, losing everything to gain the only thing that really mattered, God. The king came into a saving knowledge of God through tribulation, which could have been avoided. But due to failing to heed the warning, met with repentance, salvation was now only obtainable through humiliation. The same will be repeated for this generation, in the very near future, for the same reason.

CHAPTER SEVEN

PART ONE

'The Little Horn'
(vv. 1-8)

Following the chronological order of the book, chapter seven should be considered directly after chapter four. Chapter four addressed the pride, humiliation, and restoration of Nebuchadnezzar. Within twenty years after the king's restoration, he expired and was succeeded by his son, Belshazzar (7:1). Interestingly, through chapter three, Nebuchadnezzar is seen as a type of antichrist, promoting himself as a god, demanding worship. Chapter three is comparable with chapter seven which narrows in on the antichrist to come. The difference is, the antichrist to come will be unrepentant and therefore cast into hell (Rev. 19:20-21, 20:10), whereas Nebuchadnezzar did repent and was restored (4:34-37).

At the time of chapter four, Daniel was around fifty years old; now, he is about sixty-eight years old in chapter seven. Between chapters four and seven, some eighteen more years have passed, and another fourteen years will pass before the event of chapter six, where Daniel is thrown into the lion's den.

Before going into the events of chapter seven, it is essential to note the historical, literal, and prophetic nature of the book as confirmed by Jesus (Matt. 24:15). While all twelve chapters provide a literal and historical account of what happened some 2500 years ago, chapters two, seven, eight, nine, ten, eleven and twelve, are prophetic and historic, pointing towards a future event, still yet to take place in our time. For example, chapters two (v. 28) and ten (v. 14) use the words "latter days," referring to the end (cf. Lu. 21:24). Likewise, chapter seven reveals what will occur later, as do chapters eight, nine, ten, eleven, and twelve. Like chapter two (vv. 29, 45), chapter seven (vv. 6, 7, 24) uses the words "after this." Chapter two doubles up using the phrase "what is to be" (vv. 29, 29, 45).

As mentioned above, both Nebuchadnezzar and Daniel saw in a dream the very last days, ushering in the return of Jesus Christ. For both Nebuchadnezzar (2:45) and Daniel (cf. 8:17, 26, 12:4, 7, 9), not only will the dream be fulfilled well after their time, but well after the reign of the Babylonian kingdom, confirmed in verse forty-four, "In the days of those kings." This reference refers to those conquering Babylon, who will be defeated along with any other earthly kingdom followed by 'God setting up a kingdom that shall never be destroyed, nor shall that kingdom be left to another people' (v. 44a). The statement refers to the kingdom that Jesus establishes upon His return, confirmed by the words, "It shall stand forever" (2:44b). Chapter seven picks up the same referencing the future millennial kingdom (vv. 13-14, 18, 27), following the judgment and destruction of the last earthly dominion and kingdom (7:12, 26).

Before the final kingdom is established, Daniel saw four others, first described as 'four winds' (7:2). The word 'winds' also translated as 'spirits,' which is seen numerous times elsewhere in scripture (Jer. 23:19, 49:36, 51:1, Zech. 6:1–6, 7:14, Rev. 7:1–3), providing insight into God's dealing with humanity, through angels. In the dream, Daniel saw that the four winds were stirring up the great sea, which is the Mediterranean Sea (Num. 34:6–7, Josh. 1:4; 9:1, 15:12, 47; 23:4, Ezek. 47:10, 15, 20, 48:28).

The importance of mentioning the great sea provides the specific location where the prophetic events will occur - the Mediterranean world, yet still impacting the whole world (7:6, 23, Rev. 3:10). Three of the predicted events have already come to pass; the fourth is about to be fulfilled and will be in the same literal manner the first three were.

Alongside the four winds are four great beasts, which came up out of the sea (7:3). Again, the specific location is significant, particularly when interpreting the last, yet to be fulfilled fourth beast. Verse seventeen reveals that the great beasts are kings. Verses four to seven provide information as to who they were, and history discloses what they did. Scripture and history confirm the beasts were literal men, which debunks the idea that the coming fourth beast will be a system and not a man, as some suggest. The dream's interpretation narrows in on the fourth, yet to be fulfilled and revealed, beast (vv. 17-25), who is the man of sin (2 Thess. 2:3), the antichrist to come, sharing the same qualities of the three beasts preceding him (Rev. 13:2).

The first of the three beasts preceding the fourth was like a lion (power), having eagles' wings (swiftness). Interestingly the lion and eagle were both symbols of Babylon (cf. Jer. 4:7, 13; Ezek. 17:3). The first beast lost its wings (swiftness) and took on the appearance of a man, which could suggest that it became more humane, which was undoubtedly the case with Nebuchadnezzar, as seen in chapter four. Contrary to Nebuchadnezzar, a type of antichrist, the coming antichrist will become more beasty, possessed by Satan (2 Thess. 2:9, Rev. 13:3-4).

The second beast was like a bear (strength), following the lion. As stated above, the lion (first) and the bear (second) will be eventually succeeded by the fourth beast, which is the little horn (7:8, 8:9). The little horn is the Satan (serpent) empowered and resurrected antichrist. Amos

(5:19) describes what the tribulation will be like for those left behind, interestingly referring to the lion, bear, and serpent. However, before the antichrist, a third beast was like a leopard (fast and swift). The first beast was Babylon, the second Medo-Persia, and the third was Greece. When Greece conquered Medo-Persia, it did so with great speed. A few years after Alexander died, his kingdom was divided into four parts (cf. Dan. 8:8, 22). Greece was later succeeded by Rome, which was the sixth king at the time of John's writing (Rev. 17:10). Unlike John, Daniel does not address the kingdoms before Babylon or after Greece, apart from the ten nations and the little horn. John's reference refers to the:

1. Egyptians
2. Assyrians
3. Babylonians
4. Medo-Persians
5. Greeks
6. Roman Empire
7. Revived Roman Empire
8. The antichrist

On both accounts (Daniel and John), it is the fourth beast (7:7, 19, 23) and the eighth beast (Rev. 17:11) that they narrow in on. The fourth and eighth beasts are the same, being the antichrist to come. With each of the four beasts (kings), Daniel describes who they are and how they operate. The first three beasts mentioned were incredibly powerful, conquering kings and kingdoms at ease. However, they will all be dwarfed by the fourth. The fourth is likened to a mongrel-mix of the others (Rev. 13:2), yet different again, having the dragon's (Satan) power (2 Thess. 2:9, Rev. 13:4-5).

So consumed with the fourth, Daniel was not interested in the first three beasts. The fourth was overwhelming in that it was different from the rest, being terrifying, dreadful, and exceedingly strong (7:7). A unique characteristic of the fourth beast was its horns, particularly the little horn that came up among the others (7:8). So powerful will this fourth beast be, nothing, and no one will stand in its way (7:19). And, not surprisingly as it is God who sends him (7:5b, 2 Thess. 2:11). The antichrist will be God's servant, in the same way Nebuchadnezzar was when God sent him to punish Judah (Jer. 25:9, 27:6).

The ten horns of the fourth beast represent ten kings (7:24), from which the little horn (antichrist) will rise (7:25). Again, these kings rise up from the Mediterranean region. Sometime after formation, shortly, the little horn will uproot three of the ten horns/kings. The term 'little horn' signifies an insignificant beginning. The antichrist will appear insignificant and humble initially. Still, he will not remain that way for long, evident by his quick rise to power and ability to uproot three other kings. Alongside his strength/power, the little horn is also known for his intelligence (it had the eyes of a man) and his blasphemous claims (7:8, 11, 20, 25, 2 Thess. 2:4, Rev. 13:5-6), providing further support of a literal man, not a system.

Although little is mentioned of the coming antichrist today from most pulpits, the Bible has much to say about him. Several names and titles throughout scripture know the antichrist. These names provide a glimpse into the many facets of his diabolical character. For example, he is the beast (Rev. 13:1); the man of sin (2 Thess. 2:3); the lawless one (2 Thess. 2:8); the abomination (Matt. 24:15); the little horn (Dan. 7:8); the prince (of darkness) who is to come (Dan. 9:26); the vile person (Dan. 11:21); and a king [who does] according to his covenant, commencing the tribulation. While no one knows who the antichrist is yet, we can confidently assume that he is very much alive and active today (1 Jn. 2:18-19), preparing for a time, times, and a half a time (7:25).

Alongside the book of Daniel, the period of a time, times, and half a time, is also mentioned in the book of Revelation, chapter twelve, verse fourteen. According to Revelation twelve, verse six, this time equals 1,260 prophetic days times twice, equalling seven years. In Bible prophecy, one prophetic day equals one literal year (cf. Num. 14:34; Ps. 90:4, Ezek. 4:6, 2 Pet. 3:8), implying, the little horn will reign supreme for 1,260 days, or forty-two months times twice, dividing up the first and second part of the tribulation. Revelation, chapter eleven (vv. 2-3), and chapter thirteen (v. 5) support the same. In sum, the antichrist will rule for a total period of seven years (Isa. 26:15, 18, Dan. 7:6b, 25, 9:24-27, 12:7, Rev. 12:14), which is the entire duration of the tribulation.

The coming antichrist will have dominion for seven years. However, he will not be revealed until after the rebellion comes first (2 Thess. 2:3), which is the great falling away, leading into the tribulation. The great falling away refers to the apostate church, mainstreaming worldly worship, the absence of God (cf. church of Laodicea), yet, for a time, promoting (another) Jesus, (2 Cor. 11:4) conditioning followers for the counterfeit-Christ to come (Matt. 24:5, 23-26, Rev. 3:15-20).

The most significant sign of the antichrist's time is the great apostasy of the church, resulting in the apostates being 'left behind,' due to not being ready (Matt. 24:44, Lu. 12:25, 40, 47), therefore missing the rapture. The rapture will remove the obedience, ready believers (2 Thess. 2:7), which will reveal the antichrist in and through the tribulation. The commencement of the tribulation will be triggered by the signing of the (false) peace treaty (Isa. 28:15, 18, Dan. 9:24-27) simultaneously occurring alongside the rapture. During the tribulation, the antichrist is identified by several key characteristics.

The following lists twenty-seven deeds and characteristics of the Antichrist:

1. He comes from among ten kings in the revived Roman Empire; his authority will have similarities to the ancient Babylonians, Persians, and Greeks [Dan. 7:24, Rev 13:2 / Dan. 7:7]

2. He will subdue three kings [Dan. 7:8, 24]
3. He is different from the other kings [Dan. 7:24]
4. At first, he will appear to be insignificant, a "little horn" [Dan. 7:8]
5. He will speak boastfully [Dan. 7:8; Rev 13:5]
6. He will blaspheme God, [Dan. 7:25; 11:36; Rev 13:5] slandering His Name, dwelling place, and departed Christians and Old Testament saints [Rev 13:6]
7. He will persecute the saints [Dan. 7:25; Rev 13:7]
8. He will change the calendar, perhaps to define a new era, related to himself [Dan. 7:25]
9. He will change the laws to suit himself [Dan. 7:25]
10. No other earthly ruler will succeed him, but Jesus Christ alone [Dan. 7:26-27]
11. He will confirm a covenant with "many", i.e., the Jewish people [Dan. 9:27] This covenant will likely involve the establishment of a Jewish Temple in Jerusalem [see Dan. 9:27; Matt 24:15]
12. He will put an end to Jewish sacrifice and offerings after 3 ½ years and will set up an abomination to God in the Temple [Dan. 9:27, Matt. 24:15]
13. He will not answer to a higher earthly authority; "He will do as he pleases" [Dan. 11:36]
14. He will show no regard for the religion of his ancestors [Dan. 11:37]
15. He will not believe in any god [except himself] [Dan. 11:37]
16. He will have "no regard for the desire of women": The fact that he has no regard for the one desired by women suggests he repudiates the messianic hope of Israel. [Dan. 11:37]
17. He will claim to be greater than any god [Dan. 11:37; 2 Thess. 2:4]
18. He will claim to be God [2 Thess. 2:4]

19. He will rule like a Roman "god" of war. His whole focus and attention will be on his military. He will conquer lands and distribute them [Dan. 11:39-44]
20. His arrival on the world scene will be accompanied by miracles, signs, and wonders [2 Thess. 2:9]
21. He will claim to be the Christ [Matt 24:21-28]
22. He will claim that Jesus did not come in the flesh or that Jesus did not rise bodily from the grave [2 John 7]. He will deny that Jesus is the Messiah [I Jn. 2:22]
23. He will be worshipped by many people [Rev. 13:8]
24. He will destroy any competing religion, even the one that helps establish him [Rev. 17:16-18]
25. He will appear to survive a fatal injury [Rev. 13:3; 17:8]
26. His name will be related to the number six hundred and sixty-six—but not necessarily in an obvious fashion [Rev. 13:17-18].
27. He will be empowered by the devil himself [2 Thess. 2:9, Rev. 13:2]

Again, from the list above, it is clear that a coming antichrist is a literal man, not a system. The antichrist is a counterfeit Christ; in the same way, Jesus Christ was a literal man. The antichrist will be too, again, revealed by successfully signing a false covenant of peace within the Middle East, triggering the tribulation. He will break this (false) peace treaty forty-two months later, essentially, halfway through the seven years (Dan. 9:27b).

To summarise and add to the antichrist's characteristics as listed above, during the tribulation, he will rule the world (Dan. 7:23, 8:19-23; Rev. 13:7; 17:12-13). He will come in his own name (Jn. 5:43b); he will be eloquent and persuasive of speech (Dan. 7:20); he will be a leader of great charisma (Dan. 8:23), and he will operate in supernatural signs and wonders (2 Thess. 2:9; Rev. 13:13; 16:16; 19:20). The antichrist will have no regard for the God his fathers, being any god at all; neither will he have a desire for women (Dan. 11:37). Having no desire for women does not characterise him as a homosexual, but rather anti-women regarding the messianic hope (Gen. 3:15). Furthermore, the antichrist will rise up from the Mediterranean world, and he will be a Jew, not a Muslim, as some suggest, for a reason, Jews will only accept a Jewish Messiah. Therefore, I would argue, the antichrist is of Jewish heritage, living and or even born in the revived Roman Empire (Dan. 7:8, 24).

A great example of the above-mentioned is Emmanuel (meaning: God is with us). Macron, the French President, is said to have both Jewish ancestry and mysterious ties to Rome (Catholicism) and the Assyrian Empire. The linked characteristic of the antichrist is he is known as 'the Assyrian' dispatched by God (Isa. 10:5) to chasten Israel as the rod of His anger and the club of His wrath. Isaiah's prophecy was partly fulfilled and is yet to be fully fulfilled in the tribulation.

Another interesting reference is where Macron was questioned about being the 'Savior of Europe' by The Economist (2017), pictured walking on water (like Jesus). Time Magazine (2017) called Macon the 'Next leader of Europe.' Also, there have been numerous references to Macron as the potential new world leader, recently going on record to nominate himself for global leadership, starting by calling for a worldwide ceasefire (2020). Yet, amusingly, in 2017, Macron said he wanted to be a "Jupiterian" leader, unchallenged and detached from trivialities, like the Roman God of the skies. In 2018, Emmanuel Macron also said he would bring together a ten-nation coalition (ten toes, horns, kings), which is ongoing. In support, Macron has strong backing from the United Nations, which stated, 'Indeed, it would appear that the world could use a new leader in this time of crisis - one who is prepared to put global interests above personal or political aggrandizement' (2020). Macron also received the blessing of Pope Francis as a proposed new world leader

(2020). Another thought-provoking observation is the collective words' Macron Beast,' equalling 666 in English Gematria (cf. Rev. 13:18).

The purpose of the above-mentioned is not to state that Macon is the antichrist, but rather to point out some fascinating, 'box-ticking' similarities. As stated earlier, no one will know who the antichrist is until the tribulation commences, and then, only the wise will be able to identify him (12:10, Rev. 13:18) and warn others about him (11:23, 12:3).

Adding to the above, further evidence toward identifying the antichrist, at the mid-way point of the tribulation, is the antichrist suffers a deadly wound from which he will be resurrected (Rev. 13:3, 12-13) to do his father's (Satan) will (Dan. 11:36). Simultaneously, forty-two months into the tribulation, he demands to be worshipped (Rev. 13:14-15), proclaiming to be God (2 Thess. 2:4). He will do this from the tribulation temple (Rev.11: 1-2). This act of defilement will fulfil the prophecy of the 'abomination of desolation (Dan. 11:31; 12:11: Matt. 24:15-17; Mk. 13:14, 2 Thess. 2:4).

In sum, with the opening paragraph, of this section, I drew attention to the prophetic nature of the book of Daniel. It considers and characterises kings and kingdoms past and future, revealing patterns from the past to provide an understanding of the future through the use of double referencing. Double referencing can refer to the duplation of a literal event closer to the time of writing and a prophetic event even ahead of our own time. Double referencing can also refer to the same prophetic event taking place in two or more parts. For example, like with the Assyrian (Isa. 10:5), in the following chapter Antiochus IV Epiphanes (8:9, small horn) was a literal and predicted type of antichrist (second century B.C.), preceding the antichrist to come (7:8, 11, 19-26, 8:17, 19, 23, 11:36, 2 Thess. 2:4, 1 Jn. 2:18-19, Rev. 13:1-10).

In the same way, the prophecy was fulfilled (in part) with Antiochus; it will be fulfilled fully with the coming antichrist. From the historical event of Antiochus, we can learn something about the future events involving the coming antichrist. For example, Antiochus attacked Israel, overthrew Israel's high priest, looted the temple, and replaced God's worship with his gods. The antichrist to come will do the same thing (9:25-27, 11:31, 36, 37, 12:11, Matt. 24:15, 2 Thess. 2:4, Rev. 13:6), going many steps further, evening proclaiming to be God.

In conclusion, the coming antichrist will be similar, yet different, to other kings before him. King Nebuchadnezzar, from Daniel chapter three, is an excellent example. The difference being, Nebuchadnezzar acknowledged God and came to repentance, whereas the antichrist will not. The Assyrian is another type of antichrist, sent by God to punish Israel. Antiochus is yet another again, joining the ranks of those before him, and after, such as Hitler and so many more.

Despite the silence from most pulpits today, the antichrist is alive and well, and the spirit of the antichrist is very active within the church, which is why so many have gone astray. Churches today have gone astray, negatively fulfilling Bible prophecy. One of the most significant end-time signs leading up to the revealing of the antichrist is the great apostasy, which is the falling away from sound biblical doctrine.

Part Two
'The Books were Opened'
(vv. 9-12)

Following the short rule and reign of the antichrist, totalling seven years, Jesus will return and take away his temporary dominion (7:6, 26), setting up His everlasting dominion (7:14, 26, 27). Before Jesus established His everlasting kingdom, God told each of the four beasts to arise (7:6), which includes the coming antichrist who will be in the company of three others (Zech. 1:7-17, 6:1-8, Rev. 6:1-8). The antichrist will arise at his appointed time (8:19, 11:27, 29, 35). Remember, each beast is appointed by God to do and execute His will.

First, there was God's servant Nebuchadnezzar (7:4, Jer. 27:6, 43:10), followed by God's shepherd and anointed, Cyrus (7:5, Isa. 44:28, 45:1), then there was Alexandra (7:6, 8:5-7), who will be lastly followed by the antichrist (7:7, Rev. 6). When the antichrist comes on the scene, he will rise up quickly, having dominion for seven years (7:25), and then Jesus will destroy him (7:11, 26), casting him down into the lake of fire (Rev. 19:20, 20:10). Through the rising up and tearing down of the antichrist, God's sovereignty is absolute. Remember, "He (God) changes times and seasons; He removes kings and sets up kings; He gives wisdom to the wise and knowledge to those who have understanding" (2:21).

The opening scene of this section (7:9-12) uses the same imagery John used in the book of Revelation (1:14). So frightening was the image of the returning Christ, John fell to the ground as a man dead (Rev. 1:17). Chapter nineteen of John's revelation provides further detail of what Jesus' return looks like. Needless to say, the returning Jesus is not the same, so many are worshipping today (cf. 2 Cor. 11:4). John's image of Jesus Christ is one of a Holy God who is to be, and will be, feared and reverently worshipped (cf. Rev. 14:6-7).

Despite the religious rhetoric today, Jesus is not your lover, your boyfriend, your homie, your means to gain; He is not on your side or at your beck and call; He is your eternal judge! Daniel's vision confirms that very point - Jesus is the judge. Although man has been given an opportunity and an appointed time to dominate the earth, that time will, and is coming to an end with the return and appearance of Jesus Christ (Rev. 1:7).

Ezekiel also experienced the image of God's appearing, accompanied by the four living creatures (Ezek. 1:4–28). Instead of angels, however, Daniel's vision narrowed in on the saints; a thousand thousands and ten thousand times ten thousand of them (7:10). The number refers to a significant number that cannot be numbered. John picks up the same in chapter seven of the book of Revelation (v. 9), stating the number of saints is so great that they cannot be numbered. The saints that John refers to are those who the antichrist has slain during the tribulation due to refusing to worship him (Rev. 13:15, 14:13, 20:4), instead, 'washing their robes, making them white in the blood of the Lamb' (Rev. 7:14). Through death, the slain saints 'conquered the devil by the blood of the Lamb and by the word of their testimony, for they loved not their lives unto death' (Rev. 12:11). The same group of slain saints are first mentioned in chapter six of John's revelation, under the judgement of the fifth seal (vv. 9-11). Again, these saints had been slain for 'the word of God and for the witness they had borne' (6:9). The one who kills them is the coming antichrist, released by Jesus with the opening of the first seal (Rev. 6:1-2).

Similar to Daniel's vision, where God told the beasts (including the antichrist) to 'arise, devour much flesh' (Dan. 7:5b), John's revelation, through the form of a vision (Rev. 1:9, 9:17), also reveals that Jesus releases the antichrist to conquer (Rev. 6:2). Paul's letter to the

Thessalonians reveals that God sends the antichrist (the strong delusion) to those who refused to hear what the Spirit is saying to the churches (cf. Rev. 2:7, 11, 17, 28, 3:6, 13, 22), that they would continue to believe what is false so that all would be condemned (2 Thess. 2:11-12).

Paul's previous statement reveals that the deceived are the apostates who have fallen away from sound biblical doctrine (2 Thess. 2:3). These are those who departed from the (true) faith, following doctrines of demons (1 Tim. 4;1), due to not enduring sound biblical doctrine. Therefore, they have departed from the truth, they have drifted away, having itching ears, wanting to hear teaching that suits their passions (2 Tim. 4:3). The apostates have drifted away from salvation due to not paying close attention to what they have heard (Heb. 2:1-3, 3:7-15, 5:11-13-6:8, 10:26-39).

The warnings point to the authority of scripture, not the powerless words of modern, liberal preachers. Those deceived by messages contrary to scripture will make up the number of those who are 'left behind' to endure the tribulation, for the purpose of testing and separating through repentance.

Most living today will go through the tribulation; however, many others will not, but will instead be taken out of the way (cf. Rev. 3:10, 4:1) via the rapture (1 Thess. 4:17, 1 Cor. 15:51-52), escaping the wrath to come (Rom. 5:9, 1 Thess. 5:9). The removed/raptured saints are seen by John, making a distinction between those in heaven and those remaining on the earth to endure the tribulation. John first mentions the raptured saints in chapter five of his revelation, seen singing a song to Jesus (vv. 9-10), there are millions of them (v. 11). The song refers to Jesus establishing His kingdom on the earth, following the rule and reign of men, concluding with the antichrist's appointed time (cf. Dan 7:27).

The fact that Jesus is only now preparing to set up His kingdom on earth, after the tribulation, completely debunks kingdom now 'theology,' which will be discussed in greater detail in the following section. The heavenly singing saints now 'see' the coming kingdom, singing another similar song nearing its commencement in chapter eleven of John's revelation (vv. 17-18). The heavenly resurrected saints are later joined, in song, by the martyred saints in chapter fifteen (vv. 3-4), and again in chapter nineteen (vv. 1-3).

To summarise: the above-mentioned first group of saints addressed those raptured, while the second group addressed those who have been slain and saved through the tribulation. During the tribulation, at some point, both groups are in heaven with Jesus, seen by John and Daniel. Again, Daniel numbers this great mass of people as a thousand thousands and ten thousand times ten thousand (7:10, cf. Rev. 5:11). However, there is still another group indirectly picked up by Daniel who will be judged upon the opening of the books (7:10b). John saw the same vision, recording the event in greater detail in chapter twenty in the book of Revelation (20:11-15). This event is known as the Great White Throne Judgement, where the books are opened alongside the book of life. Those standing at this judgement will not have their names written in the book of life; therefore, they will be judged by what they have done (their works) against the Law of God (Rev. 20:12). Anyone whose name is recorded in the book of life will be judged by the works of Jesus (Eph. 2:8-9, 1 Pet. 2:22-24), again, everyone standing that the Great White Throne Judgement is judged by the Law (Ten Commandments) and will be found guilty (Rom 3:23, Ja. 2:10), and without excuse (Rom. 2:15-16, 3:19).

Following the millennial reign, every guilty person will be cast into the lake of fire, alongside Satan, where the antichrist and the false prophet have been for one thousand years (Rev. 20:10). The antichrist and the false prophet have been in the lake of fire for one thousand years already, annihilating the annihilation theory.

Annihilation theory (false theology) suggests that once a person is cast into hell (the lake of fire), they are instantly annihilated. Annihilation theory is based on a false perception of God's love, grace, and mercy, stating that a loving God would not condemn anyone to an eternal state of suffering. Scripture, however, refutes annihilation theory confirming that the rebellious will experience everlasting destruction (Matt. 10:28, Mk. 9:43-48, Lu. 16:22-28), and unending suffering (Rom. 2:6) where the whole body is eternally burned in hell (Matt. 5:29-30, Lu. 12:4-5). John's letter prewarns those left behind in the tribulation with the same; hell is forever, it is unending, eternal suffering and torment (Rev. 14:11, 19:20, 20:10).

Paul puts an end to the unbalanced view that 'God is Love' (full stop) by stating He is both kind and severe (Rom. 11:22). God is harsh to those who have fallen (away) but kind to obedient believers, providing they continue (remain). Most, however, do fall away (2 Thess. 2:3), which is one of the most significant end times signs. Therefore, most will end up in hell due to rejecting or disobeying Jesus Christ (Isa. 5:14, Matt. 7:13-14, 7:21-23). The same warning was given to the seven churches of John's revelation (Rev. 2-3), seventy percent of them were in danger of judgement for 'falling away.'

In sum, the Bible talks about two resurrections, one for the just (righteous) and the other for the wicked unjust (Dan. 12:2, Jn. 5:28-29, Acts 24:15). The first takes place upon the rapture, where faithful believers (the just) have their names written in the book of life (Phil. 4:3, Rev. 3:5, 21:27). Anyone having their name in the Lamb's book of life will be removed from the hour of trial coming to test the whole world (Rev. 3:10). These, alone, have secured eternal life (1 Cor. 15:52-53, Phil. 3:21a). When raptured, the awake (Lu. 21:34-35) and the ready (Matt. 24:44) will receive a resurrected and glorified body (1 Cor. 15:42-44, cf. 1 Jn. 3:2), and they will go before the judgement seat of Jesus Christ (1 Cor. 3:10-15). The judgement seat is also known as the Bema Seat (2 Cor. 5:10).

The 'Bema Seat' translates into 'court' or 'tribunal' and is associated with a raised seat allowing the judge full vision to judge without restriction, and therefore, without error. For example, in the Olympic arena, there was an elevated seat allowing the judge unrestricted, unhindered vision. The same is true with the judgement seat of Jesus Christ, where individual members of the bride of Christ are judged and rewarded according to their works in Christ Jesus (cf. Lu. 14:14). On the other hand, anyone who does not have their names written in the book of life (Rev. 13:8, 17:8, 20:12, 15) will go before the latter judgement, which is the Great White Throne Judgement. The Great White Throne Judgement is reserved for the unjust where they too will be resurrected. They also will receive a glorified body for the purpose of everlasting torment and destruction, as stated earlier.

Again, the Great White Throne Judgement occurs at the end of the millennial dispensation, or the Messianic reign of Jesus Christ. Until that point, the unjust are held in hades (Lu. 16:19-31), which is still a place of torment but is not comparable to the eternal lake of fire.

The statement "hades gave up the dead" (Rev. 20:13) refers to the sleeping (but not the resting) unsaved, again, who are resurrected and reunited with their physical, glorified bodies for the purpose of everlasting torment (Matt. 5:29-30, 10:28, Mk. 9:43-48, Rom. 2:6). While hades is a place of torment in itself (Lu. 16:19-30), the last and eternal degree of suffering is still yet to be announced.

In the final judgement, there will be different levels or degrees of punishment. The worst degree is reserved for those who led others astray when given the responsibility to teach scripture (Matt. 23:14, cf. Ja. 3:1). The next degree is for the servants of Christ who knew His will but disobeyed (Lu. 12:47-48). The degree following is for those who received the gospel yet fell away (2 Pet. 2:20-22), and also for those who heard and saw the power of the gospel and did not respond (Lu. 10:14-15).

As stated earlier, evidently, the Great White Throne Judgement will be the experience for most (Matt. 7:13-14, Lu. 13:23-34), including many confessing Christians and pastors (Matt. 7:21-23). Regardless of the degree of suffering in the lake of fire, any who face the Great White Throne Judgement, due to not having their names written in the Lamb's book of life, end up in the same eternal place of torment and everlasting, unending suffering.

Remember, the lake of fire is not God's will for humanity, which is why He has delayed the judgement desiring that all would repent and that none would perish (2 Pet. 3:9).

Part Three
'Dominionism'
(vv. 13-14)

Following the dominion of man (7:6), specifically the man of sin, the antichrist, Jesus will then return to establish His kingdom on the earth. As previously mentioned, this takes place at the commencement of the millennial dispensation, which follows the judgement of the antichrist and the false prophet (Rev. 19:20).

On the subject of Jesus' return, the prophet Zechariah spoke into this by prophesying the crucifixion of Jesus Christ, and John proclaims the fulfilment of the prophecy, directly quoting Zechariah, 'Whom they pierced on the cross' (Zech. 12:10, Jn. 19:37). The prophecy is picked up again in John's revelation (Rev. 1:7). Like John, the prophet Zechariah did not stop with the crucifixion of Jesus but instead looked well past that day, more than 2000-years further, to the return of Jesus at the conclusion of the tribulation. Verse eleven provides confirmation with the phrase, "On that Day…"

Throughout prophetic literature, 'That Day' always refers to Jesus' second coming and His judgement. On that day, everyone who had previously rejected Jesus will recognise Him. The event will take place at the plain of Megiddo (Zech. 12:11b), which is the location of the Battle of Armageddon. The Battle of Armageddon has been further described in chapter fourteen of Zechariah and the book of Revelation, chapters sixteen and nineteen.

During the tribulation, many Jews will come to faith in Jesus (Rev. 7, 14), producing mass evangelism and revival, converting multitudes from every nation, tribe, peoples, and languages (Rev. 7:9, cf. Dan. 7:14).

The tribulation revival will be ongoing throughout its duration of seven years, concluding with Jesus' return. Even at this late point, leading right up to Jesus' return, the remaining population will still be able to repent due to God's extended grace and mercy. According to Zechariah, chapter twelve (v. 10), even when Jesus is seen with the naked eye, at His appearing, salvation is still on offer (cf. Zech. 12:10-13:1).

By way of some background information, the prophet Zechariah came on the scene after Judah was released from Babylon. After seventy years of captivity due to idolatry and failing to observe the Sabbath, Judah returned to their sins, which is why the prophet commenced his book with the words, "Return to Me, says the Lord of host and I will return to you" (1:3). The fact is, Judah never broke away from their sins, therefore never returned to the Lord, even while in captivity, and still have not to this day. But they will do, through the coming tribulation, as prophesied by Daniel, Zechariah, and John. Israel, as a nation, and individuals of that nation and every other nation will call on the name of the Lord (Rev. 7:1-9-10).

As seen in Zechariah, chapter twelve (vv. 10-14), at the appearance of Jesus (v. 10), individual response is required through repentance and mourning. Such a response secures salvation (cf. Matt. 5:4), confirmed by Zachariah, chapter thirteen (v. 1), which states, "Where comes the cleansing of sin and uncleanness." Meaning, forgiveness is granted to repentant sinners due to God's grace and mercy, also confirmed by Peter (2 Pet. 3:9).

As mentioned above, the appearance of Jesus is expanded by John in the book of Revelation (1:7), "He is coming with the clouds, and every eye will see Him— even those who pierced Him. Moreover, all the tribes of the earth will mourn because of Him. So shall it be! Amen." The word 'mourn' is also seen in Zachariah, chapter twelve (v. 11), eschatologically supporting the phrase "On that Day," pinpointing the time of the prophesy's fulfilment.

Again, on the return of Jesus, contrary to the response of the rebellious (cf. Rev. 6:14-17), where they call for the rocks to fall on and hide them from the Lamb, multitudes will be collectively and individually saved. This fact is made evident by Zechariah's words, 'families' and 'wives,' and by 'themselves,' suggesting that many will respond to Jesus' invitation to salvation.

In sum, when Jesus returns, the whole world will see Him; they will repent, or perish, and worship Him (7:14, Matt. 24:30, Rev. 1:7). On Jesus' return, His appearance (7:9-10) will be as described in John's revelation (Rev. 1:12-17), as one coming on the clouds (7:13, Matt. 24:30, 26:64, Mk. 13:26, 14:62, Lu. 21:27, Rev. 1:7), to judge the nations. Psalms (2:6-9) provides a description of that day. "As for me, I have set my King on Zion, My holy hill." I will tell of the decree: The LORD said to me, "You are My Son; today I have begotten you. Ask of Me, and I will make the nations your heritage and the ends of the earth your possession. You shall break them with a rod of iron and dash them in pieces like a potter's vessel." So frightening will that day be when John saw the image of the returning Christ, he fell to the ground as a man dead. In other words, John was frightened to death! John saw Jesus doing what He threatened to do through the letter to the seven churches (Rev. 2-3). The threat was, failure to respond (repent) would result in suffering the consequences. The consequences for us are in two parts, 1). The tribulation, and 2). The judgement. When Jesus returns to the earth, He will first deal with the antichrist, casting him into the lake of fire (7: 11, 26, Rev. 19:20), and then He will judge the nations (Matt. 25:31-46).

Once the antichrist has been removed from the earth (7:11), his dominion will then be taken away (7:12, 26) by Jesus. Jesus will then have dominion on the planet (7:14, 27) and share His dominion with His heirs, His co-ruling saints (7:22, 27). The saints, then, rule with Christ forever and ever (7:18, cf. 6:26). Note the deliberate repetition of the word 'then,' implying, later, not now! (cf. 1 Cor. 15:24-28).

Before the coming kingdom of Christ Jesus is established on the earth, the earth-dwelling saints will be persecuted (7:21, 25). The persecution of the saints is a sign of the end times (Matt. 24:9), signifying the end is nearing and nearer. As we draw closer to 'that day,' persecution will increase, not decrease. Persecution will not only be directed towards the saints but towards any and all within the whole world refusing to follow and worship the fourth beast (7:23), who is the antichrist. John's revelation states the same; the saints will be persecuted this side of Jesus' return (Rev. 1:9, 5:9-11, 7:13-14, 12:11, 13:10, 15, 14:13, 16:6, 19:2, 20:4). However, on the return of Jesus, they will be delivered, and then they will rule and reign with Him. This is confirmed by John, "And you have made them a kingdom and priests to our God, and they SHALL reign on the earth" (Rev. 5:10).

To understand the verse above (Rev. 5:10), Revelation, chapter one (v. 6) must first be taken into consideration: "And has made us kings and priests to His God and Father." The context of chapter one revolves around the returning Christ, whom every eye will see, and the whole earth will wail (Rev. 1:7).

Many today have overlooked this simple fact, expressly evident through dominionism, which teaches Christians are to rule and reign here and now, which is entirely false for several reasons, as stated in my second book, 'The Revelation, Explained and Proclaimed.'

The first reason dominionism is false is that it fails to take into consideration the immediate context, or more comprehensive text and the source from where the quote is first found, which is Exodus, chapter nineteen (v. 6) and again later in Isaiah, chapter sixty-one (v. 6) Furthermore, the quote is also found in the book of Revelation, chapters five (v. 10), and twenty (v. 6). When considering these supporting verses, the reader gains an understanding of the timing Jesus is, referring to, and following certain events, namely false teaching, trouble, and persecution.

Secondly, starting with the verse itself, the better translation is 'a kingdom of priests' (ESV), and we are that because we have been reconciled to God through Christ Jesus, the King of kings (v. 5). That being the case, our priesthood and rulership fall directly under Jesus' rulership. That simple fact and statement alone should do most of the work for us in establishing 'when' we rule on the earth. That would be when Jesus returns (Dan. 7:13, Zech. 12:10, Matt. 24:30, 2 Thess. 1:7b-9, Rev. 19:11-21), with us (2 Thess. 1:10), just before the millennial dispensation. From that point onwards, Jesus sets up His rule and reign on the earth (Zech. 14:6-11, 16-21), and the saints will share in that under His Kingship. To clarify, see Revelation, chapter eleven (v. 15b), "The kingdom of the world has become the kingdom of our Lord and of His Christ, and He shall reign forever and forever." Clearly, the fulfilment of this verse is set for a later date.

Thirdly, from the wider text, we learn from the book of Revelation, chapters five (v. 10) and twenty (v. 6), the saint's rule with Jesus after this dispensation (church age and tribulation period) is complete. At the close of this age (tribulation), the so-called kings of this world are being slaughtered, which has been the case since Jesus was crucified. Christians are still being slaughtered today, and this will continue and increase leading up to and during the tribulation (Matt. 24:8-9, 21). During that time, the coming earthly king, the antichrist (Dan 7:24, Matt. 24:15, Rev. 17:10-13), will target both Jews (Rev. 12:15) and Christians (Rev. 20:4), killing them on an unprecedented scale.

After taking into consideration the scriptural support as mentioned above, the delusion that we are ruling and reigning here and now as kings on the earth overlooks the fact that Satan is the current god of this world (2 Cor. 4:4), and its ruler (Jn. 14:30, 1 Jn. 5:19). This is why he was able to offer Jesus all of the kingdoms of the world when tempted in the wilderness (Matt. 4:8).

Furthermore, when comparing the account recorded in Exodus and Revelation, if we are to rule and reign here and now, we need to ask some questions. Whenever did Israel rule and reign on the earth following their deliverance? They never did! And they will not until Jesus returns. And, even then, only those who have called on His name, confessing (Matt. 23:39) and committed to His Lordship (Rev. 14:4-5), and enduring until the end (Matt. 24:13) will rule during the millennium.

Another verse besides Exodus, chapter nineteen (v. 6), in need of consideration, is Isaiah, chapter sixty-six (v. 6). Here, the passage is broken up into two prophetic parts: 1). The arrival of Jesus (vv. 1-2a), confirmed by Luke (4:19-19), and 2). The return of Jesus (2b). On Jesus' return, He will set up His kingdom on the earth, which is described in verses two (c) to eleven. Within those verses, verse six clearly falls and remains to be fulfilled, during the millennium.

As for what John, through the book of Revelation, chapter one (v. 6) implied, 'in the here and now,' consideration of the original source and quote (Exodus 19:6) is required. In the Exodus event, Israel had been delivered, set free, or freed from slavery at the hand of Egypt. They were set free to be covenant people of God. When comparing that event with Revelation, chapter one (vv. 5-6), we see a repeat of the same: We are set free from slavery/sin, redeemed to God (Rom. 6) by being brought into the covenant. For us, this was achieved through Jesus Christ's finished work on the cross; therefore, our ruling and reigning here and now is over sin (Rom. 5:17). As freed people, we are commissioned to bring others into the same (Matt. 28:18-20) by preaching repentance and offering the forgiveness of sin in Jesus' name (Jn. 20:23).

In sum: Revelation, chapter one (v. 6) should be understood in two parts, 1). We are being delivered from sin through Jesus Christ. As such 2). We are a kingdom of priests under the Kingship of Jesus. As for the here and now, we are called to be ministers of the new covenant, reconciling the lost to God by preaching repentance and the forgiveness of sin. And, in the not-too-distant future, we will be caught up to meet Jesus in the air, then seven years later, we will return with Him to rule and reign on the earth under Him.

In conclusion: Daniel, Zechariah, and John saw the return of Jesus Christ, coming on the clouds to judge the nations and take dominion over the earth. The event will follow the appointed time of the antichrist, lasting seven short years. Soon the antichrist will be revealed, shortly afterward he will be destroyed, and THEN true believers will rule and reign on earth under Jesus forever.

Part Four
'Anxious and Alarmed'
(vv. 15-28)

So far, for chapter seven, we have looked at the 'little horn' (the antichrist), the 'books' that will be opened at the Great White Throne Judgement, and 'dominionism.' Each section considered a different period. The first is specific to the tribulation, the second follows the millennial dispensation, and the third addresses the time of man, ending with the man of sin, the antichrist. This fourth part will serve to recap, providing more of an overview of what has been said previously.

Starting with verse fifteen, after seeing the things to come, Daniel was anxious and alarmed, similar to John when seeing the image of the returning Christ (Rev. 1:7). After seeing the things to come, John falling to the ground is mentioned twice in the book of Revelation (Rev. 1:7, 19:10). The same is seen three times in Daniel (7:15, 8:17-18, 10:9-10, 15).

Although both Daniel and John's vision reveals Jesus' victory over the devil, the events leading up to that outcome are what terrified them both. Today, we hear plenty of rhetoric of God winning, with accompanying statements like, 'I have read the end of the book (Bible), and guess what, God wins, therefore we do too.' While there is truth in these statements, and the intentions are good, the proclaimer overlooks the point. Before Jesus conquers the antichrist and sets up His dominion on the earth, all hell is going to break loose, literally. Before Jesus returns, the end-time events must first take place (Matt. 24:6, Mk. 13:7, Lu. 21:9). During the coming tribulation, hell will open up and swallow multiple millions for all eternity (Rev. 6:8). Even before the tribulation, Jesus told the believer, in this world, you can expect trouble (Jn. 16:33).

Yet still, it was not hell that terrified Daniel and John; it was God, and the angels of God (8:17-18, 10:9-10, 15, Rev. 1:7), which is why both the book of Daniel and Revelation focus on fearing and worshipping God, alone (Rev. 14:7, 15:4). Having a fear of God leads to reverent worship, which is seldom seen in the church today. Due to a lack of fear of God, many have gone astray, preaching liberal, watered-down messages designed to attract and retain numbers by entertaining and tickling ears.

Besides both Daniel and John having a fear of God installed in them through the imagery of the returning Christ, the imagery of the tribulation also produced great fear, precisely due to the activity of the coming antichrist (7:7, 19, 23, Rev. 13:1-4, 17:12-14a). The purpose of the tribulation is specifically to produce fear, resulting in reverent worship, through repentance. The church of Thyatira was especially warned of this due to its members tolerating the so-called prophetess, Jezebel, and her teachings. Unless Jezebel repented, both she and her followers would be thrown into the great tribulation that the churches would know that Jesus searches the mind and heart, giving each what they deserve (Rev. 2:20-23).

The warning was given to the literal church of Thyatira and any other today doing as they did. A similar notice was given to the church of Sardis, where Jesus warned its members that they would be 'left behind' if they did not repent (Rev. 3:3). The church members were also told their names would be removed from the book of life (Rev. 3:5). Anyone left behind to go through the tribulation will not have their names written in the book of life. Those that do will be raptured before the tribulation commences, as confirmed by Daniel, "At that time Michael, the archangel who stands guard over your nation, will arise. Then there will be a time of anguish greater than any since nations first came into existence. But at that time, every one of your people whose name is written in the book will be rescued" (12:1). Those going through the tribulation are not rescued but delivered through death, following repentance.

The mystery of the coming antichrist, and the tribulation, for Daniel (7:16, 8:15) is not so mysterious today. One of the end times signs is the increase of knowledge (12:4) which refers to technological advancements and Bible prophecy. While Daniel and even John had no way of understanding how the events they saw would be fulfilled, we do. Anyone equipped with basic eschatological knowledge will understand the signs of the times, putting together current events and ancient prophecy. Furthermore, when the believer has knowledge of the end times, they are also defined as being wise (12:2). Here lies the danger with unwise churches ignoring Bible prophecy, making up thirty percent of scripture. By failing to proclaim, they fail to warn, therefore prepare.

Furthermore, failing to preach the prophetic text fails to correctly and contextually handle and preach the remainder of the text. Unless the preacher understands prophetic literature, they will fail to present the remaining seventy percent accurately, which always points to Jesus and His return in the New Testament. Knowing biblical prophecy helps the believer to remain focused and discerning of the signs of the times. Arguably, the observant believer is also one who has a healthy fear of God, the very thing lacking in five of seven of the churches addressed in the book of Revelation (Rev. 2-3).

The same is true today, where we would confidently state seventy percent (most) of the church does not know the fear of God, evident in their lukewarmness, meaning that they are saved (cf. Matt. 7:20-23).

Today, scripture, namely prophetic literature, is being fulfilled right under our noses, particularly with the fulfilment of the increase of knowledge (12:3). Never before in the history of man has anyone before this time been able to understand the ancient prophecies as we can today. This fact makes us more accountable, not less (Lu. 12:48) - even more accountable than those penning the predictions. To support, consider the words of Jesus:

"Then Jesus began to denounce the cities in which most of His miracles had been performed because they did not repent. "Woe to you, Chorazin! Woe to you, Bethsaida! For if the miracles that were performed in you had been performed in Tyre and Sidon, they would have repented long ago in sackcloth and ashes. But I tell you - it will be more bearable for Tyre and Sidon on the Day of Judgrment than for you. And you, Capernaum, will you be lifted up to heaven? No, you will be brought down to Hades! For if the miracles that were performed in you had been performed in Sodom, it would have remained to this day. But I tell you that it will be more bearable for Sodom on the Day of Judgement than for you" (Matt. 11:20-24).

While, in the text mentioned above, Jesus was talking about healing and deliverance miracles in plain sight, we have the miracle of two-thousand-year-old (plus) prophecy coming to pass right in front of our eyes. Yet, still, many preachers are positioned to warn and proclaim fail! Some even go as far as to dismiss biblical prophecy altogether, thereby fulfilling it in a negative way (2 Pet. 3, Jude 18); Woe to those who do!

Scoffers in the church are a sign of the end-times indicating the nearness of the prophecy being fulfilled, relating to Jesus' return. As mentioned earlier, scoffers are not only ignorant of Bible prophecy, but they go as far as to dismiss it, leading their hearer astray.

Rick Warren's book, Purpose Driven Life, selling thirty million copies, is an excellent example of a well-known celebrity preacher misleading multitudes by dismissing Bible prophecy, which is precisely what he does. Furthermore, Warren suggests that the book of Daniel is a book about healthy living. Through Warren's book, 'Forty Days to a Healthier Life,' he promotes diet, over devotion, and deity. The book has little (good) to say about spiritual health but instead promotes physical health through dieting. For the little Warren does have to say about spiritual health, he involves neo-Gnosticism promoting breathing exercises, meditation, and yoga, void of mentioning God. Needless to say, Warren's view of Daniel's diet is the furthest thing from the central theme of the biblical book of Daniel, which points to remaining faithful in the trouble to come and to the return of Jesus Christ.xx

Consequently, Warren's dietary book is better aligned to the diet (assembly) of worms (Roman Empire/Catholicism), only instead of standing up against the heresy of the Roman Catholic Church as Luther did (1521), Warren embraces and promotes it. Warren, on numerous occasions, has affirmed Catholicism under the banner of ecumenicalism. Under ecumenicalism, Warren's deception runs deep with the 'third wave of neo-Pentecostalism' chiefly expressed through the New Apostolic Reformation (NAR). The NAR promotes a new age of apostles and prophets who, apparently, have new revelation. Out of this new revelation comes kingdom now 'theology' (dominionism), which suggests everything is getting better, not worse. Warren's alignment with dominionism is made evident with throwaway statements like, 'the best is still before us.' Warren believes the best is yet to come, in this life, due to being ignorant of eschatology.

On the grounds of the above-mentioned, Warren is an excellent example of a preacher who, due to being ignorant of Bible prophecy (30 percent of the Bible), fails to interpret the rest of scripture (the remaining 70 percent of the Bible) correctly. Sadly, Warren is not alone; in these last days, there are more like him than not, which is also a fulfilment of Bible prophecy (2 Thess. 2:3, 1 Tim. 4:1, 2 Tim. 4:3), conditioning people for the strong delusion (2 Thess. 2:11), the antichrist to come.

Today, many fail to correctly interpret scripture, and hold fast to it, this side of the coming tribulation. However, during the tribulation, the left behind will have another opportunity to get it right with Jesus through repentance. Jesus confirms this fact by quoting Daniel, saying, "When you see the abomination of desolation spoken of by the prophet

Daniel, standing in the holy place, let the reader understand" (Matt. 24:15).

Where the reader failed to understand previously, now, during the tribulation, some will understand. The first thing they will understand is, they have been left behind. Then, during the tribulation, the left behind will wake up to the fact, things are not getting better but worse, much worse, which will force them to examine scripture exegetically, revealing the signs of the times and the antichrist. The event Jesus is referring to (Matt. 24:15) is that of the antichrist standing in the third, rebuilt tribulation, temple, proclaiming he is God (9:27 11:31, 12:11, 2 Thess. 2:4), otherwise known as the abomination of desolation (Matt. 24:15, Mk. 13:14). Only the left behind will witness the fulfilment of this prophecy from the earth.

As mentioned previously, when Daniel had the visions, he was unable to understand, therefore interpret them; however, God gave Daniel revelation through the angel Gabriel (8:15-16, 9:21). Again, Daniel's visions referred to the things to come, which terrified him. The things to come are terrifying, particularly for those left behind! Daniel makes the point clear; the left behind will be persecuted like never before (7:21, 25, 8:24), and that the coming event is like nothing before, or will be repeated again (12:1, cf. Jer. 30:7, Matt. 24:21, Rev. 16:18).

This biblical revelation of the things to come runs in the opposite direction to the new revelation of dominionism. Right up until Jesus returns and sets up His millennial kingdom, we are under what is known as the time of the Gentiles (Lu. 21:24). The time of the Gentiles means man ruling, dominating, in particular over the nation of Israel.

The coming end of the time of the Gentiles is revealed through the signs of the times, one of which is the reformation of Israel. Jesus taught on this, as recorded in the gospel according to Matthew (Matt. 24:32-34). The parable Jesus taught refers to Israel being reborn as a nation. The prophecy was fulfilled against all odds (Isa. 66:7-9). Israel became a nation again in 1948. When teaching, Jesus said the generation that sees Israel reborn would also see His return (Matt. 24:34). According to the book of Psalms (90:10), humanity can expect between seventy to eighty years, in general. Some live less, and some longer, but in general, seventy to eighty years is the expectation. When applying the expected number of years against the parable of Jesus, we can conclude that time is very short.

Today, in 2021, Israel is seventy-three years old. From Daniel, we also know the time of the antichrist is seven years (7:25, 9:27), which is supported by John (Rev. 11:2, 12:6, 13:5). Remember, the church will not be on the earth during the tribulation (Rev. 3:10). When putting the facts, as mentioned above, together, with potentially only seven years left before the generation that saw Israel's rebirth reach the total number of expected years, less the seven-year tribulation, the rapture/removal of the church could happen in 2021. While scripture says no one knows the day and the hour (Matt. 24:36), we should know the season by the signs of the times (cf. 1 Chron. 12:32, Matt. 16:3-4), specifically through prophetic literature, being Bible prophecy.

As mentioned earlier, another great sign of the times is the rise and increase of false teachers and teachings. Jesus warned these would be the greatest end-time signs (Matt. 24:4, 11, 23-26). Due to an increase of false teaching, many will fall away (2 Thess. 2:3). The great falling away, or apostasy, is not related to people leaving the church so much as it is about whole denominations rejecting sound biblical doctrine, thereby preaching another Jesus (2 Cor. 11:4) through a different gospel (Gal. 1:6-7).

The church of Laodicea was guilty of doing this, to the point Jesus was no longer in their midst (Rev. 3:20). While they were 'meeting in His name,' He was no longer among them. Jesus is the one who holds the seven stars and walks among the seven golden lampstands (Rev. 1:20). According to Jesus, the stars and lampstands are the churches, and while all started on the right foot, seventy percent of those addressed were in serious trouble due to false teaching resulting in false worship (Rev. 2-3). The letters to the seven churches apply to the universal church up until Jesus returns. After that, the universal church shares the same conditions, good and bad, addressed through the seven letters. The last, Laodicea, being the worst, prophetically points to us - the last church before Jesus returns. The last church will be vomited out and into the tribulation unless repentance comes first (Rev. 3:16).

Leading up to and during the tribulation, the antichrist will deceive many and has done already. He will come as a friend to Israel (9:27a). The antichrist will appear to be the long-awaited Jewish Moshiach (messiah), who will appear at the end of days (Num. 24:14). In Talmudic literature, the title Moshiach, or Melech HaMoshiach (the king messiah), is reserved for the Jewish leader who will redeem Israel at the end of days; therefore, the coming antichrist will be a Jew, not a Gentile.

Today, the Jews are looking for their Messiah, who will be made known by bringing peace to the Middle East by rebuilding the temple and bringing the Jews back into Israel. The Jewish Messiah will also be recognised by the whole world and will have dominion over the world (7:6, 23). When such a man comes, the Jews will accept him as their Messiah, therefore be deceived into accepting, receiving, and following the antichrist. The Jewish-awaited Messiah is the antichrist.

Again, the antichrist will occupy Jerusalem as the capital of his empire (11:45) for three and one-half years (Rev. 12:6; 13:5). A time, times, and half a time (cf. Dan. 12:7; Rev. 12:14) refer to the three and one-half years of the great tribulation, with "a time" meaning one year, "times" two years, and "half a time" six months. This equals the one thousand and sixty days mentioned in the book of Revelation (12:6) and the forty-two months, also mentioned in Revelation (11:2; 13:5). After a total of seven years, the antichrist's dominion is taken away from him and taken up by Jesus (7:26), who shared it with the saints (7:27), confirming the believers' kingdom is then (when Jesus returns), not and never now!

As mentioned at the beginning of this section, as exciting as Jesus' return will be, the preceding events terrified Daniel (7:15, 28). Daniel was not focused on the kingdoms before the antichrist and not even on the one following. The coming antichrist consumed Daniel's thoughts, further expanded on in the following chapters of Daniel's book through other visions.

Chapter Eight

Part One
'The Four Winds'
(vv. 1-14)

In the previous chapter, Daniel reintroduced the antichrist. He is reintroduced in chapter seven due to the first mention of him revealed through Nebuchadnezzar's dream in chapter two (vv. 40-41). Like Nebuchadnezzar, Daniel's dream foretold of the antichrist to come, albeit Daniel's vision contained much more information. While chapter seven focuses heavily on the antichrist, Daniel's revelation of the coming man of sin does not stop there. Chapters nine through twelve have plenty more to say, providing additional information about the end of the age, of which the antichrist has absolute global dominion. Chapter eight alludes to the antichrist but does not directly address him in the same way the other chapters do.

Two years after Daniel's vision, recorded in chapter seven, Daniel received another (8:1-2), recorded in chapter eight. In the dream, Daniel was in Susa, at the Ulai canal (8:2). From there, he saw a ram with two horns, yet one horn was higher than the other. The higher horn came up after the first. The vision of the ram with unequal horns is similar to the lopsided bear seen in the previous vision (7:5). Like the bear (7:5b), the ram was very powerful, where none could stand up to it, or be rescued from its power (8:4), The bear and the ram are the same, being Medo-Persia, who conquered Babylon, as recorded in chapter five (v. 30) of Daniel's book, fulfilling prophecy.

Following Medo-Persia is Greece, which is seen in the next verse, symbolised by the male goat who came from the west across the face of the whole earth (8:5). Although the ram was powerful, where none could stand up to it or be rescued from its power (8:4), one did! The male goat was faster than the ram (and bear), so fast that its feet did not even touch the ground (8:5). Due to the speed and strength of the goat, the ram was powerless against it. More so, the ram was powerless due to a divine transfer of power; God raises up one power (horn) and then later replaces it with another (2:21, 7:6). At the appointed time, the goat rose to power fast (8:8), and with great wrath it defeated the ram; there was no one to rescue it (8:7-8). Whereas before, there was no one to rescue anyone from the ram (8:4).

However, the goat's reign was short lasting in the current state. The conspicuous horn between its eyes (8:5) was broken and replaced by four more conspicuous horns (8:8). In a like manner where the ram was paralleled to the bear of chapter seven (v. 5), the goat was also likened to the leopard of chapter seven (v. 6); the leopard had four heads, and the goat ended up with four horns. The heads and horns represent four kings or rulers (7:24). The goat defeated the ram, namely due to its speed (8:5), which is characteristic of the leopard seen in chapter seven (v. 6).

Out of the four horns grew another, a little horn, which grew exceedingly great (8:9). As mentioned in chapter seven, part one, the little horn represents an insignificant or humble beginning (cf. 7:8). Like with the appointed time of the ram and the goat, where none could be rescued from them, the same will be true of the next (8:9-10). The little horn will think so highly of himself; he will even go up against God by killing the saints (8:9-10), even claiming to be God (not a god), (7:20-21, cf. 2 Thess. 2:4).

Chapter eight reveals that the little horn focuses on the glorious land (Israel), particularly Jerusalem, where the temple is located (8:9-12). Like with the bear and the leopard of chapter seven symbolised as the goat and the ram of chapter eight, the little horn of chapter seven is similar to the same little horn of chapter eight. Similar, but not the same!

Essentially, the vision of chapter seven was repeated in chapter eight, with a slight difference, which will be fully addressed later. Briefly, however, the difference between the vision in chapters seven and eight is, the little horn in chapter seven is the antichrist to come. In contrast, the little horn in chapter eight is a type of antichrist that prophetically points to the actual antichrist. The antichrist-type of chapter eight foreshadows the end time antichrist, who will be revealed in and through the tribulation (cf. 2 Thess. 2:6-8). Antiochus IV Epiphanes historically fulfilled the antichrist-type seen in chapter eight.

To qualify that statement, the difference between Antiochus and the antichrist is a distinction seen with each period allowed to operate. Antiochus was given two thousand, three hundred evenings and mornings (8:14), while the antichrist will be given two thousand, five hundred and twenty (7:25). Additional evidence of the distinction, separating one from the other, will be provided in the following section.

Again, although the visions of chapters seven and eight were similar and were given only two years apart (8:15), Daniel had difficulty understanding them (8:15, 27) and was unable to interpret the visions (7:16, 8:15). Interestingly, on this occasion, it seemed that Nebuchadnezzar, the forgetful, had a better memory than Daniel. When Nebuchadnezzar received a similar dream (chapter 2) to Daniel's (chapters 7 & 8), some twenty years later, he remembered it well enough to replicate the image of the head of gold, representing him, with the golden image, of himself, that the whole world was to fall down and worship (chapter 3). Again, as with chapter seven, in chapter eight, the angel Gabriel provides the interpretation (8:16-26). Before moving on to the interpretation, however, it is worth first considering the four winds.

As with the similarities mentioned above, there is another from chapter seven to chapter eight, which involves the four winds (7:2, 8:8). The four winds of heaven are mentioned three times in the book of Daniel (7:2, 8:8, 11:14). Zechariah also mentioned them (Zech. 2:6, 6:5). The events revolving around the four winds that the prophets saw through dreams and visions, are seen again through John's revelation (Rev. 7:1). The difference between Zechariah's prophecy and John's is that in John's vision, the winds were being held back, while in Zechariah's, they were being sent forth.

The theme of Revelation, chapter seven, revolves around salvation proclaimed through the sealed Jewish evangelists (vv. 3, 17). Jesus also references the winds (Matt. 24:31, Mk. 13:27), which refers to salvation.

At the end of the seven-year tribulation, Jesus will return to rescue the remaining saints from the ruling antichrist in the same way He rescued Daniel and his friends (3:29, 6:27) from the antichrist type, Nebuchadnezzar. During the tribulation, none will be rescued from the antichrist outside of the sealed Jewish evangelists (Rev. 7, 14). In the same way, none could be rescued from the 'wind carrying' ram or the goat; the antichrist will also be an unstoppable force, that is, until Jesus returns.

The term 'four winds' is a metaphor describing an event covering the whole earth and the heavens (Jer. 49:36). As mentioned previously, the word 'wind' is also translated, 'spirit.' The same Hebrew word (rûaḥ) as seen in Genesis (1:2), referring to God. Whenever the four winds are mentioned in the Bible, it refers to a time of great trouble (Ezek. 37:9, Dan. 7:2, Zech. 2:6).

For example, the four winds (Zech. 6:5) that Zechariah was referring to (Zech. 2:8, 6:2) are the four apocalyptic horsemen, of which the antichrist is one, seen again in John's revelation (6:1-8). The activities of the four apocalyptic horsemen will be carried out by men yet driven and influenced by spirits (demons). For example, the antichrist is a literal man, as established previously, yet will be led and empowered by Satan (a spirit being). The same is true for each of the kings (horns) referenced by Daniel (7:17), with the last still yet to come, who is the antichrist (7:23-25).

The importance of understanding the abovementioned comes with the recognition of the spirit world, which is often overlooked. In fact, the spirit world is almost forgotten by most churches today, who are instead fixed and focused on worldly materialism. Witches, however, have a much better understanding and appreciation of the unseen yet very real spirit realm, like the magicians' (sorcerers) did of Daniel's day. The so-called 'wise men' (sorcerers) of Daniel's day are mentioned numerous times in chapters two, four, and five of his book.

Contrary to sorcerers, even known today in some circles as 'Christian' clairvoyants, true wise men, of a biblical standard, are those who fear God and understand the signs of the times, and seasons of God concerning the end times biblical calendar (cf. Matt. 2:1), Having discernment (cf. Phil. 1:9, Heb. 5:14) and understanding (cf. 1 Chron. 12:23, Dan. 2:21, 2 Tim. 3:1) of the times is, however, even available to the ungodly when tuned into the spirit realm (cf. Est. 1:13). The difference is, the wise, in Christ, not only recognise and understand the signs of the times (12:10), being very much aware of the spirit realm, but also warn others, preaching repentance and the forgiveness of sin (Lu. 24:47, cf. Dan. 11:33, 12:3). Still, the wise are not immune to the predicted trouble, the birth pangs, ushering in the return of Jesus Christ (11:35, cf. Rev. 2:9-10).

The future trouble will affect everyone across the entire globe, as predicted by the metaphor, 'four winds.' In fact, the whole world is already under judgement, evident with recent events, which will only intensify (i.e., birth pains) as the day draws nearer to Jesus' return.

In sum, the reference to God sending and holding back the four winds (spirits) supports His absolute sovereignty over heaven and earth. Four times Daniel references 'the appointed time' (8:19, 11:27, 29, 35), which states God, and God alone controls what happens, when, where, how, to who, to what degree, and for how long. God is in absolute control, never man, and not even the devil. Again, and as always, the current events, and those to come, are orchestrated by God, designed to bring about salvation through repentance, that humanity would know God and make Him known. When we overlook the signs of the times, we neglect the point and purpose, which is the danger of being eschatologically ignorant. Those scoffing at end times teaching bear the fruit of ignorance, leading to fulfilling the great end-time apostasy (2 Thess. 2:3).

Right now, the winds are being held back, but soon, very, very soon, they will be released upon the earth, which will result in the coming tribulation, revealing the antichrist, as seen by Daniel and John. When the antichrist is revealed, he will be given absolute, global dominion for seven years before Jesus returns. When Jesus returns, He will defeat the unstoppable antichrist and take away his dominion.

In the limited remaining months/years left, the wise are very much aware of the things to come and the season through the signs of the times. Making the most of the remaining days (Eph. 5:16), the wise warn others, turning many to righteousness (Dan. 12:3). Fools, and scoffers, on the other hand, ignore and even dismiss Bible prophecy.

Part Two
'The Appointed Time of the End'
(vv. 15-27)

As mentioned in the previous section, the four winds (spirit) patrol the earth, awaiting their appointed time. Each of the symbolic references (ram, goat, and little horn) Daniel saw in the vision have been completed with the last partly fulfilled and yet to be fully fulfilled. The last was fulfilled, in part, by Antiochus, pronounced Anti-o-chus, who was a type and shadow of the things to come. Antiochus is a type of antichrist, providing insight into the activity and behaviour of the coming antichrist. So terrifying would be the activity of Antiochus and the coming antichrist (7:7); at the time of the vision, Daniel fainted (8:27). The vision made Daniel sick to the guts (8:27), although he could not fully understand the meaning (8:15, 16, 17). Even after Gabriel gave the interpretation (8:16), he still could not get his head around the vision (8:27).

When comparing Nebuchadnezzar's dream (chapter 2) with Daniel's (chapters 7 & 8), the visions refer to the same end-time event; Nebuchadnezzar understood the end-time mystery (2:45-47), while Daniel did not. On both occasions, the foreseen age-concluding event would take place long after Nebuchadnezzar and Daniel were gone (2:45, 8:26). When receiving the dream and vision, both Nebuchadnezzar and Daniel were troubled (2:1, 3, 30, 7:15). Again, Daniel remained troubled even after realising the prophecy would be fulfilled well after his time (7:28, 8:27, 12).

Daniel was continually frightened by the vision and by the appearance of Gabriel (8:17), yet was later told not to fear (10:12, 19). The angel

Gabriel told Daniel not to fear when seeking to understand the vision of the latter days (10:14).

Contrary to Daniel, many today have no interest in the end-times; they have no (godly) fear, therefore no wisdom (Ps. 9:10), and subsequently they fail to see and discern the season we are in, the end-times. According to scripture, only the wise will understand (12:10), and only the wise will make many others understand (11:33, 12:3), turning them to righteousness (12:3). Understanding the end-times produces godly fear, humility, and righteousness, whereas fools lacking (godly) fear lack humility and, therefore, lack understanding (cf. 10:14).

Even though we live on the cusp of the end-times, Nebuchadnezzar and Daniel both saw, most are too foolish, prideful, and therefore too blind to see it. Being spiritually blind, they are likened to the members of the church of Sardis, which had a reputation of being alive but were spiritually dead. (Rev. 3:1-6). Like Sardis, many today are conditioned and consumed by this world and even worldly preaching (e.g., Your Best Life Now), being conformed to the culture of this world. Like Sardis, unless the 21st-century sleeping church wakes up, they will be left behind.

Unlike the sleeping church, Daniel sought to understand the dream and vision, referring to the appointed time of the end (8:17, 19, 23, 26). Although he still had difficulty understanding the last part, he made sense of the first. Unlike Daniel, we have the advantage of scripture, history, prophecy fulfilling supernatural wisdom (12:10), and knowledge (12:4). Therefore, the church is held to a greater account (cf. Lu. 12:48).

From scripture and history, we understand that the vision of the appointed time includes Babylon being conquered by Media and Persia (8:20), followed by Greece (8:21), which started with one horn (Alexandra, cf. 11:3). Alexandra was the prominent horn (8:5) who died prematurely of malaria, and had no heirs; his kingdom was divided up among his four generals, who are the four horns (8:8, 11:4). One of which is Antiochus (8:23-25), who rose up, invaded, and conquered the

Jews through cunning and deceit (8:25). Although he seduced many with flattery, that is, those who violate the covenant, those who remained faithful to God stood firm and revolted (11:32). As a result, they were persecuted, and many died, fulfilling prophecy (7:18, 22, 27, 8:10, 24). Many died, but some were successful, such as the Maccabees.

The Hebrew word Maccabees can be translated as 'hammer,' which fits this priestly family of Jews. The Maccabees made history by organising a revolt against Antiochus after he defied the temple. They were successful in raising up a resistance which eventually took back Jerusalem. Under the order of the Maccabees, the temple was cleansed, and the idols were removed. However, the revolt cost many Jews their lives, as many as one thousand in a single day. The same will be repeated in the coming tribulation; however, that event will dwarf anything before it (12:1).

While Antiochus was in Jerusalem, he warred against the revolting saints and even against the God of Israel (8:25). During that time, Antiochus desecrated the temple for a little over six years (8:14), setting up pagan idols, changing the laws regarding temple sacrifices, and forcing the Jewish people to defy God. By conforming, the Jews would come under the divine penalty of death. This time is known as 'the time of wrath' (8:19). The actions of Antiochus were likened to waving his middle finger at God, even daring Him to respond. God did respond by sending Antiochus insane, in which state he died. God, not man, destroyed Antiochus.

History has it that Antiochus' friends called him Epiphanes 'the Illustrious One'. The name Antiochus in Greek is broken up into two parts, anti, meaning 'against,' and ochus, meaning 'support.' Put together, his name implies, 'against support' (being independent of man and God). The name Epiphanes is the Greek word meaning 'god manifest,' which he loved. Interestingly, Jesus is also known as Emmanuel, which means 'God with Us;' being, God manifest! Thus, Antiochus and the coming antichrist both are counterfeits by name and by nature.

Perhaps for this reason of counterfeiting God, the Jews called him Epimanes 'the Madman'. The madman is also fitting due to him dying insane in Persia in 163 B.C. Again, Antiochus became insane by the hand of God (8:25) in the same way Nebuchadnezzar did (4:28-33), the difference being, Nebuchadnezzar came to his senses, humbled himself through repentance, giving glory to God (4:34-37). Antiochus never did. Therefore, like his rise to power is not his own doing (8:24), his downfall was not by human means either.

As mentioned earlier, while the prophecies recorded in chapter eight have been fulfilled, ending with Antiochus, in part, the prophecy goes well beyond this antichrist-type. Antiochus was a type of antichrist who foreshadows the antichrist to come. The paralleled predictions of Antiochus and the coming antichrist are many. They include rising to power supernaturally (8:22, 23), promising (false) peace, and prosperity (8:25, 9:24-27) through seduction and flattery (11:32), operating independent of man, being empowered, and controlled supernaturally, (8:24), focusing on Israel (8:9), setting himself up as the authority (God) in Jerusalem (8:24-25), which includes defiling the temple by changing the laws regarding worship (7:25).

Antiochus changed the laws by forbidding the observance of the Sabbath, practicing temple sacrifices, and reading the Law of Moses. Antiochus even banned circumcision in an attempt to cut the Jewish people off from their God. Circumcision is what separated the Jews from the rest of the world's population (Jer. 4:4), in the same way Christians are to be separated through the circumcision of the heart (Rom. 2:24-29).

However, like today, at the time of Antiochus, many Jews under Jason the High Priest took the easy way out by conforming. Those who resisted and rebelled against Antiochus' redirected worship (cf. 11:32), he made war against them (8:10, 24, 11:33). Again, the self-professed god (Antiochus) even warred against God (8:25), in the same way, the coming antichrist will do (Rev. 13:7, 17:14), which did and will result in their supernatural deaths (8:25, Rev. 19:20), not by the hands of men but by God.

As mentioned earlier, the prophetic visions of chapters seven and eight are set to be fulfilled in the time of wrath, which falls within the time of the Gentiles (Lu. 21:24), covering the period from Nebuchadnezzar to Christ's return. The period between Nebuchadnezzar and Jesus is where Israel is undergoing divine discipline for disobedience, although they did have another opportunity when God appeared in the flesh through Jesus (Mk. 1:15), which was extended through Paul (cf. Acts 20:20-21); however, the invitation was largely rejected.

Until the tribulation commences, the people of the book (Israel) will not even see that they are under divine judgement until the fullness of the Gentiles has come in (Rom. 11:25). When the last Gentile has come in (salvation), then the church will be removed/raptured, and then Israel's eyes will be open, in the tribulation, seeking redemption for themselves (Rom. 11:26-32). At that point, they will call on the name of the Lord, and Jesus will return (Mt. 23:39).

Paul's letter to the saints in Rome (Rom. 1:7) further explains God's divine plan of salvation for the Jews. Now, those inheriting salvation, are saved from the wrath (tribulation) to come (Rom. 5:9, cf. 1 Thess. 5:9). Following the commencement of the tribulation, the Jews are first to be redeemed (Rev. 7:1-8) then as a result of their ministry (Rev. 14:1-5), multitudes are saved (Rev. 7:9-17). At the same time, many more remain blind to the signs of the times.

During the tribulation, the message of salvation is available to all (Rom. 10:8-13). The gift of salvation is always on offer regardless of the dispensation. The verse and phrase "the gifts and the calling of God are irrevocable" (Rom 11:28) provides confirmation, contextually referring to the gift of salvation, not charismatic gifts, such as tongues and prophecy, as some suggest. The gift of salvation is irrevocable, even while in the tribulation! ANYONE who calls on the name of the Lord (cf. Acts 4:12) by believing in their heart and confessing with their mouth shall be (not 'might be') saved (Rom. 10:8-10). Redemption is the point and purpose of the coming tribulation.

In conclusion, as mentioned earlier, the prophetic passage of chapter eight is to be considered dualistically, interpreted both literally and allegorically. The purpose of the passage serves to prepare, not scare, the reader. Judgement came to Israel due to disobeying God. Judgement will also come to the church for the same reason (Rom. 11:22). The judgement of God serves to test and separate one from another, such as the Maccabees; the God-fearing, God seeking remanent will separate themselves from the rest.

When Antiochus took authority over Jerusalem, God allowed him to have dominion for a time, which lasted a little longer than six years. When the antichrist comes, he will act in the same manner Antiochus did, and God will allow him to for seven years (7:25, 9:24-27). God not only allows the antichrist to persecute the Jews and anyone else who refuses to worship him, for seven years, but also sends him (2 Thess. 2:11). God will send the antichrist (strong delusion) due to confessing, yet apostate (2 Thess. 2:3), 'followers' refusing to love the truth, and take a stand, to be saved (2 Thess. 2:10).

Contrary to the teaching of the false 'once saved always saved' (hyper-grace), gaining and maintaining salvation always follows holding fast to confession and repentance, and making a lifestyle of it. An excellent example of a lifestyle of confession and repentance is in the next chapter, where Daniel prays, acknowledging God, repenting of sin, and asks for forgiveness (9:1-19). Daniel's prayer is addressed in the section following chapters five and six. While Daniel struggled to understand the vision of the end times, his mind was never too far away from it, which caused him to fear and draw near to God and warn others also.

Only the wise will understand (12:10) and only the wise will bring understanding to others (11:33, 12:3).

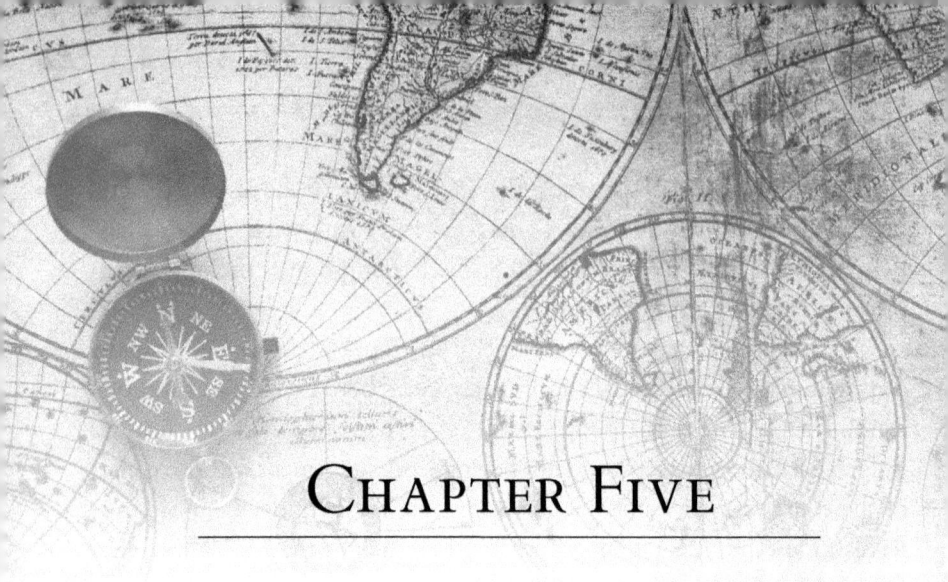

Chapter Five

Part One

'The Enemy is at the Gate'
(vv. 1-12)

In the previous section (chapter eight), we talked about the importance of discerning the signs of the times. Yet today, most cannot, even though as appointed watchmen (cf. Ezek. 3:17, 33:7), they have the responsibility to hear and warn. Worse again, instead of a warning, many who are positioned to proclaim Christ, by pointing to His return, distract and deceive with empty talk of hyper-grace, security, and prosperity. Unlike these dumb dogs (prophets/pastors) that do not bark, Daniel warned, like any other biblical prophet and watchmen. Isaiah sums up the problem then, and now, very well with the following verses:

"Israel's watchmen are blind; they are all oblivious; they are all mute dogs, they cannot bark; they are dreamers lying around, loving to slumber. Like ravenous dogs, they are never satisfied. They are shepherds with no discernment; they all turn to their own way, each one seeking his own gain: "Come, let me get the wine, let us imbibe the strong drink, and tomorrow will be like today, only far better!" (Isa. 56:10-12).

The dogs are dumb due to being distracted and deceived through empty dreams and dissipation. You will recognise them by the silly sayings they love so much, such as, 'Your best life now,' or 'The best is still before us' (cf. "tomorrow will be like today, only far better!" Isa. 56:12). Jesus warned about this, recorded in the book of Luke (12:13-21), and again when teaching on the signs of the end times (Lu. 21:34-36). There, verse thirty-four (Lu. 21:24) includes the word, 'dissipation' which warns against 'overindulgence.' Those caught up in overindulgence, 'living for their best life now,' are distracted, looking in the wrong direction, They will soon will be trapped in the 'day' (tribulation) that will suddenly come upon the whole world, catching any and many who are not awake, therefore, not ready (Lu. 21:36). This is precisely what happened to Belshazzar.

To recap:

Chapter five chronologically follows chapter eight, which concludes the rule and reign of the lion (7:4), being succeeded by the bear (7:5). We know the lion represents Babylon and the bear represents the Medes and Persia, being lopsided due to Persia being more significant than the Medes. Medo-Persia is also symbolically depicted in chapter eight as the ram where one horn is greater than the other. Again, the difference with the horns represents the level of power, Persia being more powerful than the Medes.

In the same way, God gave Nebuchadnezzar greatness (5:18), whereas all peoples, nations, and languages trembled and feared before him (5:19), God also gave Medo-Persia greatness. 'None could stand before them, and none could be rescued from their power. So Medo-Persia did as they pleased and became great' (8:4), as Nebuchadnezzar did (5:19), as God allowed for a time and a season (2:21).

God gave Medo-Persia dominion over Babylon (7:5) due to Belshazzar's pride (5:23). Even though he knew how God dealt with his grandfather (4:28-33, 5:22), he repeated the same and did not humble himself. However, his grandfather eventually did humble himself after the tribulation (4:34-37, 5:21).

Nebuchadnezzar died shortly after being restored, ruling Babylon for forty-three years. Babylon remained under the rule of the Babylonians for another twenty-three years before being conquered by Persia. Chapter five sees the transition of power, where Persia commenced its regime over Babylon from chapters six, nine, to twelve. At the point of chapter five, Daniel is in his eighties.

According to history, Dwight Pentecost (1985) states that after Nebuchadnezzar died, he was then succeeded by his son Merodach who ruled for two years (562–560 B.C., 2 Kings 25:27–30; Jer. 52:31–34). Merodach was murdered by Neriglissar, who was Nebuchadnezzar's son-in-law. Neriglissar then ruled four years, receiving a brief mention by the prophet Jeremiah (Jer. 39:3, 13). At his death, his young son Labashi-Marduk, succeeded him and ruled only two months (May and June) before being assassinated and succeeded by Nabonidus, who reigned seventeen years (556–539 B.C.). Nabonidus was committed to restoring Babylonian pagan worship, moving well away from Nebuchadnezzar's confession (4:1-3, 37). Belshazzar was Nabonidus' eldest son and was appointed by his father as his coregent (co-ruler). Nebuchadnezzar refers to Belshazzar's grandfather (5:2, 11, 13, 18; cf. v. 22). This coregency explains why Belshazzar was called king (5:1) and exercised kingly authority even though Nabonidus held the throne. The chart below summaries those as mentioned above.

Babylonian Kings	Reign	Relation to Nebuchadnezzar	Book of Daniel
Naborpolasar	621- 605	Father	
Nebuchadnezzar	605-562 B.C.	Self	Chapters 1 to 4
Evil-Merodach	562-560 B.C.	Son	
Neriglisar	560-556 B.C.	Son-in-law	
Laboroarchod	556-556 B.C.	Grandson	
Nabonidus Belshazzar	556-539 B.C. 553-539 B.C.	Son-in-law Grandson	Chapters 7,8, 5

Returning to the opening statement of this section, like many today, boastful Belshazzar had no fear of God. His foolishness was evident in his actions towards his enemies. Even though the Persians were at the gate, besieging Babylon, Belshazzar threw a party for one thousand lords (5:1). Instead of repenting and returning to what he once knew (5:22), he pridefully remained in his sin. Instead of warning those he was responsible for, he distracted and deceived them further with false hope by throwing a praise party.

Like Antiochus, Belshazzar waved his middle finger at God, daring Him to respond by calling for the vessels his father, Nebuchadnezzar, had taken from the Jewish temple (5:2). Not only did Belshazzar use the sacred vessels to get drunk from, but he also praised his gods of gold and silver, bronze, iron, wood, and stone (5:3-4). These useless gods were the same Nabonidus, Belshazzar's father, reimplemented within the Babylonian religion. Belshazzar's 'boldness,' however, was short-lived.

Belshazzar's actions dared God to respond. Using the items from Solomon's Temple to praise the Babylonian gods, foolish Belshazzar was making a direct challenge to the God of the Jewish temple, being the God of Israel. He literally dared Him to do something, all the while overlooking the grace of God extended towards him, providing an opportunity to repent.

Due to forgetting God, forsaking God, and replacing God, when the opportunity for repentance presented itself, Belshazzar did not see it, and therefore could not seize it. The opportunity was presented by the enemies being at the gate. You could say the writing was on the wall then, but still, Belshazzar was too blind to see. Instead of repenting, he pushed the envelope further, as far as it would go, by defiling the sacred vessels while praising his useless gods of stone and wood (cf. Rev. 9:20-21, 16:8-10).

Although 'brave' Belshazzar, fuelled by drunkenness (Dutch courage), was more than willing to challenge God, he was not ready for the response, as seen in verses five and six. Immediately a mysterious hand appeared and began writing on the wall. Brazen Belshazzar went white, and his limbs went weak with fear. Still, instead of falling on his face in repentance (remember, he knew of Nebuchadnezzar's experience), he called for the sorcerers, like Nebuchadnezzar did (2:2-3, 4:6-7, 5:7-8). Although the sorcerers, when summoned, on each occasion proved to be useless (2:10, 4:7, 5:8), just like the false gods were, made of metal, stone, and wood. And even though great reward awaited the one who could reveal the mystery, including being promoted to the third ruler of the kingdom, none of the useless sorcerers could.

As mentioned previously, the position of the third ruler was the next position under Belshazzar as a co-ruler; his father, Nabonidus, was the king. When the sorcerers could not read the writing on the wall, the king's colour changed some more (5:9). It was then, like with Nebuchadnezzar (4:8), Belshazzar was reminded that Daniel was able to interpret mysteries (5:10-12). So evident was the king's distress, his mother (or grandmother) said, "let not your thoughts alarm you, or your colour change" (5:10), followed by "king, live forever" (5:10), reminding her grandson of Daniel. The woman attempted to first comfort the king by dismissing the threat (like many today) by casually pointing out that Daniel can interpret. The woman was most likely to be Belshazzar's grandmother due to her familiarity with Nebuchadnezzar and Daniel's relationship. She also knew that Daniel had within the spirit of the holy gods (cf. 4:8–9, 18; 5:14). She knew of his insight, intelligence, wisdom (5:11), knowledge, understanding, and ability to interpret dreams (5:12). Because of Daniel's ability to solve mysteries, Nebuchadnezzar made him chief over the magicians (5:11). Knowing this, the king's grandmother advised Belshazzar to call for Daniel (5:12).

It was while Belshazzar was ruling Babylon (7:1, 8:1) that Daniel had visions of the time of the end (8:17, 19, 23, 26), which also turned him white and made him sick with fear (7:28, 8:27). The difference being, instead of seeking the counsel of foolish men, as Belshazzar did (5:7), Daniel sought to understand the mystery, from God, through prayer (see chapters 9 & 10).

Unlike Daniel, many today repeat the foolishness of Belshazzar by forgetting and forsaking God, surrounding themselves with foolish counsellors (so-called prophets, or 'Christian' clairvoyants – charlatans!), and will continue to do so even in the tribulation. In fact, during the tribulation, most will be deceived by the cunning craftiness of false prophets (Matt. 24:24).

Also, like Belshazzar, many today are 'throwing a partying' (worldly self-help church services, resembling motivational Ted talks and imitating nightclubs), despite the enemy being at the gate (cf. Gen. 4:7). This will result in judgement, executed through the tribulation. The tribulation is on the other side of the gate, knocking even now evident through the signs of the time, primarily through an increase of false teachers and false teaching, resulting in lukewarmness and apostasy.

Other signs indicating the nearness of the tribulation include everything Jesus predicted, which is now daily news (Matt. 24, Mk. 13, Lu. 21). Still, most are failing to hear and warn, likened to the dumb dogs Isaiah spoke of, that refuse to bark. Instead of warning, the dumb dogs distract with Christless preaching, promoting false peace and prosperity (e.g., Your Best Life Now). Instead of preparing, they throw a praise party. The church of Laodicea (Rev. 3:14-22) is an excellent example of this, serving as an end-time warning to the last church (us) before Jesus returns. Laodicea claimed to have everything and no need for anything. While they had everything the world could offer, they did not have Christ, and therefore were in danger of being vomited out. The 21st-century church is the prophetic fulfilment of the Laodicean church. Unless repentance comes first and fast, this lukewarm, apostate church will be vomited out and into the tribulation (cf. 2 Thess. 2).

The modern church represents blind Belshazzar, who could not see the writing on the wall with the enemies at the gate, and neither could he read the writing on the wall. Even when Daniel was summoned to reveal the mystery, he seemingly still did not realise its severity, promoting and rewarding Daniel (5:29), with only hours left to live.

When Daniel interpreted the writing on the wall, unlike many today, Daniel did not attempt to flatter or distract with empty words. Unlike when dealing with Nebuchadnezzar (cf. 4:19, 27), Daniel spoke plainly, informing Belshazzar he had been weighed and found guilty. Time had run out, and the judgement would be executed swiftly. The same is true for this generation. Time has just about run out, and many will soon be weighed and found guilty, in the same way the church of Laodicea was. The difference will be, this generation will not be given another opportunity to repent before judgement, due to wasting and even perverting grace (Jude 1:4). Soon, most will be vomited into the tribulation.

The enemy is at the gate, and the writing is on the wall, right now, yet still, most cannot see it. Instead of warning, most distract with praise parties. Even in Christ's name, due to a departure of sound biblical doctrine, churches are competing with nightclubs, conducting services void of the biblical Jesus. But soon, like with Belshazzar, the writing will appear on the wall, or even in the sky (Rev. 6:14-17), where the left behind apostate church who once knew God will realise that they have been weighed, found guilty, and judged. When that day comes, like Belshazzar, the left behind will go white with fear, and their limbs will go weak in terror. Replacing boastfulness will be brokenness, which is the point and purpose of the tribulation.

This was predicted by Jesus (Matt. 7:21-23) and Paul (2 Thess. 2:3), also seen through the seven letters to the churches (Rev. 2-3, where 70 percent of the churches were in trouble). Most will go through the coming tribulation, not escaping the wrath (judgement) to come.

Today, the carnal church, like Belshazzar, is partying while the enemy is at the gate. Like with Belshazzar, the enemy did not need to scale the walls or break down the gates. To penetrate the walls of Babylon, Persia diverted the Euphrates River and came in under the gates. The river had previously been the source of life for the Babylonian people.

In the same way, the biblical Jesus proclaimed through the gospel (sound biblical preaching), has been the source of life for the church. Yet, through a departure of sound doctrine, the enemy has done the same as Persia did; he has diverted the Word of God from our churches. The departure from truth, absolute truth, has allowed the enemy to creep in under the gates. In contrast, the sleepy church has been preoccupied and distracted with worldly hype, namely prosperity preaching.

In sum, chapter five is compared to chapter four, with a reminder and an ominous warning to this generation, of Nebuchadnezzar's closing words, "And those who walk in pride, He is able to humble" (4:37, 5:21). God judged prideful Nebuchadnezzar for seven years, and for seven years, God will soon judge this generation through the coming tribulation. In the same way, Belshazzar knew the stories yet failed to respond; the church does likewise, especially through the letters to the seven churches (Rev. 2-3). The church was warned yet ignored and dismissed the warnings in the same way Belshazzar did. In the same way, Belshazzar was judged, so will the apostate church be.

Part Two
'The Writing on the Wall'
(vv. 13-30)

From part one of this chapter, we are reminded that chapter five follows chapter eight chronologically. Chapters seven and eight are very similar, predicting the succeeding empires ruling over Babylon, concluding with the antichrist (cf. Rev. 13) governing the Babylonian religious and political system during the tribulation (Rev. 17, 18).

While Daniel struggled to understand the events and activity of the concluding ruler, he did understand the vision regarding the Medes and Persia and Greece, who would conquer the Babylonian empire. Daniel did not understand the end times, as we can, but he certainly did connect the dots regarding Persia when the enemy was at the gates. The evidence of that statement was seen where he changed the word PARSIN (5:26) to PERES (5:28), referring to Persia.

While Belshazzar was partying with his lords, wives, and concubines (5:2), the city was besieged by Medo-Persia, the enemy at the gate. Although God was about to hand the Babylonian kingdom over to Persia (5:28), as prophesied (7:5), Belshazzar was too blind to see it; blind drunk, and spiritually blind as well. Thus, instead of walking in humility and surrounding himself with godly counsel, Belshazzar was blinded by pride (5:22) and by the fools who surrounded him (5:7), as Nebuchadnezzar had been and done previously. Nebuchadnezzar did, however, repent after God humbled him (4:37). Unlike Belshazzar, Nebuchadnezzar also held Daniel in high esteem (2:46-48); conversely, Belshazzar did not.

While Belshazzar was blind drunk and challenging God (5:3-4), likened to waving his middle finger at God, God's finger appeared and began writing on the wall (5:5), MENE, MENE, TEKEL, and PARSIN. The witting was a language familiar to the king (cf. 2:4), written in Aramaic. Still, the writing remained a mystery; therefore, Belshazzar summoned his foolish 'wise men' to interpret. Proving to be useless (5:15) as with every other time (2:10, 4:7) the (not so) wise men could not read the writing on the wall. Still ignorant of the meaning and growing increasingly concerned (5:6, 9), the king summoned Daniel after being reminded of him by his grandmother (5:11-12). The king's grandmother was most likely to be Nebuchadnezzar's widow. When Daniel was summoned, Belshazzar greeted him with the words, "You are Daniel, one of Judah's exiles" (5:13). The address was one of contempt. Belshazzar treated Daniel with the same level of contempt he did the God of Israel (5:2-4). After belittling Daniel, the king relayed the queen's words (5:14, cf. 11-12).

As mentioned in the previous section, Daniel's feelings for Belshazzar were seemingly mutual. Instead of wishing the king well (cf. 4:19), he rebuked him (5:22-23). Daniel rebuked Belshazzar after summarizing what he already knew about God's dealings with Nebuchadnezzar (5:18-21). God humbled Nebuchadnezzar for his pridefulness (4:30, 37); after being allowed to repent (4:27), he failed to heed the warning, resulting in judgement (4:20-26). Showing further contempt for the king, Daniel rejected the going reward and position of third in the kingdom for interpreting the writing on the wall (5:17). Daniel was not interested in the reward, or the promotions of men, unlike the wise men were. Neither was Daniel interested in keeping corrupt company (cf. 1 Cor. 15:33), unlike the unwise king.

Another thing that separates Daniel from the rest is that on each occasion, the (not so) wise men were summoned, Daniel was not among them (cf. 2:2, 4:6-7, 5:7) even though he was the chief of the magicians

(2:48). He did not waste his time hanging around fools, and he wasted no time flattering the foolish king either when summoned, unlike the useless wise men (cf. Ps. 5:9).

Again, chapter four considered Daniel's address and the respectful exchange between Daniel and Nebuchadnezzar (4:19). No such offering is made or seen between Daniel and Belshazzar, who refused to humble himself (4:22), and who foolishly and openly challenged God. He would now hear and learn of his fate, and that his very breath was in God's hands (4:23). It is with this statement, "But the God in whose hand is your breath" (4:23b), wrapped in the rebuke, that the reader could detect Daniel's disdain for the king. The God Belshazzar has mocked is not just the God of the Jewish Temple, therefore the God of Israel alone, but He is the God of heaven (4:22), and the God of earth, and everything in it (cf. Ps. 146:6).

Nebuchadnezzar made this known previously (4:34, 37, cf. 4:1-3, 2:47). Therefore, Belshazzar had no excuse, knowing this to be the case (5:22). Consequently, he was judged for sinning against knowledge, thus more severely (cf. Lu. 12:48). Belshazzar would have been better off never knowing about God than to have heard and not remained (cf. 2 Pet. 2:21).

Like all of us, Belshazzar's life was in God's hand, which was the same hand that wrote on the wall (4:24). Instead of turning to God in humility through repentance, pleading for deliverance from his enemies who were at the gate, like David did (cf. Ps. 31:15-17), Belshazzar mocked God. The foolish king put his trust in useless gods, that knew nothing (5:23), made by man's hand rather than in God, in whose hand his very life-breath was. Now, not only would God take Belshazzar's life, but He would also end the Babylonian rule.

This was the judgement written on the wall, MENE, MENE, TEKEL, and PARSIN, meaning, MENE, God has numbered the days of your kingdom and brought it to an end (4:26). TEKEL, You have been weighed in the balance and found wanting (4:27). PARES, Your kingdom is divided and given to the Medes and the Persians (4:28).

Belshazzar had been weighed and judged, and he had fallen short of God's required standard, like all of us (cf. Rom. 3:23), without Christ. Although Belshazzar predates the cross by half a century, like all of us, he still had an opportunity to repent by the of grace God. Grace is evidence in every dispensation, followed by judgement. The worst will follow this dispensation of grace (Eph. 3:2), with the tribulation (12:1, Matt. 24:21).

Regarding Daniel's interpretation of Belshazzar's judgment, notice when interpreting, Daniel changed PARSIN to PARES, which refers to Persia. Due to Belshazzar's lack of humility, God would now take away his kingdom and give it to the Persians, which was fulfilled that very night (5:30). The story of sudden judgement is not unlike another, found in the book of Acts, chapter five (vv. 1-11). The story refers to Ananias and Sapphira who were suddenly judged and stuck dead as a result of lying to the Holy Spirit. The sudden judgement served as a warning to the church, producing godly fear (Acts 5:11). The tribulation will do the same thing for those left behind (cf. Rev. 2:22-23).

Sadly, godly fear departed the church long ago, which is the reason that most have strayed. A lack of godly fear was also the root cause of Belshazzar's behaviour, costing him his life and his kingdom. Hours later, Darius took Babylon and killed Belshazzar. While Belshazzar's life ended, Daniel would continue to prosper under the new God-appointed ruler of Babylon, Darius (6:1-3).

The defeat of Babylon fulfilled not only the prophecy Daniel made earlier through chapters seven (v. 5) and eight (vv. 3-4) and again that same night (5:28) but also a prophecy given by Isaiah (Isa. 47:1–5). The rule of the Medes and Persians was the second phase of the times of the Gentiles (cf. Lu. 21:24). The events in chapter five illustrate that God is sovereign and moves according to His predetermined plans. Thus, the events assure the reader, biblical prophecy is 100% accurate and reliable. The events of chapters seven and eight also anticipate the final overthrow of all Gentile world powers that rebel against God during the coming tribulation. The coming judgement, predicted in Psalm, chapter two (vv. 4–6) and Revelation, chapter nineteen (vv. 15–16), will be fulfilled at the Second Advent of Jesus Christ to this earth.

Before Jesus returns to judge the nations, one final warning will be given to those trusting in the false gods of the Babylonian (world) system. Revelation, chapter eighteen, pronounces judgement on Babylon (vv. 1-3) with the last call to anyone having ears to hear, "Come out of her my people" (Rev. 18:4a). The consequence of remaining in Babylon results in sharing in her judgement (Rev. 18:4b). The same warning was given to five of the seven churches (Rev. 2-3). If you continue to do what displeases God, namely practice false worship, you will share in the final judgement. Every letter to the seven churches concluded with, "He who has an ear to hear let him hear what the Spirit is saying to the churches." The message is timeless; the warning is accurate, reliable, and relevant for us today; especially for us, being the last church before Jesus returns.

Like with Belshazzar, where the judgement of God was executed swiftly, the same will be repeated for those remaining in rebellion during the tribulation. During the tribulation, the rebels will be given the opportunity to repent. Every plague is designed to produce repentance, yet still, most will not respond positively.

Instead of repenting, like Belshazzar, the rebels will continue to worship false gods (Rev. 9:20-21), and while doing so, they even curse the God of heaven (Rev. 16:8-10). Again, like with Belshazzar, when God does respond, judgement will be swift. In a single day (Rev. 18:8) and a single hour (Rev. 18:9, 17, 19), the Babylonian world system will be destroyed. Once more, like with Belshazzar, Babylon will be no more, no more, no more, no more, no more, no more (Rev. 18:22-23, x6).

Due to a lack of fear, Belshazzar provoked God in the same way many churches do today. Churches that are watering down and twisting scripture, producing false worship, even blessing abortion clinics, celebrating same-sex relationships, and adopting gender fluidity, provoke God to anger.

Scoffers do likewise (2 Pet. 3:3, Jude 1:18). Scoffers mock God by ignoring and dismissing the prophecies. Instead of looking to Jesus, longing for and living for Jesus, they twist the scripture to support their worldly lifestyles. Because of this, the church is now unrecognisable from the world, and runs in the opposite direction to the gospel (cf. Rom. 12:2). The church and Babylon have become one, which is why God says, "Come out of her My people," or else (Rev. 18:4a).

The enemy is at the gate, and the writing is on the wall, yet few can see it and even less announce it. Instead of having eyes to see and ears to hear, most are drunk with worldly passion (Rev. 18:3). From out of the same cup Babylon drinks, the wrath of God will flow in double portion (Rev. 18:6). When Belshazzar drank from the golden cup, he touched God's glory and thereby drank the wrath of God unto himself (5:2-5).

The wrath poured out during the tribulation is the same wrath Jesus drank unto Himself (Lu. 22:42). Jesus drank the wrath of God that we may never need to. However, if you do not come to God and remain in God through the requirement of repentance and obedience, then you too will share in the cup of wrath. Anyone during the tribulation who rejects God by accepting and committing to false worship and accepting the 'mark' of the beast (666), will drink from the cup of wrath for all eternity (Rev. 14:9-11).

In sum, an important takeaway from Daniel, chapter five, is that our lives and very breath are in God's hand (5:23b). The same hand will either save (cf. Ps. 31:15-17) or slay (4:30 cf. Rev. 2:16, 19:11-16), depending on how we respond. Paul clarifies that the one true God is both kind and severe, kind to those who remain but severe to those who fall (Rom. 11:22). Your response to God will determine your experience of Him and your eternal destination. As it was for Belshazzar and Ananias and Sapphira, so will it be for the left behind lukewarm 21st-century church, unless repentance comes first, and fast. The writing is on the wall and the enemy is at the gate – soon it will be too late.

Chapter Six

Part One
'Daniel Prospered'
(vv. 1-5)

The previous section, chapter five, concluded the Babylonian reign, succeeded by Persia, as prophesied in chapters seven (v. 5) and eight (vv. 3-4). Chapter two also referenced Persia's succession to the Babylonian Empire (v. 39). Chapter five (v. 30) sees the fulfilment of that prophecy, stating that Darius, the Mede received the kingdom after conquering Babylon and killing Belshazzar. Chapter six commences with Darius' arrangement of his new government, in much the same way we see any newly elected governmental official arrange their government when coming into power. The freshly arranged government included Daniel being positioned with distinction (6:2-3).

Due to having an 'excellent spirit' (beyond what is normal), Daniel was set up over the whole kingdom (6:3). Daniel was a faithful man, with no error found in him (6:4), making him unusual and untouchable. It is not the first time Daniel has stood out among his peers, for in chapter one, none was found to be equal with Daniel when tested before king Nebuchadnezzar (1:19); Daniel was ten times better than the rest (1:20). As a result, he was prominently and permanently positioned within the Babylonian kingdom until the first year of king Cyrus (1:21). Chapter two sees Daniel promoted again, rewarded with gifts, and made ruler over the whole province (2:48). Due to Daniel's request, his companions were also promoted (2:49). In confirmation of chapter one, verse twenty-one, while Belshazzar was ruling Babylon, Daniel was still positioned within the kingdom and known to be chief of all the wise men (5:11).

In the same way, Daniel was positioned to be ruler over the whole province by Nebuchadnezzar (2:48), he was again by Darius (6:3). Chapter one (v. 21) notes Daniel would rule until the first year of king Cyrus and then did likewise from the first year of Cyrus. Darius and Cyrus are co-ruling kings of Persia, therefore refer to the same time.

Some say Darius is another name for Cyrus (cf. 6:28). Others say Darius was appointed to rule over Babylon by Cyrus (cf. 9:1). Ezra (6:14b) clears up the confusion, however, listing Cyrus, Darius, and Artaxerxes, as the kings of Persia. Still, both Darius and Cyrus are interconnected, referring to the same event and the same time.

During that time, Daniel prospered under the reign of Darius/Cyrus (6:28). Due to Daniel's faithfulness to God (6:4), he prospered regardless of the circumstances. It did not matter who was ruling and reigning over Babylon; God still promoted and prospered Daniel over and above any other. Even when Belshazzar was on the throne, who had little regard for Daniel (cf. 5:13), Daniel was still rewarded with great wealth and promoted to the third ruler in the entire kingdom (5:29), despite not pursuing it (5:17).

Further evidence of Daniel not pursuing position and prosperity is in chapter one, where he refused to eat from the king's table (1:8), which could have resulted in his death (1:10). Also, in chapter two, Daniel was not among the wise men (2:2) when summoned to interpret Nebuchadnezzar's dream. The sorcerers knew the king would reward the one who could do as he asked (2:48-49). The same is true of Daniel's companions; they risked losing their position of prominence (2:49) and even their lives (3:17) by refusing to bow down and worship the golden image (3:8-18). Daniel did the same when opening up the window, openly praying to God (6:10, 13) when instructed to only worship Darius, for just thirty days (6:7). Daniel refused to compromise, even for just thirty days; he was not interested in pleasing man, pursuing or maintaining prosperity and position.

Yet, Daniel prospered (full stop). The 'full stop' is where many within the charismatic camp stop. They do so by reading the likes of Daniel, chapter six (in part and out of context). By doing so, all they see is that Daniel prospered. DANIEL PROSPERED! God made Daniel rich, so rich that it prompted others to jealousy. God not only made Daniel rich, but He also promoted him, and He protected him from danger! Not only was Daniel rich beyond measure, but he was also untouchable! God foiled the plans of evil men who would do him harm and even shut the mouth of lions (6:22, cf. Heb. 11:23). Therefore, if He did it for Daniel, He will do it for us; After all, God is no respecter of persons (Acts 10:34) - right?

What was meant for evil was used for good (cf. Gen. 50:20). The very thing the satraps used to destroy Daniel was used to kill themselves (6:24). The story should remind us of Haman, who also planned to harm one of God's servants by hanging Mordecai (see Esther, chapter five). Verses nine to fourteen of Esther, chapter five, tell the story. However, God turned around what was meant for evil, for good; instead of Mordecai being hung, Haman was (Est. 6:7-10). The same thing happened with Daniel's accusers (6:24); therefore, according to Word of Faith teaching, the same is true for us. God will make us rich beyond measure, promote us above our peers. God will also protect us from man and beast; after all, that was Daniel's experience; therefore, it should be ours also - right?

I have given three references (cf. Matt. 18:16, 1 Cor. 13:1) for this occurrence (Gen. 50:20, Est. 5-6, Dan. 6); therefore, it must be true. Having these three references is proclaimed as sound biblical truth! Furthermore, Paul confirms that God gave him divine protection from those opposing him by shutting the mouths of lions (2 Tim. 4:17). Paul's reference to the mouths of lions referred to those seeking to do him harm (2 Tim, 4:14).

Based on the above, as taught by the Word of Faith movement, God wants us to be rich and walk in divine protection, including protection from sickness. Happy, healthy, and wealthy, that is their gospel! But is that the gospel? Is that what Daniel, chapter six is all about? And is that what other chapters and passages are talking about? We already know that the answer is a definite no!

Daniel suffered, yet due to his faithfulness in suffering, God sustained him to make God known through him (2:47, 4:1-3, 27, 34-37, 5:17-26, 6:25-27). The same was true of Paul. Although God did, on occasion, deliver Paul, Paul still suffered greatly for the sake of the gospel (Acts 14:19, 16:22, 2 Cor. 6:5, 11:16-33). Paul ended his time on earth by being beheaded. He seemed to be anticipating his soon demise when writing: "For I am already being poured out as a drink offering, and the time of my departure has come. I have fought the good fight, I have finished the race, I have kept the faith. Henceforth there is laid up for me the crown of righteousness, which the Lord, the righteous judge, will award to me on that Day, and not only to me but also to all who have loved His appearing" (2 Tim. 4:6-8).

Like with Paul, who was opposed and challenged from within (1 Cor. 4:19), chapter six confirms, Daniel's life was not without challenges (vv. 4-5). When setting up his new government, Darius appointed one hundred and twenty satraps, provincial governors in the ancient Persian Empire (6:1). Nebuchadnezzar did the same thing (3:2-3), and it was these satraps who caused a problem for Shadrack, Meshach, and Abednego (3:8-13), yet to no avail (3:27). Repeating chapter three, in chapter six, it is the satraps who seek to destroy Daniel, probably due to jealously (6:4-5). Whatever the reason, their accusation was malicious (6:24). Due to not finding fault in Daniel, the satraps devised a plan to eliminate him (vv. 6-9); the plan was strategically connected to his uncompromising faithfulness to God (6:5).

As mentioned above, Daniel was delivered from the devilish plans of men, like Paul was (2 Tim. 4:17) on occasion; however, that does not mean we will experience the same deliverance. Sometimes, deliverance is gained through death, as it was ultimately for Paul and many countless others (cf. Rev. 2:10). Deliverance through physical death was the twelve apostles' experience also, except for John.

However, countless millions have been persecuted, even to death, over the centuries, which is set to get worse, not better, leading up to Jesus' return (Matt. 24:9). During the tribulation, persecution resulting in death will be the only means of escape (Rev. 6:9-11, 7:13-17, 13:10, 15, 14:13, 16:6, 20:4). Trusting God is our only hope, now, as it will be during the tribulation for those left behind.

Daniel trusted God (6:23), regardless of the outcome. Shadrack, Meshach, and Abednego did the same (3:17). Hebrews, chapter eleven refers to the same again. Yet, many perished trusting God (Heb. 11:36-40), recognising this world is not our home (Heb. 11:13-16, 10).

The reward of trusting God is not the riches of this world, but instead having an opportunity to bear witness for God, even in and through persecution, like with the church of Smyrna (Rev. 2:8-11). Smyrna literally means 'myrrh.' When myrrh is crushed, it releases a sweet aroma. When crushed through persecution, even unto death (Rev. 2:10) the church of Smyrna released a sweet aroma of faithfulness unto

God. The only charge Smyrna received from Jesus was to remain faithful to God unto death, and then they would receive the crown of life (Rev. 2:10). When taking a stand for God, you are more likely to be crushed, or thrown into the lion's den, or a fiery furnace, than to be rewarded by and in this evil world.

The gospel, as mentioned earlier, puts God front and centre by dying to self (Gal. 2:20), while the prosperity gospel (another gospel, cf. 2 Cor. 11:4) focuses on self, 'me and mine in the here and now.' That 'gospel' was designed to distract, therefore deceive, and ultimately disqualify from the eternal prize. The prize is not earthly reward and riches; it is Jesus (Phil. 3:13-14).

Many today are willing to sacrifice Jesus for materialism, such as Judah, (Matt. 26:14-16) and Demas did (2 Tim. 4:1). Others cannot sacrifice materialism to follow Jesus, such as the rich young ruler (Mk. 10:17-27). Instead, they do as the church of Laodicea did (Rev. 3:14-22); they consume themselves with so much materialism that it replaces Jesus. The evidence is where you can no longer tell the difference between the church and the world.

The prosperity gospel, as taught by many, is a false gospel. God gives us prosperity for purpose, being that He will supply your "need" in accordance with His calling (Phil 4:19; Matt. 6:25-34), not self-centred greed or fleshly desire. Prosperity for many is an idol of the heart (Ezek. 14:1-11). Modern-day idols are fleshly desires which can quickly lead us astray (Mk. 4:19; 2 Pet. 1:4b). Unsurprisingly, scripture has plenty to say about those who preach and chase after prosperity (2 Cor. 2:17; 1 Tim. 6:3-10, 3:3b; Jude 11b). Scripture clearly states not to toil to acquire wealth (Prov. 23:4; 28:20), neither desire it, love it or put your trust in it (Matt. 6:19; 1 Tim. 6:9-10; Heb. 13:5).

Running hand-hand with the idea that God wants His followers to be wealthy is the false ideology that the believer in God deserves to be happy. However, Solomon, through Ecclesiastes (9:2-3a), and Luke

(13:1-5), and Matthew (5:45), reveal that all are subject to good and evil while living in a world compromised by sin (Rom. 8:19-22). Peter has plenty more to say on the matter of the suffering believer (1 Peter), confirmed by James (1:2), John (16:33), and Luke (Acts 14:22), to list but a few. The Bible tells us that sinful man yearns for money, pleasure, security, significance, health, food, self-righteousness, worth, power, knowledge, and happiness - every sort of blessing squandered at the Fall. Yet, God's children should seek, long for, and thirst after Him, alone (Ps. 42, Lu. 11:9-13, Rev. 3:18, 22:17).

Many today claim that the followers of God deserve to have a good life and that God wants believers to have the desires of their heart, and that God has destined His children to reign in this life (by twisting scripture). But, God does not owe anyone a prosperous existence, either materially or culturally. In fact, as mentioned above, Jesus promised His followers the exact opposite (Jn. 16:33), which is why He said we must endure (not enjoy) to the end if we want to be saved (Matt. 10:22, 24:13).

When taking into consideration the above mentioned, Daniel chapter six is descriptive, more over-prescriptive. The book as a whole, however, sets up the framework for a 'suffer now/glory later' gospel, contrary to what Kingdom Now theology proposes. As mentioned previously, Kingdom Now theology (ideology, or better still, idiocy) claims the believer in God is to dominate this world until Jesus returns. By doing so, believers are to reign as kings, to prosper in this life with health, wealth, and happiness. That idiotic teaching runs in the opposite direction to what the Bible teaches.

Daniel chapter twelve clarifies this by pointing to the everlasting prosperity reserved (alone) for those who refuse to compromise. The promise is not rewarded to the likes of Judas and Demas, who looked to this world for comfort. The same is true for many prosperity preachers who peddle the gospel for greedy gain. The true believer in God does not lay hold of the wealth here and now, any more than what is described at the end of Daniel, chapter six, but rather that of chapter twelve. "You shall rest and shall stand in your allotted place at the end of the days."

In chapter twelve (v. 13), God gives a pre-resurrection promise to the delivered (12:1) and to the resurrected (12:2). As seen through these verses, our ultimate prosperity is eschatological. The promised prosperity begins now only with the promised end-time Holy Spirit being poured out, (Acts 2), which puts spirit against the flesh, heightening the same dangers to prosperity that Daniel faced, as we face today.

The eschatological promise is that we shall stand in our allotted places at the end of days. WE SHALL STAND! The future prosperity forms our attitudes towards the enticing lure of the kingdom now, prosperity now teaching. Without sound biblical knowledge, particularly a good theological/eschatological framework, many will be deceived in these last days by 'another gospel,' namely one that promises prosperity now at the expense of prosperity later. Those who fall for it, prosperity now will be their gospel, and their god, causing them to fall down to any image and give homage to any power promising it. Essentially, they are being conditioned (see Rev. 18) for the coming events of Revelation, chapter thirteen, where they will bow down and worship the beast (Rev. 13:11-17). Hence the need for an angel flying overhead with the eternal gospel, saying with a loud voice, "Fear God and worship Him" (Rev. 14:6-7). Those words are sounding even today, loud and clear, for any with ears to hear. Like with Daniel, only the humble (11:12), wise (1210), and the faithful (6:4, Rev. 2:10, 13) will hear and hold fast (Rev. 2:13, 25, 3:11).

Part Two

'All People are to Tremble and Fear Before God' (vv. 6-28)

As concluded in the previous section, Daniel, chapter six has about as much to do with prosperity as it does petitioning God to deliver (declare and decree, command and demand). Instead of prosperity and protection, the chapter focuses on trusting God and fearing Him more than man. Daniel's fear of God is evident in his outworked faithfulness towards God (6:10, 23); and even towards the king (6:5, 22). The king reciprocated Daniel's faithfulness (6:16, 18). God did likewise (6:22). The passage ends with the king's proclamation for all people to fear and tremble before God, eventuating through his newfound commitment of faith in God (6:25), resulting from Daniel's faithfulness.

Like Daniel's companions (3:16-18), his faithfulness to God was unwavering, regardless of the outcome (6:10, 22). The story of Daniel and the lions' den is a repeat of chapter three, where Shadrack, Meshach, and Abednego were tested by fire. Both stories revolve around false worship and the attempt to cause faithful worshippers to fall. Again, both stories revolve around a man setting himself up as a god, demanding to be worshipped (3:1-7, 6:7, 12). In the case of Darius, all agreed with the decree (6:7), except for Daniel (6:10). Daniel responded like Shadrack, Meshach, and Abednego, who stood alone in their faithfulness to God (3:12).

Following the failed attempt to cause the faithful to fall comes persecution. On both accounts, the faithful few were heavily outnumbered by their accusers, which were on each occasion, the satraps. For

Daniel, it was a case of one hundred and twenty against one (6:1). The satraps set out to destroy God's faithful remanent (3:8-12, 6:4-5, 11-13, 15). Again, on both accounts, the faithful few faced the ultimate test involving being thrown into a fiery furnace and thrown into the lions' den. The difference being, Shadrack, Meshach, and Abednego had an opportunity to recant (3:15), whereas Daniel did not (6:16). Regardless, none shrank back (cf. Heb. 10:37-39).

The test was a direct attack on God and His ability to save, as seen with Nebuchadnezzar, when he said, "Who is the god who will deliver you out of my hands?" (3:15). Nebuchadnezzar responded to his rhetorical statement at the close of the chapter, stating, "Blessed be the God of Shadrach, Meshach, and Abednego, who has sent his angel and delivered his servants, who trusted in him, and set aside the king's command, and yielded up their bodies rather than serve and worship any god except their own God" (3:28). Darius came to the same conclusion (6:27) after being tricked into changing the law, which prohibited any worship, but the worship of Darius (6:7).

To trap Daniel, the satraps manipulated the king into establishing a law (6:7) that cannot be changed (6:8, 12), not even by the king (16:15). The malicious satraps tricked Darius into making the decree (cf. 6:6-9, 24). Once the decree had been made, the satraps went (lit. rushed) to where Daniel was praying. They could not get there fast enough. The trap had been set, and now it was time to collect. Sure enough, they found Daniel faithfully praying, as previously (6:10). The satraps reported the matter to the king, belittling Daniel as one of the exiles from Judah (as Arioch and Belshazzar had done; cf. 2:25; 5:13).

Although Daniel was not given the opportunity to renounce his faith before being thrown into the lions' den (6:16), he was not prepared to 'shelve' or 'hide' his commitment to the law of God in any way (6:5), not even for just thirty days (6:7). As Daniel had done previously, he went home to pray when he heard about the decree (6:10). Daniel prayed three times a day to God (6:13). Daniel's prayer was one of petition (6:11, 12, 13), thanksgiving (6:10), and guidance (6:11). Contextually, Daniel was praying for help when faced with having to disobey the king's decree, being instead required by the law of God to fear and obey God rather than man (cf. Acts 5:29). Much more can be learned from chapter nine about what Daniel prayed, which revolved around humility, confession, and repentance.

Contrary to the false teaching from the Word of Faith movement, Daniel was not declaring and decreeing, demanding, and commanding (petitioning) as some, pointlessly, do today. The idiotic idea that we can command of God comes from twisting the words of God, spoken through Isaiah (45:11). The Word of Faith camp practises exegetical gymnastics when misquoting the verse from the KJV, which says: "Ask Me (God) of things to come concerning my sons and concerning the work of My hands command ye Me." However, the ESV translates it this way: "How dare you question Me about My sons, or instruct Me in the work of My hands?" Paul picks up the same idea in Roman's: "But who are you, O man, to answer back to God?" Read Romans chapter nine (vv. 1-29) for context. The context of Isaiah's reference is where God is using His shepherd (Isa. 44:28) Cyrus, the anointed (Isa. 45:1), to discipline Israel due to them replacing God with false gods. Due to being disciplined, Israel questions God (Isa. 45:9), and God rebukes them (Isa. 45:11). Through discipline, God points the rebellious back to Himself as their only Saviour (Isa. 45:15) which will be repeated in the coming tribulation. Interestingly, the passage (esp. Isa. 45:5-7, 18) makes the same proclamation that Darius did at the conclusion of Daniel, chapter six (cf. Isa. 45:23b, Dan. 6:26).

Unlike unfaithful Israel, through a testing time, Daniel thanked God, who was able to deliver him. Shadrack, Meshach, and Abednego responded similarly when threatened with the fiery furnace (3:17). They trusted God to deliver them, either in the fire or through it. Darius also hoped God would rescue Daniel (6:16).

The difference between King Nebuchadnezzar and King Darius is that Darius was humble, to some degree, and loving towards Daniel; the evidence in verse fourteen: "Then the king, when he heard these words, was much distressed and set his mind to deliver Daniel. And he laboured till the sun went down to rescue him." While Nebuchadnezzar said, none can rescue from my hand, Darius tried to save Daniel. He also hoped that Daniel's God would, as seen in verse sixteen: "May your God, whom you serve continually, deliver you!" The following morning, Darius inquired of Daniel, whether or not God was able to deliver him (6:20), and later proclaimed to all people, nations, and languages that the God of Israel delivers and rescues; He works signs and wonders in heaven and on earth, He who has saved Daniel from the power of the lions."

Darius' proclamation is the actual evidence of his humility; however, he was initially prideful enough to accept the idea that he should be worshipped as a god (6:7). Thus, all people were to worship Darius as a god, even though he could not change the law once decreed, and he could not save Daniel as much as he wanted to (6:14).

In addition to the story of chapters three and six, which started in the same way, the chapters also ended in the same way; God delivered Daniel (6:22) and his companions (3:17). Both times God's angel delivered them, as Daniel said, He had kept the lions' mouths shut. Perhaps this "Angel," like the One in the fiery furnace with the three young men (3:25), was the pre-incarnate Christ. Both times, the deliverance of the faithful Jews resulted in both kings stating, "No other god can rescue in this way" (3:29, 6:27).

The faithfulness of Daniel and his companions resulted in king Nebuchadnezzar, and King Darius acknowledging God, praising Him, and proclaiming Him (3:28-29, 6:25-27). Lastly, with both accounts, Daniel and his companions prospered after first being tested by fire and by lions (3:30, 6:28). His accusers, who were fed to the lions, did not share the result for Daniel. Not only did they meet their fate in the jaws of lions, but their entire families also, indicating some five hundred lost their lives due to trying to discredit and destroy one single soul. That day, fathers, mothers, and their children were crushed in the mouths of lions before they even hit the ground (6:24).

In the same way, Daniel had no opportunity to plead before the king; the satraps were neither afforded it. The same will be repeated when Jesus, the Lion (Rev. 5:5), returns, taking vengeance on the wicked for persecuting the righteous (2 Thess. 1:5-12, Rom. 12:19).

The faithful prospered after first being tested, but the application of the passage had nothing to do with prosperity and protection in the here and now. But it rather applies to faithfulness under threat and through persecution.

The application implies the same for us today. God will deliver His faithful remnant in and through times of trouble, the worst of which is yet to come (12:1). The greatest time of trouble the world has ever seen or will see again is still before us, not behind us (12:1, Matt. 24:21, Jer. 30:7, Rev. 16:18). The proclamation of increasing trouble runs in the opposite direction to false teaching, suggesting the best is still before us (cf. Isa. 56:10-12).

To arrive at this conclusion, biblically illiterate preachers twist the likes of Jeremiah (29:11). The promise of peace and prosperity for the believer in Jesus Christ is set for the other side of this world, the millennial kingdom, where God will have everlasting dominion (6:26).

In the same way, Nebuchadnezzar and Darius set themselves up to be worshipped; another would in the coming days. Then, any 'left behind' who refuse to worship the antichrist will be slain. During the tribulation, the newfound faithfulness of the tribulation saints will be tested in the same way that Shadrack, Meshach, Abednego, and Daniel were. Daniel, chapter eleven states, "He (the antichrist) shall come into the glorious land (Israel). And tens of thousands shall fall, but these shall be delivered out of his hand: Edom and Moab and the main part of the Ammonites" (v. 41).

During the tribulation, the antichrist will not only control the holy city, but he will also control many other countries as well (11:30). The antichrist will persecute the saints when given dominion, where countless millions will only be delivered through death. For seven years, the antichrist will control most of the world by setting up a new world order, made up of a one-world religion and a one-world government. Any who refuse to worship him will be slain (Rev. 13).

As for us, this side of the coming tribulation, we are to remain faithful in the same way the members of the church of Smyrna were, through tribulation (Rev. 2:10), or else be tested in the tribulation. Those who hold fast will avoid the tribulation (Rev. 3:10). Holding fast involves fearing God more than man. As with Daniel and his companions, the uncompromising faithful remnant will fully commit to God; therefore, only a few, by comparison, will escape the wrath to come (cf. Lu 21:34-36). Then, through tribulation, the lukewarm left behind will have another opportunity to fear God and worship Him alone (Rev. 14:6-7).

Darius, the once decreed and discredited (false) god, evidently arrived at this point where he rightly proclaimed, "All people (cf. 3:4, 7; 4:1; 5:19; 7:14) are to tremble and fear before the God of Daniel" (6:26). Darius continued that the God who created everything is the only living and eternal God; everything else is false and useless (6:26-27). This living God is the God who delivers through signs and wonders (6:27, cf. 4:2-3). The greatest signs and wonders are reserved for the coming tribulation, purposed to test, sift and separate one from the other.

Chapter Nine

Part One

'We Have Sinned'
(vv. 1-19)

As with chapter six, chapter nine was written in the first year of Darius (6:1, 9:1). Darius conquered Babylon, killing Belshazzar (5:30) in the seventh year of Judah's captivity, confirmed by Jeremiah's prophecy (Jer. 25:12). Judah was in Babylon as a result of being exiled from the Promised Land for a total of seventy years, as prophesied by Jeremiah:

"Therefore, thus says the LORD of hosts: because you have not obeyed my words, behold, I will send for all the tribes of the north, declares the LORD, and for Nebuchadnezzar the king of Babylon, my servant, and I will bring them against this land and its inhabitants and all these surrounding nations. I will devote them to destruction and make them a horror, a hissing, and an everlasting desolation. Moreover, I will banish from them the voice of mirth and the voice of gladness, the voice of the bridegroom and the voice of the bride, the grinding of the millstones and the light of the lamp. This whole land shall become a ruin and a waste, and these nations shall serve the king of Babylon seventy years. Then after seventy years are completed, I will punish the king of Babylon and that nation, the land of the Chaldeans, for their iniquity, declares the LORD, making the land an everlasting waste" (Jer. 25:8–12).

When Darius conquered Babylon, Daniel knew the times, by the signs, and through the scriptures. Daniel was aware of Jeremiah's writings (9:2), knowing the exile would be for a total of seventy years (9:24). He also knew that the Medes and Persians would succeed the Babylonian rule through the vision God gave him (7:5, 8:2-4, 20). Finally, Daniel knew, being the seventh year, Judah would be allowed to return to Jerusalem under the new kings Darius, and Cyrus (read 2 Chron. 36:22-23, Ezra 1:1-11, 2:1-70, Ps. 126, 147, Ezra 3:1-13, 4:1-5).

Daniel's awareness of the times, through the signs and the study of scripture (9:2), led him to pray. However, Daniel's prayer was not likened to today's neo-Pentecostal proclamation of prosperity and praise, by claiming now, the future (millennial) promise (Isa. 11, 60). Instead, Daniel's prayer was a plea for mercy (9:3) accompanied with a confession. Daniel confessed his sin and the nation's sins (9:3-15, 20), followed by a petition to God. (9:15-19).

Judah's sin was that they had failed to obey God (Jer. 25:8), and after seventy years of captivity, nothing much had changed, hence Daniel's prayer, "We have sinned" (9:5, 8, 11b, 15b). Likewise, all of Israel had rebelled against God (9:9) by refusing to obey His voice (9:11, 14b), expressly heard through the Law of Moses (9:11, 13). The sins that Daniel confessed are specifically those of the forefathers (9:6, 8), but also include the sins of the generation in Daniel's day. Jeremiah prayed the same prayer before the exile (Jer. 3:25, 8:14, 14:7), and during it (Lam. 5:16), describing the event as tribulation (Lam. 3:5).

Following confession and repentance, Daniel acknowledged God's righteous response (9:7, 16) towards Israel's sin (9:11), which confirmed His words, "For under the whole of heaven there has not been done anything like what has been done against Jerusalem" (9:12). The words confirming God's righteous actions against Jerusalem fulfil the prophecy given by Jeremiah, who said, "Behold, I will fulfil My words against this city for harm and not for good, and they shall be accomplished before you on that day" (Jer. 39:16b). Daniel's words also fulfil Ezekiel's prophecy, in part, "And because of your abominations I will do with you what I have never yet done, and the like of which I will never do again" (Ezek. 5:9b).

The fulfilment of Ezekiel's words was set for the coming tribulation (12:1, Jer. 30:7, Matt. 24:21). The part-fulfilment of the prophecy is mentioned again by Jeremiah in the book of Laminations, "Look and see if there is any sorrow like my sorrow which was brought upon me which the Lord inflicted in the day of His fierce anger" (Lam. 1:12). To understand what the day looked and felt like, read Lamentations. There, Jeremiah notes the 'tribulation' (Lam. 3:5) of Judah, where all hope is wavering (Lam. 3:18, 21, 24, 29), if not completely lost (Lam. 5:21-22). Judah's experience, then, will be dwarfed by what is coming. The worst is yet to come.

As mentioned earlier, Daniel was fully aware of Jeremiah, and Ezekiel's writings, having personally experienced the fulfilment, in part, of God's words towards the rebellious nation. Daniel remembers their sin, prompting him to pray and petition God with fasting and sackcloth and ashes (9:3, cf. Gen. 37:34; Neh. 9:1; Es. 4:1, 3; Isa. 58:5; Jer. 49:3; Ezek. 7:18; Joel 1:8; Matt. 11:21, Rev. 11:3). While praying, Daniel references the prophets and the Law of Moses by saying:

"To the Lord our God belong mercy and forgiveness, for we have rebelled against Him and have not obeyed the voice of the LORD our God by walking in His laws, which he set before us by his servants the prophets. All Israel has transgressed Your Law and turned aside, refusing to obey Your voice. And the curse and oath that are written in the Law of Moses the servant of God have been poured out upon us because we have sinned against Him" (9:9-11).

Daniel's confession narrows in on Deuteronomy, chapter thirty. The big idea of Deuteronomy, chapter thirty, is obedience (Deut. 30:2, 8, 18, 20) by keeping (Deut. 30:10, 16) and holding fast (Deut. 30:20) to the Law of God (Deut. 30:10). Obedience results in peace and prosperity by inheriting and remaining in the Promised Land (Deut. 30:9, 16, 20). However, failing to obey, keep, and hold fast to the Law of God results in disqualification from the Promised Land (Deut. 30:17-18). Only two of the original company of Israelites leaving Egypt entered the Promised Land due to grumbling and disobedience (Num. 14:30). Exodus, chapter twelve (v. 37) reveals that about six hundred thousand men on foot left. Taken at face value, this would indicate somewhere between two and three million Israelites altogether left, counting women and children.

Due to disobedience, Israel was later removed from the Promised Land. Disobedience resulted in the discipline where Israel would be subjugated to Gentile powers (Deut. 28:48–57, 64–68). Judah's experience in Babylon was the outworking of this principle. For the curse (9:11) to be lifted, Israel had to return to God, that God would return to them (9:16). Unfortunately, Israel never did fully return to God, and has not, even to this day.

Due to Israel's disobedience, they lost what they once had; hence they were disqualified from the Promised Land. However, through repentance (Deut. 30:2) and forgiveness (Deut. 30:3), they can be once again returned and restored. By referencing Deuteronomy, Daniel knows repentance and forgiveness are never far off but are as close to anyone as the words in their mouth (Deut. 30:12-14, cf. Rom. 10:6-8). None need to go anywhere or do anything special for God to hear and forgive them, but rather confess their sins and receive forgiveness.

Paul picked up on the same, stating that none need to ascend into heaven (bring Christ down) or descend into the abyss (bring Christ up), but rather release the words from their mouth (Rom.10:6-9). Believing and confession (repentance) results in salvation (Rom. 10:10). Keeping the Law, and holding fast to God, ensures the believer that the promise of salvation remains.

Daniel's prayer included himself in the nation's great and awful sin (9:16, cf. Jer. 30:14-15); and acknowledged God's mercy, greatness, and awesomeness (9:3, 4, 9, 15, 17, 18). While praying, Daniel remembered God's deliverance from Egypt (9:15) and pleaded that God, through His mercy, might do it again (9:17). Not because of Israel's righteousness, but due to God's righteousness and great mercy (9:18). Daniel's prayer was that God would listen (9:19), forgive (9:9, 19), and quickly (19:19) turn away His wrath and anger from Jerusalem, His holy hill (9:16). Jerusalem is God's city (9:24) and His holy hill (9:20; cf. Joel 2:1; 3:17; Zeph. 3:11).

Remember, Israel was once secure within God's holy hill but lost what was already theirs by disobeying God. Judah was warned many times by the prophet Jeremiah over forty years, that judgement would come, but they did not listen, 'having not ears to hear'.

The same is true today for the church, prompting the warnings given by Jesus to the seven churches (Rev. 2-3). The seven churches represent the church throughout the church age, sharing the same conditions, good and bad. Even before Jesus addressed the churches (Rev. 2-3), the church was warned by Paul (Rom. 11:22), and Peter (1 Pet. 4:17), and the writer of the book of Hebrews.

The book of Hebrews' central theme could be summed up as, 'Do not neglect such great salvation' (Heb. 2:3, 5:12-6:20, 10:19-39). Said another way, 'Do not drift away!' (Heb. 2-4). The author of the book of Hebrews compares the church to Israel, warning not to do as Israel did, resulting in disqualification from the Promised Land (Heb. 3:1-4:16).

The Promised Land for the church is heaven, temporarily, and then the earth under Jesus' reign.

In the same way Israel was disqualified from the Promised Land, the church can be too, which prompts the statement, "Strive to enter in" (Heb. 4:11). Jesus said the same, "Strive to enter through the narrow door" (Lu. 13:24). Jesus' comment was in response to the question asked of only a few being saved; Jesus confirmed this to be true; only a remnant will be saved. Like with Israel, only a few will get in (Lu. 14:22-30), hence the many warnings.

Hebrews, chapter two (v. 1) is the first of five warnings within the book, with the other four found in chapters three and four, five (vv. 11-6:20), ten (vv. 19-39), and twelve (vv. 3-17, 25-29). The first is the lightest of the five, however, the intention is to sober you up! Here is the message: Pay Attention: "Pay much closer attention to what we have heard, lest we drift away from it" (v. 1). Chapter four, (v. 2) warns of those who heard the message but did not benefit because they were not united by faith with those who believed/received it. They did not mix what they heard with faith (cf. Heb. 11:6). The consequences of failure do not refer to a loss of reward, as some suggest, but to death (Heb. 3:11, 4:3, 5, 10:27).

Like Israel, the warning given in the book of Hebrews is towards the congregation of believers, some who have believed and experienced God (Heb. 6:4), have drifted away, or are in danger of drifting away. Specifically, the writer warns against such apostasy (Heb. 5:11-12), and in some cases further warns apostasy is impossible to restore (Heb. 6:4-8, 10:26-27, 29). Chapter three reinforces the requisite of remaining: "We have come to share in Christ IF we hold firmly to the end the assurance, we had at first" (Heb. 3:14. cf. Matt. 24:13). Note the conditional IF, which is seen three more times in chapter three (vv. 6, 7, 15).

Chapters three and four reference the fate of Israel, who went astray (Heb. 3:9b) and fell away from God (Heb. 3:12) due to failing to remain in faith and obedience to warn the church. Again, like Israel, the church can lose what it once had (Heb. 4:11) by 'drifting away' (cf. 1 Jn. 2:28). Although Hebrews chapter four (v. 1) states the promise to enter God's rest stands; most will fail to reach it. In the same way, only a remnant of Israel was and will be saved (Rom. 9:27, 11:1, 5, cf. 11:22). This is based on seventy percent of the churches addressed by Jesus being in danger (Rev. 2-3), and Jesus' warning (Matt. 7:21-23. Lu. 13:22-30), most will not make it. Remember, only two from Israel's Egypt departing congregation entered the Promised Land, and only two of seven churches addressed by Jesus were positioned to enter heaven.

In conclusion, Daniel understood the times through the signs and the scriptures. His understanding of the times brought about repentance, pleading for mercy and forgiveness. Likewise, the church should be doing the same, praying, "We have sinned." We have sinned against God through rebellion and apostasy by drifting from Him and His word. The church has replaced the word of God with worldliness. As a result, the lukewarm church will soon experience the same thing Judah did, as prewarned by Jesus, unless repentance comes first (Rev. 2-3). For Judah's sin, they suffered tribulation (Lam. 3:5), just as God forewarned. Soon, the lukewarm church and remaining Israel will experience the same, only much worse than anything previous, through the great tribulation.

The church has become lukewarm due to drifting away from the word of God, specifically, from sound biblical doctrine, like Israel did (9:11-15). The problem stems from losing the fear of God. Israel lost the fear of God; in the same way the fear of God is no longer evident in most churches today. Yet, there is still a remnant, like Joshua and Celeb, Jeremiah, and Daniel, who have godly fear, understanding the consequences of sin. Darius came to the same conclusion. Taking heed to the words of Darius, the apostate church now needs to tremble, and fear before God (6:26), this side of the tribulation, or else be reminded to do it again in the tribulation (Rev. 14:6-7).

In the words of Paul, who, like Daniel (9:11, 13), cites Moses, God (therefore forgiveness), is as near to us as the word in our mouth (Rom. 10:10). Jesus said, "He who has ears to hear, hear what the Spirit is saying to the churches" (Rev. 2-3). The author of the book of Hebrews puts further urgency on Jesus' words (cf. Rev. 1:1, 3b, 7, 22:7, 12, 20), saying, "Today, if you hear His voice, do not harden your hearts" (Heb. 3:7, 8, 4:7). Paul agrees, by warning not to receive God's grace in vain (2 Cor. 6:1b), "Now is the day of salvation" (2 Cor. 6:2). Now is the time to confess, "We have sinned and done wrong and acted wickedly and rebelled, turning aside from Your commandments and rules" (9:5). By praying this prayer, our hope, like Daniel's, is that God would be merciful toward us and forgive us (9:3, 9, 17, 18, cf. Heb. 4:16). Remember again, God (therefore forgiveness) is as near to us as the words in our mouth (Deut. 30:12-14, cf. Rom. 10:6-8).

Daniel saw the things to come (8:17), which terrified him (7:15, 28, 8:27). That which terrified Daniel also terrified John (Rev. 1:17), and should also frighten us, producing godly fear. Like Daniel, the wise know and understand the times (12:10), warning others (11:33). However, most are blind and refuse to hear; therefore they will soon experience what Daniel and John saw. Remember, like Israel, only a few will hear and repent and bear the fruit of repentance (hold fast and remain), therefore by default, most will go through the coming tribulation. The coming tribulation will make Judah's tribulation (cf. Jer. 25:8–12, Lam. 3:5) look like a tea party, by comparison.

Part Two
'One Micro Minute to Midnight' (vv. 20-27)

Chapter nine is consumed mainly with Daniel's prayer. Daniel was praying a desperate plea for God to forgive Israel's sin without delay (9:19) in response to his misunderstanding of the times signs and scriptural consideration. Daniel's plea was that God would act quickly in mercy due to knowing through the writings of Jeremiah, the seventy years of captivity had concluded (Jer. 25:11-12). Therefore, he falsely assumed God would judge the nations and set up His Messianic Kingdom. Daniel's reference to God's holy hill and city (9:16, 19, 20) refers to his understanding of the Messiah ruling from Jerusalem (Isa. 65:17-25, esp. v 25). Remember, Daniel saw Jesus taking dominion over the earth in chapter seven (vv. 9-14, 26-27), causing him now much anxiety (7:15, 28, cf. Heb. 10:31).

For this reason, Daniel was pleading with God for forgiveness. How much more should we be praying like Daniel today! Unfortunately, what Daniel thought to be happening next for him is happening next for us. In fact, the event is even knocking at the door.

Despite Daniel's devotion to God and dedication to the scriptures, he misunderstood the timing of the end times events, which is why the angel Gabriel came. This was the second time Gabriel was sent to Daniel (8:16) to help him understand the vision of the signs of the times (8:17, 27, 9:22, 23, 25). God wanted Daniel to understand the scriptures and the signs of the times in the same way He does for us today (cf. 10:10-11). Although Daniel did have some understanding of scripture and the vision (10:1), he gained more understanding of his times through the angel Gabriel (10:11, 14), and yet was still not able to fully comprehend it (12:8). We, however, live in the day Daniel saw and can, therefore, fully understand the prophetic scriptures (12:2) through the signs of the times (12:10). By doing so, we are also responsible for warning others (11:33). Only the unwise and wicked are to remain ignorant in these last days (12:10).

While Daniel was still praying for mercy by confessing sin, Gabriel swiftly came at the time of the evening sacrifice (9:20-21). Although Daniel was not in the Land, having no Temple, he still observed and obeyed the Law of God, the very thing Israel had neglected (9:5). Daniel continued to follow the Law regardless of where he was, who was in power, and what laws were in place (cf. 6:10). Due to Daniel's commitment to God, God sent Gabriel to answer him while still praying (9:20-21).

Gabriel was sent to confirm God's covenant with Israel (9:23) and clear up the matter of seventy years (9:1; cf. Jer. 25:11–12; 2 Chron. 36:21). Gabriel informed Daniel that God's plan would be fulfilled in seven seventies, not seventy years. Seven seventies amount to four hundred and ninety years. The period has to do with Israel's history (10:14, 11:14) and the holy hill (9:16, 24), not the church or even the history of the world.

By the conclusion of four hundred and ninety years, six things will happen:

1. Israel's transgression would finish (9:24)
2. God would put an end to Israel's sin (9:24)
3. God would atone for Israel's wickedness (9:24)
4. God would bring everlasting righteousness to Israel (9:24)
5. God would seal up the prophecy (9:24)
6. God would appoint the most holy place, in Israel (9:24)

The above listed six things will be fulfilled after the four hundred and ninety years are completed, taking place in the millennial kingdom. The prophecy is sealed/confirmed until that day. On that day, God will appoint Jesus (7:25-27), who will anoint the holy temple (Ezek. 41-46). Those claiming the prophecy was fulfilled fall well short on the above listed items one, two, and six. Item six fulfils Jeremiah's prophecy (Jer. 31:31-34), which is impossible to claim this side of the millennium. The closest Israel will come to fulfilling Jeremiah's prophecy this side of the millennium is in the coming great tribulation (cf. Rev. 7).

The seventy sevens begin with the decree to rebuild the temple, which commenced on March 5, 444 B.C., issued by Artaxerxes Longimanus (Neh. 2:1–8). Artaxerxes permitted the Jews to rebuild Jerusalem's city walls. The decree commenced the period Gabriel informed Daniel of (9:25). Remember, the completion of the prophecy sees in the return of Jesus Christ, who anoints the holy place (9:24). Therefore, the prophecy does not end with the first appearing of Jesus, as some suggest, but His second.

Dwight Pentecost (1985) sums up verse twenty-six this way - the sixty-two "sevens." (434 years) extend up to the introduction of the Messiah to the nation of Israel. This second period concluded on the day of the Triumphal Entry just before Christ was cut off, that is, crucified. In His Triumphal Entry, Christ, in fulfilment of Zechariah, chapter nine (v. 9), officially presented Himself to the nation of Israel as the Messiah. He was familiar with Daniel's prophecy when on that occasion, He said, "If you, even you, had only known on this day what would bring you peace—but now it is hidden from your eyes" (Luke 19:42).

Israel missed their Messiah, rejecting Him, and therefore temporarily put aside until the full number of Gentiles come into the kingdom (Rom 11:25). There is now a gap between Christ's first appearance and His second, due to being cut off after sixty-two weeks (9:26), which means there is an interval between the sixty-ninth and seventieth sevens.

Again, the gap temporarily set Israel aside (Matt. 21:42-43, Rom. 9-11) and established the church (Matt. 16:18) on the revelation that Jesus is the Messiah. On 'that' Rock (the revelation of Christ), the church would be built.

Even to this day, Israel has rejected their Messiah, but they will call upon His name in the tribulation (Matt. 23:39). Jesus will not return until they do. Amillennialism overlooks this, missing verse twenty-six, stating, the seventieth week was fulfilled with Christ's First Advent. However, He was "cut off" through crucifixion, having "nothing" (9:26). The prophecy of having 'nothing' applies to Israel's rejection of Jesus Christ (Jn. 1:11).

In-between Christ being cut off and His return, another would come, destroying the holy city and the sanctuary (9:26). The one to come was Rome, where the prince's people destroyed the city, desolating the house (cf. Matt. 23:38), leaving not one stone on another (Matt. 24:2). This prophecy was fulfilled in 70 A.D. As horrific as that event was, suffering did not end there for the Jews, for their suffering would continue until the end. The end would not come before war, and desolations came first (9:26). Israel will continue to suffer from the event of 70 A.D. until the Second Avent; only then would the Jews be delivered of Gentile dominance (cf. Lu. 21:24). The greatest time of trouble for Israel is still before them (12:1, Jer. 30:7, Matt. 24:21).

In sum, the understanding given to Daniel from Gabriel is a decree from God, revealing the things to come (9:24, 26, 27, 11:36). Although Daniel was given a detailed description of what would take place 'after this.' He was not permitted to dwell on it, as it would take place well after his own time (12:9, 13).

However, John, who received the same, and a more detailed version of the things to come, was instructed, "Not to close up the book" (Rev. 22:10). The command to John, "Do not seal up the words of the prophecy of this book," means, proclaim it, "For, the time is near, even here!"

The words "The time is near" relate to the message's urgency due to the shortness of time remaining (Rev. 1:1, 3, 7, 22:7, 12, 20).

The urgency was introduced from chapter one of John's revelation (1:1b, 3b, 7) and further communicated to the churches (Rev. 2-3). This is the reason why the seven churches were to have a listening ear (Rev. 2:7, 11, 17, 29, 3:6, 13, 22, 13:9, 21:7).

Today, however, few churches do when it comes to the message on the things to come through the period of the end times, placing more value on having 'your best life now.' Based on the instructions given to John, we should not only be reading the books of Daniel and Revelation, but every other Bible book containing prophetic literature, which includes all the major and minor prophets. These books all talk about the things to come, which, is argued to come in our lifetime. The things to come refer mostly to the great tribulation!

As mentioned earlier, the understood timing of the tribulation gives rise to great controversy, forging two sides made up of Preterists and Dispensational Futurists. While the Preterist position maintains that the tribulation events were fulfilled in 70 A.D. with the sacking of Jerusalem, Futurists believe that the predicted events are unfulfilled and will remain so until the signing of the peace treaty (Dan. 9:27). The signing of the peace treaty, not the rapture, will begin the tribulation, although the rapture is likely to coincide. The one who 'confirms the covenant' (peace treaty, see appendix) is the antichrist (Dan. 9:27), who will then be unrestrained and revealed but not to all (2 Thess. 2:9-12), by the taking away (removal/rapture) of the church (2 Thess. 2:3-8).

The book of Daniel, chapter nine, provides compelling evidence for the pretribulation position as held by Futurists by revealing the timing of the event and its duration. Again, the chapter starts by revealing that Daniel had an initial understanding, through prophecy (cf. Jer. 25:11-12; 29:10-14), of a 'seventy-year period' in Babylonian captivity (Dan. 9:2). The captivity resulted from Judah's sin (Dan. 9:4, 7, 8, 9, 10, 11,

12, 13, 15, 16, and 20). Daniel was given divine, corrective revelation of the 'actual time' in captivity (Dan. 9:22).

The determined or decreed length of time (seventy sevens) came as a result of not keeping the Sabbath-year rest (2 Chron. 36:20- 21; Jer. 25:11; 29:10) as commanded by God (Lev. 25:2-6; 26:34-35, 43). For a total of seventy sabbatical years that Judah violated, they received one year in captivity; that is, for each year within the seven; amounting to seventy sevens within a total of eight hundred years of occupation of the Promised Land.

This prophecy has been largely fulfilled: seven weeks (Dan. 9:25a) and another sixty-two weeks (Dan. 9:25b), or four hundred and eighty-three years were served from B.C. 445 (Neh. 2:1-8) to 30 A.D. (Lu. 19:28-40). Then the Messiah was "cut off," as predicted in verse twenty-six of Daniel chapter nine. Here, the passage clearly shows a gap between the sixty-ninth and seventh week, in the same way as Isaiah's prophecy (Isa. 61:1-2). Of which, (Isa. 61:1-2a) Jesus read only the first section (Lu. 4:18-19), leaving the second part out (Isa. 61:2b), indicating a future fulfilment that will take place throughout the tribulation.

As for the 'one week', or seven years of Daniel's prophecy left remaining (Dan. 9:27), this period will be divided again into two halves (Dan. 7:25; Rev. 11:2-3; 12:6; 13:5) covering the years commencing with the release and revealing of the antichrist (Rev. 6:2; 2 Thess. 2:3b) to the return of Jesus Christ (Rev. 19:11).

The final 'week' (Dan. 9:27) or seven years derived from the Hebrew word 'shavuim' would be better-translated 'sevens.' The actual term for 'week' is 'Shavuot.' Again, up until this point, Daniel (Dan. 9:2) expects the Kingdom of God to be established after the seventy weeks (years) of captivity. It is like John the Baptist (Matt. 11:3), and the disciples thought that Jesus was going to set up the Kingdom at His first appearance (Lu. 19:11); likewise did the Jews in Jerusalem (Mk. 11:9-10). As such, Daniel misunderstood not only the length of time but the gap in-between, to which God brought correction through His angelic messenger, Gabriel (Dan. 9:22-27).

To reiterate, commencing the 'seven weeks' is the signing of the covenant or peace treaty, 'guaranteeing' seven years of peace (Dan. 9:27). The signing of the peace treaty will coincide with the rebuilding of the third tribulation, Temple. The antichrist, however, will break this covenant halfway through the tribulation (Dan. 9:27; Rev. 11:1- 2). Isaiah predicts the same, calling this 'false peace treaty a "covenant of death" (Isa. 28:15). In his letter to the Thessalonians, Paul also mentions it, referencing a perceived time of "peace and security" before sudden destruction (1 Thess. 5:3).

As previously stated and supported through Paul's writings, the destruction occurs after the rapture (1 Thess. 4:15, 17). Here, the distinction between 'they' (1 Thess. 5:3) and 'those' (1 Thess. 5:7) from 'you,' 'we' (1 Thess. 5:5, 10), and 'us' (1 Thess. 5:6, 8, 10) makes it clear. As addressed in previous chapters, The true church will be removed before the coming destruction; therefore, its members will not go through the tribulation. Further support outlining the futuristic timing of this event is found in the book of Revelation, chapter seventeen.

"Here is the mind which has wisdom: The seven heads are seven mountains on which the woman sits. There are also seven kings. Five have fallen, one is, and the other has not yet come. And when he comes, he must continue a short time. The beast that was, and is not, is himself also the eighth, and is of the seven, and is going to perdition. "The ten horns which you saw are ten kings who have received no kingdom as yet, but they receive authority for one hour as kings with the beast" (Rev. 17:9-12).

The seven kings refer to seven fallen world-dominating empires (first five: Egypt; Assyria; Babylon; Medo-Persia; and Greece). "The one that is" refers to Rome, being the then ruling empire (sixth) at the time of John's writing (A.D. 95). The "other" (seventh) has not yet come and will be established under the antichrist as the next world-dominating 'prince' or world ruler (Dan. 9:26-27; 2 Thess. 2:2-4, 6-8; Rev. 13). The antichrist is both the seventh and eighth ruler in that he will bring about the 'revived Roman empire' as predicted in Daniel (Dan. 2, 7, and 9). This will be established during the antichrist's first term of three and a half years. At this time, he will co-rule alongside ten kings.

However, the second term will be somewhat different, seeing the resurrected, Satan-incarnated son of perdition (2 Thess. 2:3; Rev. 13:3-4), the antichrist (Dan. 7:25; 8:23-26; 11:36; 2 Thess. 2:3-8; Rev. 13:5-6), singlehandedly ruling over the submitting nations: "being of one mind" (Rev. 17:13), and "making war against the Lamb" (Rev. 17:14).

In support of the above, Daniel's writings were confirmed by Jesus (Matt. 24:15). What Daniel received from the angel Gabriel, as recorded in the book of Daniel, chapter nine verse twenty-seven, remains unfulfilled. It includes the "abomination of desolation," as directly quoted by Jesus (Matt. 24:15), speaking about the antichrist and his established sacrificial worship in the rebuilt tribulation Temple (Rev. 11:1–2). Daniel refers to the abomination of desolation twice more (Dan. 11:31; 12:11), indicating from that time, "one thousand two hundred and ninety days" remain until the Messianic Kingdom is established.

It then places the act of the abomination of desolation at the midway point of the tribulation, forty-two months in (Dan. 9:27), with a further forty-two months to go, plus seventy-five days more in-between the Second Advent and the millennial dispensation (Dan. 12:11-12).

Again, this creates several problems with this event having been fulfiled as Preterist claim. The obvious one, of course, is that Jesus has not returned in the manner described in the book of Revelation, chapter one, verse seven: "Every eye shall see Him."

In conclusion, it was the sense that the Messiah might come at any moment and establish His rule on His holy hill that caused Daniel to pray to God for mercy and forgiveness. Although the prophesied event was many days from Daniel's time, it is right before us, being now 'One Micro Minute to Midnight.' Due to that reality, the church should be praying as Daniel prayed (We have sinned) in the hope God will forgive us for departing from Him, and His word. Right now, the prophetic time clock has been paused, yet the next strike of that clock will commence the great tribulation. ARE YOU READY!

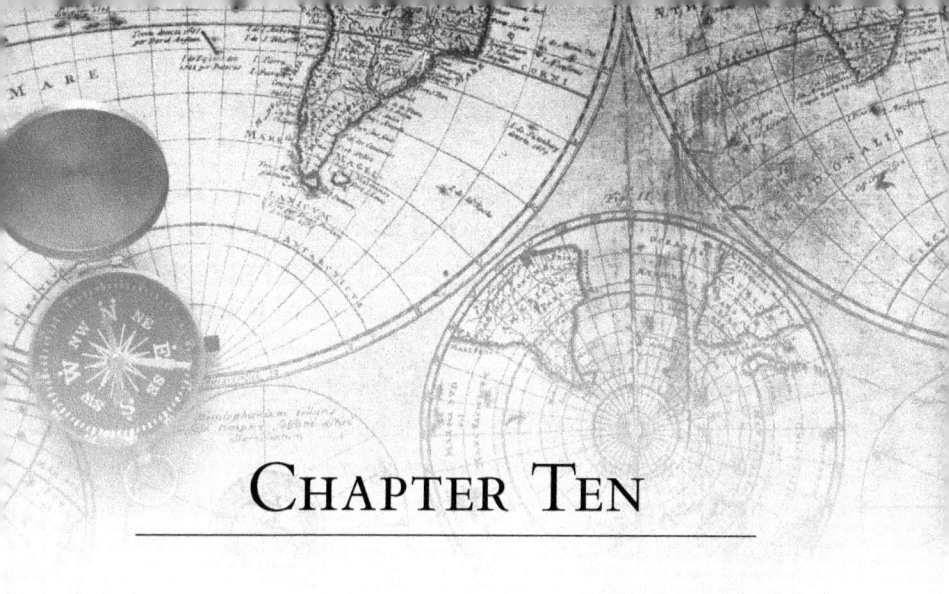

Chapter Ten

'Understanding Things Unseen, and Things to be Seen'

(vv. 1-21)

As mentioned in the previous section, chapter nine marks Judah's release from Babylon after seventy years of captivity. Judah's release also commenced the rebuilding of the temple. Ezra, chapters one to four provides information regarding the temple rebuild. Psalms (126, 147) provides further insight into Judah's joy and excitement of release after seventy years of captivity. A reflective comparison of the book of Lamentations alongside the Psalms (126, 147) causes the reader to ponder yet another Psalm, recording the words of David, "For His anger is but for a moment, and His favour is for a lifetime. Weeping may tarry for the night, but joy comes with the morning" (Ps. 30:5). For a moment, seventy years in Judah's case, there is mourning, but joy came in the morning when released.

The lasting reality of the joy to come will be actual for the church in the millennial kingdom. It will even be true for many left behind to face the great tribulation, providing they repent before perishing.

Interestingly, Psalm thirty is a song dedicated to building the first temple. Like the other Psalms (126, 147), connected with the second temple rebuild, they reveal God's merciful plan of redemption despite our many and epic failures. The third temple, rebuilt in the tribulation, will be different from the previous two, serving to promote the antichrist, from where he proclaims to be God (7:8, 9:27). However, when rebuilt, like every other time, Israel will again rejoice. Serving as a thorn in the side of the antichrist, the two witnesses will be proclaiming Jesus Christ from outside the tribulation temple for three and a half years (Rev. 11). The fourth millennial temple will once again promote reverent fear through the pure worship of Jesus alone (Ezek. 40-48).

Three years after the vision of chapter nine (10:1), in chapter ten, Daniel contemplates the word (from chapter nine), which is like the vision of chapter seven (7:15, 28). The word (9:24-27) motivated him to pray and fast, lasting three weeks (10:1-2). Daniel's prayer was heard by God, who sent an angel to help him further understand the vision of chapter nine. The angel, who was sent was so frightening that Daniel, and the others, trembled with fear (10:7). Those with Daniel hide (10:7), leaving Daniel alone, who was, due to fear, left without strength (10:8, 9, 10, 11, 16, 17).

Daniel's experience is similar to John's when receiving the revelation of the things to come (Rev. 1:17). While Judah was praising God for their deliverance, Daniel was mourning over the disclosure of the things to come; Israel's newfound peace and security would be short-lasting (9:25-26, 10:1). Daniel understood, in part (10:12), the word of chapter nine (9:22, 10:1) and the visions of chapters seven and eight, predicting Israel's future judgment. Due to Daniel misunderstanding the time of the things to come (10:14), God sent an angel to help him better understand what he was seeking to understand (10:5).

While Daniel had experienced angelic visitations before (6:22, 8:16, 9:20-21), on this occasion, the visitation was particularly frightening. The visiting messenger-angel was dressed in linen (10:5) and is quite likely to be Gabriel (8:16, 9:20-21), who is the only named messenger-angel in scripture (cf. Lu. 1:19, 26). However, the appearance of this angel (10:5-6) is similar to that of Jesus' second coming (Rev. 1:13-15, 2:18, 19:12). Again, like John (Rev. 1:17), Daniel and those with him were terrified (10:7-8). Due to the similarity of the angel's appearance to Jesus Christ, some suggest the angel is Jesus, preincarnate.

Further support for this understanding comes from the use of the word 'man' (10:5, 18, cf. 7:13, 8:15). Conversely, debunking the idea of the angel being Jesus is where he needs help from Michael due to being hindered by the prince (demon) of Persia (10:13). Jesus does not need help overpowering any demon, including Satan himself, alongside every other demon in his company combined. When Jesus returns, He will effortlessly deal with Satan and his whole company of fallen angels (Rev. 20:1) and again at the end of the millennial dispensation (Rev. 20:10). Even while Jesus was on the earth, incarnate, no demonic power came close to being a match for Him, evident where He cast out anywhere between three to six thousand of them out of one man (Mk. 5:9) with a single word (Mk. 5:13).

Clearly, the messenger-angel was not Jesus, albeit his appearance is similar. The appearance of the messenger-angel visiting Daniel is not unique to Jesus alone but is also seen in Ezekiel, chapter nine (vv. 2, 11). Ezekiel, chapter nine is a vision given to the prophet Ezekiel, where God shows him the future fulfilment of God's threat to execute judgment without pity on Jerusalem (Eze. 8:18). Ezekiel sees God's executioner, an angel, accompanied by other angel-guards (Eze. 9:1). The angelic executioner is dressed in linen; the linen clothing suggests dignity, purity, or divine origin (cf. Dan. 10:5; 12:6–7; Rev. 15:6). The angel also has a writing kit (9:2, 3) used to carry pens, possibly used for recording names and deeds, as a scribe. The angel is told to pass through Jerusalem and put a mark on the forehead of the men who sigh and groan over all the abominations that are committed (Eze. 9:4). Verse four is similar to Revelation, chapter seven, where the 144,000 Jewish evangelists are sealed (marked) on their forehead, by an angel, in the tribulation (vv. 1-8). Following those being sealed, Ezekiel hears God instruct the guards (angels) to follow the angelic scribe, killing anyone not marked, without distinction. The killing began at the temple, as judgment begins at the household of God (cf. 2 Pet. 4:17).

The sins of Israel had spread throughout the land (Eze. 8); therefore judgement would follow the same path. Judgement began with the priests, who had their backs to God, practicing and promoting false worship (Eze. 8:16). So overwhelming was the pending judgment, Ezekiel cried out, "Ah, Lord God! Will You make a full end to the remnant of Israel?" (Eze. 9:8, 11:13). Israel's sin had gotten to the point of no return, despite the many warnings to repent, but they did not. Judgement was now unavoidable and would be executed without pity (cf. Eze. 7:4, 9; 8:18; 24:14).

God would give the rebellious nation what it deserved. Only those sealed would be spared (Eze. 9:11). The same will be repeated during the tribulation to come, which is what Daniel was contemplating, producing prayer and fasting (10:1-3, cf. 9:24-27) inviting an angel to explain.

Again, the angel Daniel saw is similar to the one Ezekiel saw. The angel Daniel saw was one of judgment, yet the angel strengthened Daniel (10:15-17) in the same way Jesus strengthened John (Rev. 1:17). The angel strengthened Daniel and confirmed that he was greatly loved (10:10, 15, cf. 9:23). The angel also told Daniel, not to fear, to be at peace, be strong and of good courage (10:19), in the same way, Jesus told John not to fear (Rev. 1:18). However, the primary purpose of the angel was not to tell Daniel he was greatly loved but to bring him an understanding of the word he was praying about (10:11-12, 14, 20), from chapter nine (9:24-27). Specifically, Daniel prayed to gain knowledge of the great conflict to come (10:1, cf. 9:25-26, 11:29-12:1-13). Daniel was praying for three weeks (10:2-3) before the angel appeared. However, the angel was dispatched from the first day (10:12), yet the prince of Persia withstood him; therefore, Michael was sent to help (10:13).

Alongside losing his strength (10:15-19), being overcome with fear, Daniel also lost his ability to talk when told by the angel of the supernatural conflict in the heavenly realm. When hearing this, Daniel was speechless (10:15). The supernatural battle in the heavens would significantly bear on the earth (925-26). The revelation exanimated Daniel, leaving him completely incapacitated (10:8). Daniel was even breathless at the thought of Israel's coming judgement in the latter days (10:14, 17, 11:29, 40, 12:1).

Seen through chapter nine, the conflict between good and evil reveals how powerful demons can be, even delaying the answer to prayer. The prince of Persia is a particularly powerful demon, a demon, not a man. None of God's angels could be hindered by a mere man, especially a chief angel such as Michael, who the messenger-angel returned to help fight the powerful demon in the air (10:20). The prince of Persia was a ruling power of the air (Eph. 1:21). Michael was the only angel contending alongside the messenger-angel against the prince of Persia. Michael (meaning like God) is one of the archangels (10:13) assigned to Israel (12:1, 10:21).

Only Michael has gone up against Satan in the past (Jude 9) and will again, alongside other angels. Michael will contend against Satan during the tribulation in the not-so-distant future, casting him from the air to the ground (Rev. 12:7-9). Satan will be cast to the earth at the mid-point of the tribulation (Rev. 12:12, 14).

From there on, Israel will be persecuted like no other time before (Rev. 12:13, 15-16). Yet still, Michael will protect her, even during the tribulation, preserving a remnant. Finally, at the end of the tribulation, Michael, alongside other angels, will again defeat Satan, seizing him, bounding him, and casting him into the bottomless pit (Rev. 20:1-3).

In sum, in the same way, Michael is assigned to Israel, the prince of Persia is assigned to Persia, who warred against the messenger-angel sent to Daniel while in prayer and fasting. Again, Daniel was in intercessory prayer for Israel regarding their sin and the coming consequences (10:1-3, cf. 9:1-19), which caused a fight, lasting three weeks, in the heavenly realm (cf. Eph. 6:12). The messenger-angel was only able to come to Daniel after Michael turned up (10:13), allowing Daniel to receive the message from God about 'his' people (Israel) in the latter days (10:14, cf. 9:24, 11:29, 40, 12:1).

Daniel's revelation concerns the great conflict (10:1, 9:25-27), which will continue and increase in severity until Jesus returns (Lu. 21:24). Following the church age, the next time of peace for Israel will result from signing the false peace treaty (9:27, Isa. 28:15, 18, cf. 1 Thess. 5:3), albeit only lasting three and a half years (7:24). True and lasting peace will only come in the millennial dispensation once Jesus has returned to rule and reign over the earth. Any hope of peace before the millennial dispensation is a false peace, thoroughly debunking dominionism (kingdom now 'theology').

Understanding the difference between true and false peace draws an interesting contrast between the passage and supporting scripture passages. While Judah was celebrating (Ps. 126, 147), Daniel was mourning (10:2). While Judah was praising God over their deliverance, Daniel was praying and fasting over the coming judgement. While Judah had a false sense of confidence, thinking God would overlook their sin and not judge them, again, Daniel was shaken at the sight of the angel of judgment, having the same attire as Jesus, when coming to judge the nations. So frightening was this manifestation, the angel had to strengthen Daniel's lifeless body.

Needless to say, standing before an angel of this nature is a terrifying thing, even for the likes of Daniel. He fearlessly confronted kings (chapt. 2, 5) and went into the lion's den without blinking an eyelid (chapt. 6). After the messenger-angel had strengthened Daniel and gave him understanding (11-12), on departure he said he must return to fight against the prince of Persia, and then, the Prince of Greece will come. The prince of Greece is another powerful demon, which will be addressed in the following chapter.

In conclusion, chapter ten has one primary purpose: An angel sent by God tells Daniel, what he was mourning over is set for the latter days (10:14). However, from this chapter, we learn much more:

I. Over each nation and region of the earth, there are angels and demons assigned.
II. Michael is the prince over Israel (10:21).
III. Angels and demons battle in the heavenly realm, resulting from our prayers (Eph. 6:12).
IV. The spiritual warfare in the heavenly realm and on the earth will be ongoing until Jesus returns. Not only ongoing but will increase with intensity as the end draws nearer.

Subsequently, our prayers and conduct on the earth have significant influence and are being influenced by the heavenly realm. When continuing in sin, we come under the influence of demons (Eph. 2:1-3). When submitting to God, angels are activated to protect, serve and minister to us (6:22, cf. Acts 8:26, 12:7-11, 27:23, Heb. 1:14).

Such was the case for Judah and Israel as a whole. Few within the chosen nation submitted to God, therefore judgment came and will come again, yet a remnant will receive salvation. The same is true for the lukewarm church, which will soon share in Israel's fate and final judgment in the coming tribulation. Daniel saw (9:24-27), mourned, prayed, and fasted for three weeks (10:1-3) over Israel's future judgement.

Daniel's prayer resulted in an even greater revelation of the coming angel of judgment through the manifestation of that angel (10:5-21). Tribulation judgment, administered through God's holy angels, will be the experience of both Israel and the lukewarm church, alongside the entire world, soon. While some today falsely celebrate and even prophesy a time of peace and prosperity and will again through the signing of the false peace treaty (9:27) at the commencement of the tribulation, their joy will quickly turn to mourning. However, in the morning, when Jesus returns, true and lasting joy will come for those (alone) who have repented and are sealed by God.

When Jesus returns, that day will be the best day for those living, looking, and longing for Him. That day will equally be the worst day for those loving and living for this world. Their best life now will result in their worst life to come (cf. Lu. 21:34-36).

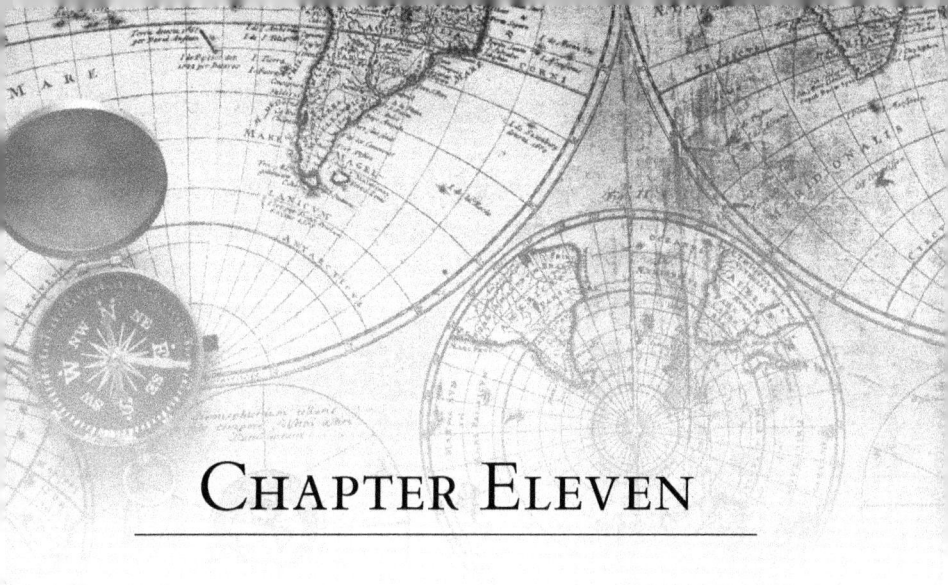

Chapter Eleven

Part One
'The Book of Truth'
(vv. 1-20)

Continuing from chapter ten (10:20-21), which will carry through until the end of the book (chapt. 12), the angel-messenger further explains to Daniel what must occur after this. Chapter ten (v. 21) and chapter eleven (v. 1) are connected with the words of the messenger-angel, "I stood up to confirm and strengthen him." The messenger-angel confirmed and strengthened Michael, contending together against the prince of Persia (10:21), since the first year of Darius. Darius is now in his third year (11:1), which illustrates how powerful this messenger-angel is to be the only one fighting alongside Michael (10:21).

Three and a half years into the coming tribulation (Rev. 12:6, 14), Michael will be supported again by other angels when he battles with Satan in the heavens (Rev. 12:7). Michael will defeat and cast Satan down to the earth (Rev. 12:9, 12). Michael is the guardian angel over

Israel (10:21, 12:1), who fights for and protects the chosen nation. When Israel is under threat, we know from chapter ten that there is an ongoing spiritual battle in the heavenly realm involving Michael and others. For Israel, after seventy years of captivity, spiritual warfare was significant due to the possibility of the Messiah appearing to deliver the Jews from Gentile rule to co-rule and reign with the Messiah over the earth. The Messiah's appearance would also conclude Satan's dominion, which was the cause of the heavenly conflict. Contrary to Daniel's understanding, the conclusion of Satan's rule is set for the latter days, where a supernatural battle is seen again through John's revelation, chapters twelve and twenty (in the book of Revelation).

Although we can learn much about spiritual warfare from the book of Daniel, chapter ten, this was not the reason the angel came. The closing question of chapter ten is, "Do you know why I have come to you?" (10:20). The answer is in response to prayer (10:2-3) regarding the things to come (9:24-27). Daniel's mind is still set on the word from Gabriel, given three years ago, in chapter nine (9:24-27), and the visions of chapters seven and eight. (10:12). Chapter eleven further explains the meanings of that word and visions, precisely the vision of chapter eight.

Again, the messenger-angel came to address Daniel's confusion, believing the Messiah would appear at any moment, confirming, therefore, the timing of the visions and word referred to what will happen to Israel in the latter days (10:14). In doing so, the angel gave Daniel an incredibly detailed account of future events, explicitly involving Greece.

Due to the astonishing insight and accuracy of future events foretold, some have said the book of Daniel was written after the events occurred for the reason that none could have such comprehensive knowledge of the future. Those making such claims (dismissing Bible prophecy) would do themselves, and others, excellent service to retire from biblical scholarship altogether and perhaps take up golf! Slicing golf balls and hacking the green is a far better option than slashing and hacking away at God's Holy Word, the Bible. While the prophecy is amazing, containing details impossible for man to know and predict, it is nothing for God. God knows the beginning from the end and everything else in-between (Isa. 46:9-10).

To recap, Daniel knew Judah's captivity, of the seventy years, ended with the death of Belshazzar, the king of Babylon, commencing the first year of Darius (10:1). Consequently, Daniel also thought this would be the same year the Messiah came. Therefore, Daniel was expecting the Messiah to come and set up His kingdom, rule, and reign on His holy hill. For this reason, Daniel was praying and pleading for the forgiveness of his and Israel's sins (9:1-19), knowing when the Messiah comes, He will judge the nations. Chapter five concludes the Babylonian world-dominating reign, where Persia succeeded them, picked up from chapter six.

The visions in chapters seven and eight are chronologically placed after chapter four. Nebuchadnezzar acknowledged God and proclaimed Him to all peoples, nations, and languages that dwell on the earth (4:1). The proclamation occurred after enduring seven years of tribulation to humble him (4:37). The vision of chapter seven majors on the seven years of tribulation to come for the purpose of humbling humanity. Those left behind would also come to know (experience, cf. Jn. 17:3) the one true God through the worst possible time the world has ever known (cf. Rev. 14:4).

Chapter eleven follows from chapter ten as one piece, going into greater detail of what Daniel had already seen in chapters seven and eight and chapter two, where he gave Nebuchadnezzar the interpretation of his dream. The future certainty and the accuracy of Daniel's visions and his understanding of Nebuchadnezzar's dream regarding the things to come are absolute, based on what was already fulfilled to date. Nebuchadnezzar's dream and Daniel's visions have been fulfilled in part; for the amount that has been fulfilled, that portion has been literally and historically and to pinpoint accuracy. That is, Persia succeeded the Babylonians, and the Greeks followed the Parisians. The next and final portion of the prophecy involves the antichrist to come.

In the same way, the fulfilled sections of the prophecy have been achieved to literal, historical, and pinpoint accuracy; the latter will also be, in the not-so-distant future. As mentioned previously, we are the generation that will see the fulfilment of what is to occur in the latter days. Although the latter-days were many days from Daniel's lifetime, they are not many days from today.

Unlike John's revelation, the latter days' events were not always given to Daniel in a mysterious way, such as through signs (Rev. 1:1), but rather in word (10:7, 9). The words given to Daniel were further explained and expanded on through the angel (9:22, 10:14) and again through the messenger-angel (probably Gabriel) in chapter eleven. Chapter eleven provides greater detail of the previous, reinforcing God's appointment of Persia over Babylon and Greece of Persia.

The preordained events were prophesied in chapters two, seven, and eight. God prearranged Darius, the Mede who would be succeeded by three others, arising in Persia, and a fourth who would stir up trouble with Greece (11:2). The three kings who ruled between Cyrus and Xerxes were Cambyses, Smerdis (pseudo-Smerdis or Gaumata, and Darius Hystaspes. The Persian king who stirred up trouble with Greece was Xerxes. Xerxes invaded Greece. Responding to the Persian invasion is the unstoppable and mighty king, Alexander, the Great, who brought an end to the Persian Empire (8:8). Alexander died a short time later in Babylon, having no successors due to his two sons being murdered; his kingdom was, therefore, broken and divided into four (7:6, 11:3-4). Alexander was succeeded by four Greek co-ruling generals (kings/horns) - one was Antiochus, a Seleucid-Greek ruler (vv. 21-24).

From verse five onwards, the chapter concentrates on the king of the south (10:5) and the king of the north (11:15). The king of the south refers to the successors to Ptolemy who ruled from Egypt, south of the Holy Land. The king of the north refers to the successors to Seleucid (Greece) ruling north of the Holy Land. Ptolemaic and the Seleucid are the focus of verses five to twenty due to this interaction with Israel. However, Antiochus is the primary focus (vv. 20-35), but not more so than the coming antichrist (vv. 36-45).

As the antichrist will be, Antiochus was well received by the Jews 'as a deliverer and benefactor.' However, Antiochus (meaning against support) was not in support of Israel; he was no friend or ally of the Jews. Antiochus was a type and shadow of the antichrist and was said to be the worst tyrant Israel had ever experienced. Antiochus' persecution of the Jews will only be outmatched by the antichrist to come.

In the same manner, the former prophecies were fulfilled regarding Israel's fate. The latter will also be – in the words of the angelic-messenger, "I will show you the truth" (11:2) about the things to come. The "truth" the angel spoke of applied to the "book of truth" (10:21) containing what will be, mapping out a prophetic pathway escalating in trouble for the Jewish nation by ending with the antichrist.

The events of chapter eleven were first written in the heavenly "book of truth" and then made available to us through another supernatural 'book of truth' which is the Bible. Chapter eleven contains much from this book, being the most prophetic passage within all of scripture. Chapter eleven provides a detailed historical account of what has happened and a reliable understanding of what will occur shortly. The "book of truth" should be compared to the book of mystery (Rev. 10), containing a sweet and bitter message.

The word consumed by John is divine revelation, to be recorded and proclaimed faithfully. The sweetness of God's word is His grace and mercy to those who believe and respond/obey. The bitterness of God's word refers to judgement, stored up for those who do not believe or disobey. God's bitter judgement will be executed in the tribulation against the rebellious and the disobedient, through the antichrist (2 Thess. 2:9-12).

Again, following a detailed account of what has been fulfilled (for us), chapter eleven's primary focus is Antiochus and the antichrist. Once more, Antiochus is a type of antichrist who will persecute Israel like none other. Contrary to false teaching (dominionism, reconstructionism, kingdom now 'theology'), the worst time in the history of mankind is still yet to occur (12:1, Jer. 30:7, Matt. 24:21). The message, 'Your worst life to come, not your best life now,' is the prophesied proclamation over Israel that alarmed Daniel so greatly (7:15, 28), resulting in repentance, pleading for mercy, and asking for forgiveness (9:1-19).

The broader scope of verses one to twenty focuses on the ongoing conflict between Persia, Greece, Egypt, and Rome, with Israel at the centre, and the point of interest (cf. Rev. 17:6b-14). Chapter ten (vv. 20-21) provides insight into the heavenly activity mirrored by earthly conflict. From the detailed prophetic account of chapter eleven, and taking chapter ten (vv. 20-21) into account, a revelation of the ongoing and intensifying spiritual warfare was gained.

Behind the scenes, battles are being fought, won, and lost in the invisible realm that we can only begin to imagine. And Israel is often at the centre of them, somewhat like a game of chess. You could say Israel is the most important 'chess piece' on the board. She always has been and always will be. During the coming tribulation, Israel will be centre stage with Jerusalem as the location of the antichrist's headquarters. At the midway point of the tribulation, the antichrist will set himself up in Jerusalem, from the third rebuilt tribulation temple, and from there, he will announce himself to be God (7:8, 9:27).

In conclusion, while the revelation of spiritual warfare made Daniel mute (10:15), the purpose of chapters ten and eleven are not to teach about spiritual warfare. Providing insight on spiritual warfare was not why the messenger-angel came. Nor was it to tell Daniel how greatly

God loved him (10:11, 18, cf. 9:23). Although God did greatly love Daniel, the purpose of the visitation was to reveal what would occur in the latter times, specifically involving Israel (10:14), as recorded in the "book of truth" (10:21). The book of truth contains pre-recorded information about events set to happen in the future shown to Daniel in advance (11:2). The Bible is the earthly version of the heavenly book of truth. Like the book of truth, the Bible also contains information about the future, being 30% prophetic.

The prophetic portion of the Bible provides us with indisputable proof, God's word is 100% reliable, accurate, and without error. Prophetic literature confirms God providing evidence, beyond any doubt, God is who He said He was and who He said He is. And God will do what He said He would do. No other 'prophet' or book has ever predicted the future with 100% accuracy. However, every fulfilled prophecy the Bible has ever given has been satisfied with pinpoint historical and literal accuracy. Not one single prediction has failed or fallen short. In the same way, every prediction the Bible has made has been fulfilled to date; those yet to be fulfilled will also be fulfilled likewise, literally and historically.

The remainder of chapter eleven focuses on the portion of prophecy to be fulfilled. The fulfilled portions serve as a template and a pattern of the things to come. Verses twenty-one to thirty-five serves as the climax of the chapter. The historical opening verses of the chapter (vv. 2–20) provided Daniel with the order of things to come. For us, they provide confirmation of things already fulfilled, which has set the stage for the prediction of an eighth Seleucid-Greek ruler, Antiochus Epiphanes. Antiochus Epiphanes is the "little horn" of chapter eight (cf. 8:9–12, 23–25). Much attention is given to him because his actions severely affected Israel and because he will be mirrored by the antichrist to come. Antiochus is also a type and shadow of the antichrist, revealing insight into his nature and activity in the coming tribulation.

Part Two

'The People Who Know Their God Shall Stand Firm and Take Action' (vv. 21-35)

As mentioned in the previous section, Antiochus is the primary focus of the next (this) portion of chapter eleven (vv. 21-35). Much more can be learned about Antiochus from the books of Maccabees. Specifically, Antiochus was a type and shadow of the coming antichrist and is said to have been the worst tyrant Israel has ever experienced to date. He, however, will be dwarfed by his successor, the antichrist, who is the coming fourth beast (7:7-8, 23-25).

The verses mentioned above covered in this section (vv. 21-35) serve as a template and a pattern of the things to come. Verses twenty-one to thirty-five serve as the climax of the entire chapter. Remember the words of the angelic messenger again, "I will show you the truth" (11:2) about the things to come, which is the reason the angel came to Daniel (10:20). The "truth" the angel spoke of applied to the "book of truth" (10:21), containing what will be after this, by mapping out a prophetic paralleled pathway, predicting an escalation of trouble for the Jewish nation and the world.

The truth is the future concerns for Israel, and the world will only conclude after the coming antichrist is dealt with by Jesus (7:11-12, 26) and not before. The coming antichrist is the eighth Seleucid-Greek ruler. Before addressing the coming antichrist, however, once again, we are reminded this section (11:21-35) handles the foreshadowed antichrist, Antiochus Epiphanes, who is also the focus, and the "little horn" of chapter eight (cf. 8:9–12, 23–25).

Following his first mention in chapter eight, Antiochus IV Epiphanes is again addressed in chapter eleven, from verse twenty-one. Verse twenty briefly references Antiochus IIIs son Seleucus IV Philopator who heavily taxed his people to pay Rome. He was subsequently "broken off," but not in battle; instead, he was poisoned by his treasurer Heliodorus. Antiochus IV Epiphanes is the son of Antiochus III. According to the first book of Maccabees, chapter one, Antiochus Epiphanes is the "a sinful root " ... "who began to reign in the one hundred and thirty-seventh year of the kingdom of the Greeks" (I Mac. 1:10). In that time, lawless men within Israel (Jews) led many more (Jews) astray by making a covenant with Antiochus. By doing so, they broke and removed themselves from the covenant with their God, and they also removed the marks (symbol and remembrance) of the covenant (circumcision).

At that time, like the antichrist will, Antiochus established himself in Jerusalem; he removed the sacred items of the sanctuary and took them back to his land. He deceitfully spoke words of peace to the Jewish people and then struck them with a severe blow, destroying many (I Mac. 1:30). Many fled Jerusalem, and the land became a dwelling place of strangers (Gentiles). Still, many other compromising Jews remained, gladly adopting Antiochus' false religion and worship, sacrificing to idols, and they profaned the sabbath (I Mac. 1:43). Antiochus forbade burnt offerings and sacrifices and drink offerings in the sanctuary to profane sabbaths and feasts (I Mac. 1:44). Antiochus also built altars and sacred precincts and shrines for idols to sacrifice swine and unclean animals (I Mac. 1:47), causing the Jews to reject and forget the Law of God. Like with the coming antichrist (Rev. 13:11-18), any people refusing Antiochus were destroyed: "And whoever does not obey the command of the king shall die" (I Mac. 1:50).

Jews joining Antiochus turned against their kind, driving the faithful remnant out of the city (I Mac. 1:53, cf. Matt. 24:10, 21). The faithless Jews also joined Antiochus, betraying their brothers and their God, erecting and desolating abominations of blasphemy upon the altar of burnt offering. The perfidious Jews burned incense to false gods, namely Zeus, and burned the books of the Law, and condemned the remaining faithful Jews to death. They were the ones who held to the word of God: "Any having the mark of circumcision (the sign of the covenant) were also killed, and their families and those who circumcised them; and they hung the infants from their mothers' necks" (I Mac. 1:61). Despite the great apostasy: "Many in Israel stood firm and were resolved in their hearts not to eat unclean food. They chose to die rather than be defiled by food or profane the holy covenant, and they did die. And very great wrath came upon Israel" (I Mac. 1:62-64).

As mentioned previously, a good portion of chapter eleven (vv. 21-35) was dedicated to Antiochus Epiphanes, the "little horn" due to being a type and shadow of the antichrist to come. As seen through chapter one of the first book of Maccabees and the book of Daniel and the book of Revelation, the deeds of Antiochus, and the betrayal of God from God's people, are repeated in the coming days.

When comparing First Maccabees with the book of Revelation and other prophetic passages, there is a clear pattern or template for the things to come that are even happening now. Like Antiochus, the antichrist will arise a contemptible person, without warning, seducing many with flattery (11:21).

Interestingly, although Antiochus had no legitimate right to the throne, he talked his way to it. He was initially accepted as a ruler due to turning away an invading army and removing Onias III, the high priest, "the prince of the covenant" (11:22). He then redistributed wealth, taking from the rich, giving to the poor (socialism), deceitfully bringing a false perception of fairness and (false) peace to gain followers and loyalty from everyday people (11:23-24).

From the book of Daniel, and the book of Maccabees, a great deal can be learned about Antiochus, and even these days, in which we live, leading up to the revealing of the antichrist. Much more can be assumed regarding the deeds of the coming antichrist regarding how he will come in, establishing (false) peace, gaining popularity and prosperity, and commanding great armies.

Like the coming antichrist will do, once Antiochus secured "peace," he attacked another power, being the king of the south, Egypt (11:25). No victory was gained from attacking Egypt, so Antiochus attempted to make (false) peace with the king of the south by professing (false) friendship. Antiochus and the king of the south shared a meal, hoping to sign an agreement, yet both were deceitful; therefore, no peace covenant was established (11:26-27).

Having failed to conquer Egypt, Antiochus departed, returning to his land; he desecrated the temple in Jerusalem (11:28). Despite his frustration, Antiochus' move against Egypt was not a total failure, as he acquired great wealth before eventually being stopped. Still, he was not content, and two years later, he attacked again (11:29-30a). The next attack was not like the last, failing due to Rome, who came against him in ships from Kittim (Cyprus). Rome told Antiochus to return home or be at war with them, which was not viable. Antiochus was humiliated by his defeat taking his frustration out on the Jews for a second time while giving favor to those who forsook the covenant (11:30b).

As the antichrist will do at the commencement of the tribulation, Antiochus made a false covenant of peace with the Jews. He then broke it and slaughtered many of them on the Sabbath day, taking women and children as slaves; he then ransacked and burnt the city. Furthermore, and as mentioned above through the record of the first book of Maccabees, Antiochus "Set up the abomination that makes desolation" (11:31) by erecting an altar to Zeus on the altar of burnt offering outside the temple, and had a pig offered on the altar. The Jews were then forced to provide a pig on the 25th of each month to celebrate Antiochus Epiphanes' birthday.

Antiochus pledged to the apostate Jews (11:30) a reward if they would forsake their God, the God of Israel, and worship his god, the Greek god, Zeus. Again, to achieve this, Antiochus "flattered" the Jews, making false promises, causing many to violate their covenant with God (11:32a). Turning their back on God, many Jews bowed down and worshipped the false god Zeus. Under the promise of reward and the threat of death, only a remnant of the Jews remained faithful (11:32b).

Only a remnant of the people who knew their God stood firm and took action (11:32b). Again, for refusing to bow down and worship the false god of Greece, the faithful Jews were persecuted, even at their own (brothers) hands (I Mac. 1:53), and many fell (11:33). Those resisting Antiochus were of the Maccabean uprising. The resistance started with just a few and quickly grew; some who joined the resistance were sincere, while others were not (11:34). The true and the false were mixed. The same is true within the church today, as Jesus illustrated with the bulk of the parables.

The parables reference sheep and goats, wheat and tares, good and bad, wise, and foolish, etc. grouped, for a time, but in the end, they will be separated one from the other. Through persecution, the faithful Jews were separated, refined, purified, and purged of sin (11:35). This is happening today within the church (cf. Rev. 2:10) and will be again for those professing Christ during the tribulation.

In sum, for Daniel, the prophecy of the things to come through Antiochus was the fulfillment of chapters eight (8:14, 23-25) and eleven (vv. 21-35), serving as a shadow for what is to come in the latter days. The latter days are unfolding now but still await the appointed time (11:35b).

Again, Antiochus is a type of antichrist, providing insight into the antichrist's activity to come. Although Antiochus and the coming antichrist are similar, they are not the same.

Chapter six of first Maccabees reveals that Antiochus died of insanity, after losing a battle in the city of Elymais, Persia (I Mac. 6:1-4), also losing ground to the revolting Jews, who tore down his idols in Jerusalem (I Mac. 6:7), he was shaken with fear and became sick with grief (I Mac. 6:9), even dying (I Mac. 6:9). Antiochus recognized he had done wrong by the Jews and was being punished (1 (I Mac. 6:12-13). Admitting fault, without repentance (unlike Nebuchadnezzar, who repented), Antiochus, the king, died in his bed, insane, in the one hundred and forty-ninth year (I Mac. 6:16).

Antiochus died acknowledging his sin, without repentance; however, the antichrist to come (7:8, 9:26) will not come to the place of admitting wrong. Instead, he will go to war against Jesus Christ before being cast into the lake of fire (Rev. 19:19-20). Like Antiochus, the antichrist will be a powerful ruler; he will be the final world ruler, coming out of the revived Roman Empire. He will first appear insignificant as the little horn, yet will quickly rise to power, empowered by Satan (Rev. 13:1-8). Like Antiochus, the antichrist will also be authorised by kings submitting to him; ten kings will advance the antichrist (11:36, Rev. 17:12-13).

The coming antichrist is appropriately addressed in the last portion of chapter eleven (vv. 36-45), covering the final seven years of the seventy sevens (9:24).

While the coming antichrist will not be revealed until the church is taken out of the way (2 Thess. 2:6-7), antichrist activity, being the spirit of antichrist (1 Jn. 4:1-6), is already at work within the church today (2 Thess. 2:7). As with the covenant-breaking Jews (11:30), many 'Christians' have already been deceived by the smooth talk and flattery of the antichrist spirit, promising peace and prosperity/security. In the same way, Antiochus promised peace and prosperity to the Jews who broke the covenant and defiled the temple by setting up idols and by participating in false worship. The spirit of the antichrist does this today through the hyper-grace prosperity gospel. When people are saying, "There is peace and security, then sudden destruction will come upon them, as labor pains will come upon a pregnant woman, and they will not escape" (1

Thess. 5:3). To "not escape" is to be 'left behind' (cf. Rev. 3:10); left behind to endure God's wrath in the coming tribulation (cf. 1 Thess. 5:9).

But those who know their God shall stand firm to God (holding to sound biblical doctrine) and will take action (11:32b). Those who know their God take action by resisting false declarations, rebuking doctrines of demons, and thereby rejecting false worship. Taking action is also by way of proclaiming the truth (when few can endure it), producing purity in themselves and others (11:35), by turning many to righteousness (12:3).

Although commonly misquoted, the great exploits of chapter eleven (action taken, 11:32b) are not as many Charismatics claim (dominating, ruling, and reigning as kings in this life) but instead refer to rejecting false worship. Specific to the verse (11:32b) was the Maccabean uprising, which resisted Antiochus with force (11:34, Zech. 9:13-16, 1 Mac. 1:52, 2:42). For us, however, it is more about standing firm for righteousness (I Cor. 15:58, 16:63, Eph. 6:11, 13, Phil. 1:27, 4:1), which includes resisting and overcoming the world by ruling over our sin (Rom. 5:17). Regardless of the situation and the pressure to buckle, we are to remain faithful to God, (Rev. 2:10), holding fast to (and proclaiming) His uncompromised Word (Rev. 3:10).

When standing firm and taking action for the uncompromised truth of God's Word, persecution, not prosperity, is promised, even from within (I Mac. 1:53, Dan. 11:33-34, 41, Matt. 24:10, 21). Persecution is the expectation in this world (Jn. 16:3), not and never 'Your Best Life Now.' Persecution will increase and will intensify until Jesus returns. Only those who endure until the end will be saved (Matt. 10:22, 24:13). Those who love this world will quickly fold, when persecution comes as the faithless Jews did under Antiochus. But those who have come out from this world will unit and get stronger, as the Maccabee's did. The purpose of persecution is to separate you from this world, strengthening you for the glory of God in preparation for the next (11:32-35).

Part Three
'The Stage is Set'
(vv. 36-39)

In part two of chapter eleven, Antiochus was the focus, being a type and shadow of the antichrist to come. Part three will address the coming antichrist, which mirrors Antiochus during the tribulation. In the same way "The Book of Truth" (10:21, 11:2) was proven accurate and reliable by history regarding Antiochus, it will be again with the coming antichrist. The antichrist will fulfil every prophecy to literal, historic pinpoint accuracy. Once more, for this purpose, the messenger angel came to Daniel (10:20), providing understanding about the end times, especially the timing of the things to come (9:24-27, 10:11-12, 14).

As explained to Daniel in chapter nine (vv. 24-27), the fulfilment of the prophecies regarding the latter days would take place in the seventieth week, following a pause between the sixty-ninth and seventieth week (9:26). The hiatus between the sixty-ninth and seventieth week is due to Christ being "cut off" through crucifixion. When He returns for His bride, the church is removed from the earth (Rev. 3:10), restarting the prophetic clock, commencing the tribulation.

Remember, the church does not go through the tribulation (Rom 5:9, 1 Thess. 1:10, 5:9), and neither will Messianic Jews (12:1, Isa. 26:20-21, Zeph. 2:3), therefore the time of trouble will not commence until the church is first taken out of the way (2 Thess. 2:6-7). The church will be removed for a duration of seven years, patterned after a Galilean wedding, where the bride is 'lifted up' and 'flown away' to meet the groom. Before appearing, the bride and groom are joined and then 'hidden away' in the wedding chambers for seven days.

Those left behind will endure the coming tribulation, which will last seven years (7:25, 9:27, 12:7, Rev. 11:2, 3, 12:6, 14, 13:5), being one prophetic week. The tribulation 'week' is the seventieth and final week, and the appointed time (11:35), where the "strong covenant" of "one week" (the Middle East Peace Treaty) will be signed, and then broken halfway through that week (9:27a, cf. Isa. 28:15, 18). After three and a half years of (false) peace, the antichrist will break his covenant with the Jews during the tribulation. At the same time the antichrist breaks his covenant of death (Isa. 28, 15, 18), he will also commit the abomination of desolation (9:27, Matt 24:15). The abomination of desolation is where the antichrist proclaims, from the rebuilt temple, at the midway point of the tribulation, that is, he is God (2 Thess. 2:4). At this point, the antichrist will also force the world's population to worship him, alone, and receive his mark (666), or else be slain (Rev. 13:11-18).

Again, the antichrist will not be revealed until the church is first taken out of the way (2 Thess. 2:6-8), which triggers the tribulation alongside the signing of the peace treaty. When the church is raptured, then the "little horn" (insignificant beginning) will appear, offering peace and security. However, like Antiochus (meaning against support), the antichrist will be independent of earthly authority, doing as he pleases (11:36), yet is empowered by ten kings (7:8, 20, Rev. 17:12-13). Through the ten kings, the antichrist will possess global political power; he will also control every religious practice, redirecting every form of worship to himself. As mentioned above, the abomination of desolation is where the antichrist claims to be God, blaspheming the one true God from the rebuilt tribulation temple (7:8, 25, 2 Thess. 2:4).

During the tribulation, right from the beginning, many will be deceived by the antichrist, who will operate with lying signs and wonders (2 Thess. 2:9, Matt. 24:24, Rev. 13:11-15). So convincing will the antichrist be, he will lead many astray, even the elect would be deceived, if possible (Matt. 24:24). For this purpose, and to condemn (2 Thess. 2:12), God sends the antichrist (2 Thess. 2:11, 'strong delusion') due to the majority falling away from sound biblical doctrine, this side of the tribulation (2 Thess. 2:3) - no longer loving, and wanting, truth and righteousness (2 Thess. 2, 10, 12). Essentially, by sending the antichrist, God gives the apostates, and the world, what they desire and deserve.

At the appointed time (11:40, 12:1), which is the commencement of the tribulation, God will appoint the antichrist, as He did with all four beasts (7:6), giving him dominion over the whole earth, as the final world ruler, for seven years. At the commencement of the tribulation, the opening of the first seal releases the white horse, who is the antichrist (Rev. 6:1-2). Then, after seven years (7:25), God will take away the authority of the antichrist (Dan. 7:11, 26; 9:27; Rev. 19:19–20), retaking authority and dominion over the earth for Himself (7:14, 26).

At the opening of the first seal (Rev. 6:2), the antichrist will appear, and he will do so out of the revived Roman Empire (7:2-3). Again, the antichrist will not be revealed until the church is removed (2 Thess. 2:6-7), which means he cannot be identified on this side of the tribulation. However, there are still some clues to who he may be. For example, the antichrist will rise from the revived Roman Empire; nevertheless, it is strongly argued, he will also have Jewish roots. Support for this argument is that the antichrist will be the false Jewish, long-awaited Messiah that Jesus warned us about. Jesus said that many false prophets would come (Matt. 24:4, 5, 11, 24, cf. 1 Jn. 2:18-19), but there is one who will come, fulfilling the prophecies regarding the antichrist (Matt. 24:25-26, cf. 1 Jn. 2:18). The Jews are looking for such a man to accept as their messiah. It goes without saying, for the one the Jews accept as their Messiah, he would have to be Jewish or of Jewish descent. Religious, orthodox Jews will never receive a Gentile Messiah, which debunks any suggestion of a Muslim antichrist, discrediting the claim of a Middle East Beast.

Although the antichrist will be of Jewish descent, he will also be Gentile. Support for this argument is where the antichrist will rise out of the sea (7:2-3), the Mediterranean Sea, or the Revived Roman Empire. Therefore, he will have to be a Gentile, like Antiochus was, with Jewish roots. As mentioned previously, Emmanuel Macron ticks many boxes, being a ruler within the region of the revived Roman Empire and is also said to have Jewish roots. Interestingly, the name Emmanuel means, 'God is with us.'

Furthermore, in English gematria, the words 'Macron Beast' equal 666, and the words 'A President' also equal 666 (cf. Rev. 13:18). Additionally, when Macron appeared on the scene, from nowhere, the Economist magazine (2017) put him on the front page and pictured him walking on water, with the heading, 'Saviour of Europe.' The case for Macron to fulfil the prophecy of the coming antichrist is further strengthened, by him, speaking loftily, claiming to be a "Jupiterian" leader that is unchallenged and detached from trivialities, like the chief Roman god of the skies. Macron said he would rule Europe like the Roman god of Jupiter. A Jupiterian leader is said to be a mix of political and religious ambition. However, Marcon is not content to rule just Europe but has much grander purposes, such as to rule the world (cf. Dan. 7:4-7, Rev. 13:2, 7).

When building a case of support for the possibility of Macron to fulfil the prophecies, consideration of his move in 2018 towards forming a ten-nation collation (ten horns, 7:7, 20, 24, Rev. 21:3, 13:1, 17:3, 7, 12, 16), is noteworthy, which gained further traction in 2020. The promoted motivation for the ten-nation collation is international security, confirmed by the German president, Frank-Walter Steinmeier (2020), saying, "We are witnessing today an increasingly destructive momentum in global politics. Every year we are getting further and further away from our goal of creating a more peaceful world through international cooperation."

Macron believes policies and processes are the answer, to resolve saying, "I do not believe in miracles, but in policies." To implement a 'peace' policy Macron called for a "Process becoming less teleological, long-winded and bureaucratic. The bloc's current review of its accession procedures should do away with the idea that progress to accession was not reversible." The word 'teleological' replaced the original word 'theological.'

Macron's 'peace' policies are not restricted to Europe, but globally, also having a vested interest in the Middle East Peace Treaty. Remember, the one who is successful in establishing peace in the Middle East, through a signing of a 'strong covenant,' is the antichrist. The peace treaty currently tabled, and gaining traction, is the Abrahamic Accord, offering 'Prosperity for Peace.'

Further to establishing peace and security, Macron has recently implemented a new policy requiring mandatory vaccinations, under the threat of fines and jail sentences for those who refuse. Any unvaccinated, untested person entering a business, or operating a business open to the public, will be fined and or jailed. Others joining France, in part, are Greece, Italy, Hungry, Kazakhstan, Russia, Saudi Arabi, Turkmenistan, Indonesia, New Zealand, Australia, Britain, Canada, and the United States, to name a few. In time, vaccinations will become a global requirement. Those who comply are praised, and those that do not are punished.

To establish stability, peace, and security, recently, in the same way Antiochus gained the trust of the Jews (11:21b-22). President Macron of France went on record, positioning himself for global leadership, starting by calling for a worldwide ceasefire (Andelman, 2020). Like Antiochus, who turned away an approaching army and then, through flattery, formed a covenant with the Jews (11:22), the antichrist will also do, followed by a false proclamation of peace.

To do so, like Antiochus, alongside Europe, Macron has strong support from the United Nations. Macron also has religious support, recently receiving the blessing of Pope Francis, positioning him as a proposed new world leader (O'Connell, 2020). As with a call for a new world order, the request of a one-world leader is nothing new: Henri Spaak, Secretary-General of NATA, said in 1957, "What we want is a man of sufficient stature to hold the alliances of all people and to lift us out of the economic morass into which we are sinking. Send us such a man, and be he god or devil, we will receive him."

"Send us such as man, and be he a god or devil, we will receive him!" As mentioned earlier, God will send such a man, releasing him at the commencement of the tribulation, being both a man and a devil, but not a god, despite claiming to be God. Although the coming antichrist will claim to be God, dismissing, and elevating himself above every other god, including the gods of his fathers (11:36-37), even operating supernaturally (Rev. 13:13-14), he will be in for one hell of a time while attempting to rule the world.

The antichrist will face many challenges in his short seven-year season, especially in the last three and a half years of the tribulation. The following and concluding section of chapter eleven, will be addressed in part four. Briefly, at the midway point of the tribulation, the antichrist demands that the whole world worships him, and in doing so, challenges God to a showdown, which he will have (Rev. 19:11-21).

The reference to the coming antichrist magnifying himself above every god, speaking things against the God of gods, and paying no attention to any other god (11:36, 37), confirms he will be deeply religious and that the end-time agenda is that humanity would worship him, as God, alone. This is also why he will "Pay no attention to the one beloved by women" (11:37). The reference, 'the one beloved by women,' refers to a Jewish virgin who gave birth to the Saviour of the world, Jesus Christ (cf. Rev. 12:1-6). The antichrist will pay no attention to the Messianic hope of the world, dismissing and rejecting God's only means of salvation, Jesus (Jn. 14:6, Acts 4:12).

Instead of acknowledging the Saviour of the world, brought forth through the virgin birth, the Satan empowered antichrist will persecute

Israel like never before. Also, any other who stands with her, who keeps the commandments of God, holding to the testimony of Jesus (Rev. 12:15-17).

Satan will be solely committed to destroying the Jews to prevent Jesus from returning. Jesus said, "For I tell you that you will not see Me again until you say, 'Blessed is He who comes in the name of the Lord.'" If the Jews were to be wiped off the face of the earth, they would not be able to call upon the name of Jesus. Therefore, He would not return; consequently, Satan's rule would not end. If Satan continued to rule as the god of this world, fallen humanity would openly worship him, which was always the plan (cf. Gen. 3, Matt. 4:9).

At the midway point of the tribulation, knowing his time is short (Rev. 12:12), Satan will desperately attempt to achieve his objective through the antichrist who will command everyone to worship him alone (Rev. 13). In the same way, Antiochus demanded the Jews break the covenant of their God by removing the marks of that covenant (circumcision), the antichrist will do the same by forcing the global population to receive his mark (666). The antichrist will demand the tribulation population reject God or be slain (Rev. 13:15-18). In sum, the antichrist will proclaim a false gospel, promising salvation, safety, and security through him, as the 'saviour of the world.'

Instead of paying attention to the Messianic hope that came through the Jews (Jn. 4:22), being Jesus Christ, the antichrist, will magnify himself (11:38). Rather than trusting Jesus, the antichrist and put his trust in "A god his fathers did not know" (11:38), who is Satan. Although and again, the antichrist will come offering peace, with a peace covenant (9:27) like Antiochus did (11:23, 32), he will break the (death) covenant halfway through the tribulation (Isa. 28:15, 18), making war against the people of God. During the tribulation, the antichrist will only honour a god of fortresses and receive help from a foreign god (11:39), referring to his political and military strength. His political position will enable him to command armies, resulting in great wealth. The antichrist will take from the uncompliant and redistribute their wealth to those who are compliant, for a price (11:39). Antiochus did the same thing, taking from those who held to the holy covenant, scattering, plundering, spoil, and goods among those that broke the holy covenant (11:22-24).

As Antiochus did, the antichrist will do, only dwarfing his predecessor in every way. Even now, the stage is set, evident under the guise of COVID-19. The 'plandemic' (not a typo), COVID-19, has brought about unprecedented (special) powers for governments of the post-modern world, uniting globalists with a plan to vaccinate, control, and corrupt (corrupting human DNA, as the days of Noah, cf. Matt. 24:37, Gen. 6-7) the global population. Soon, the noncompliant, refusing the vaccination will lose the ability to buy, sell, and travel, ultimately being unable to function within society.

As the narrative goes, due to posing a risk to themselves and others, and therefore, presenting a security threat to the global community, the unvaccinated will be put under house arrest before being jailed. Due to not having the capacity to jail everyone resisting, camps will be utilized. FEMA camps have already been set up for this purpose. Holding people in camp will be a temporary measure, requiring the need for something more permanent.

In the same way, the Jews were dealt with in World War II; the nonvaccinated will likewise be. The vaccination is the first stage, conditioning the naïve and deceived for the mark of the beast. In time, the government will repossess the possessions and the property of the unvaccinated as Antiochus did, and the antichrist will do, to be redistributed as the government sees fit. COVID-19 has set the stage for the global reset and for the mark of the beast and every other event corresponding with it (cf. Rev. 13:10, 15). Even now, most cannot see it. Only the wise will understand (12:10).

Part Four
'And they will know that I Am God' (vv. 40-45)

In the previous section, the leadup to the revealing of the antichrist was addressed, highlighting clues possibly identifying who he could be. However, the antichrist is not revealed until after the church has been removed. Therefore, any suggestion that the antichrist is this person or that, on this side of the rapture, is void of scriptural support; therefore, is purely speculative. At best, we can say, this person or that ticks some boxes.

Alongside clues as to who the antichrist could be, the previous section also considers what circumstances set the stage for the tribulation, leading into the time of trouble, and the events of the first three and a half years. This section looks at the final three and a half years, marked by the antichrist committing the abomination of desolation in the rebuilt tribulation temple. Another marker is where the antichrist breaks the Middle East peace treaty. Yet another again is where Michael casts Satan to the ground, with the help of other angels (cf. Rev. 12).

At the midway point of the tribulation, the antichrist will also enforce his mark, the mark of the beast (666). Following the proclaiming that he is God, he will demand that everyone worships him. The sign of his covenant is his mark, he will require the earth's remaining population to receive it or be slain. At that time, death will be welcomed by those resisting, escaping increased persecution, rendering the noncompliant unable to function within society (trade and travel), and delivering them from the tribulation judgement. Confirmed by the voice from heaven, during the tribulation, from here on, blessed are those who die, early (Rev. 14:13).

However, as mentioned, during the tribulation, the antichrist will be in for a hell of a time, dealing with the noncompliance, resulting in uprisings, leading to wars. He will also be subject to the judgements of God, in particular, the fifth bowl judgement, where an angel pours out God's judgement on the throne of the beast (Rev. 16:10). While all judgements are global, this one is localised, explicitly aimed at the antichrist and his followers. The fifth bowl judgement cloaks the beast's kingdom in darkness, like the ninth plague in Egypt (Ex. 10:22-23). When God covered the land of Egypt with pitch darkness, none could see anyone or go anywhere for three days, albeit the Israelites were separated (Ex. 10:23).

The thick darkness to be be poured out on the beast's throne was predicted by Joel (2:2) and John (Rev. 16:10). God's judgement of darkness, during the tribulation is a taste of the eternal state for the antichrist and his followers. As for how long the darkness lasts, once poured out through the administration of the fifth bowl, the gospel, according to Matthew, provides a clue: "From the sixth hour there was darkness over all the land until the ninth hour" (Matt. 27:45). The reference refers to the event following the death of Jesus. When Jesus died, the earth was covered in darkness for three hours, and also covered Egypt for three days.

In the same way, during the tribulation, just before Jesus returns, the earth will be covered in darkness for a period of three units, which are probably months. It could explain the reference to horses and not tanks being used in the tribulation wars (Joel 2, Rev. 9, 16, 20). It could also be argued the darkness will not end until the light (Jesus) comes, which happens in the proceeding judgement confirmed by the words, "It is Done!" (Rev. 16:17-21). During darkness, and following, those affected will curse (rather than repent) God due to their pain (16:11, 21).

The judgement of darkness refers to more than the absence of light, including electricity and the internet, without which renders the modes of modern warfare useless but is also noxious darkness resulting in physical soars and pain (Rev. 16:11). Due to cursing, God responds appropriately, divinely stoning the blasphemers with hailstones, weighing one hundred pounds each (Rev. 16:21). Death by stoning is the penalty for blasphemy (Lev. 24:10-16).

Again, the judgement of the fifth bowl is poured out on the throne of the beast, causing his followers to gnaw their tongues in anguish (Rev. 16:10). During this time of darkness, only the followers of the beast suffered pain and sores (Rev. 16:11). Something similar is seen with the first bowl, where God directs an angel to pour out judgement where harmful sores came upon the people who bore the mark of the beast and worshipped its image (Rev. 16:2).

The tribulation bowl judgements escalate in severity, ending with war (sixth bowl) before Jesus returns (seventh bowl). The sixth and seventh trumpet and the sixth and seventh bowl are the same events. There are three woes within the tribulation (Rev. 8:13), the first being the demonic locusts that torment any without the seal of God with painful stings, causing pain for nine months (Rev. 9:1-12). This is like the first woe being the fifth trumpet judgement of the tribulation. It is similar to the first bowl, resulting in physical pain for those following the beast. The second woe is the sixth trumpet of the tribulation, and the third and final woe is the seventh of the tribulation - these are also directed at the beast's followers.

The tribulation events, as mentioned above, will occur at the end of time (11:40). In context, the end of time refers to the second half of the tribulation. From the midway point of the seven years ordeal, the antichrist's new world order will be anything but orderly. The whole world will be in a state of disorder and on the brink of World War III. Verse forty of Daniel, chapter eleven narrows in on the coming world war that will conclude the time of this age, ushering in the return of Jesus Christ. The future king of verse forty, the antichrist, is at the centre of the coming war, confirmed by the concluding verses of chapter eleven. In verses forty to forty-five, every occurrence of "he" (seven times), "him" (four times), and "his" (three times) refers to the antichrist.

The same 'king' who enters through flattery, promoting peace, and establishing a covenant with the Jewish people (9:27), will single-handedly bring about World War III, otherwise known as the battle of Armageddon. Like Antiochus, the antichrist will deceive the Jews by preventing war, possibly by participating in the destruction of Damascus (Syria), fulfilling Isaiah's prophecy (Isa. 17).

Sometime in the future, Syria will attack Israel, and losing, resulting in total devastation, even ceasing to exist from that day on. On that day, northern Israel will also take a significant hit (Isa. 17:3), causing many to desert the Holy Land (Isa. 17:9). The devastation will, however, cause them to remember their God (Isa. 17:7-10). The future attack could provide an opportunity for the antichrist to establish the peace treaty, which he breaks, and then leads to Armageddon.

The campaign of Armageddon, resulting in World War III, will commence with the land of Israel being attacked, again, this time by the king of the south (Egypt and co.). While the antichrist turns against orthodox Jews, especially those following Jesus, he will fight for the land of Israel,

As mentioned earlier, through the sixth trumpet and bowl judgement, war will break out towards the end of the seven-year ordeal. War in the tribulation should be expected as an ongoing and escalating theme, being the purpose and nature of the red horse, released with the breaking of the second seal (Rev. 6:3-4). In the act of war, Damascus will attack Israel, probably just before or at the beginning of the tribulation, followed by the king of the south, who will attack Israel somewhere around the midpoint of the tribulation. Remember, Egypt is part of the

Middle East, therefore it will be in covenant with the antichrist through the Middle East peace treaty. The signing of the peace treaty triggers the tribulation. An attack on Israel will break the treaty, and through the breaking of the peace treaty, tens of thousands in the Holy Land will die (11:41).

As already established, the southern king refers to Egypt (11:5-35); therefore, the reference in verse forty refers to the same. In confirmation, Egypt is mentioned twice more (11:42-43) yet will not be alone in the attack against Israel. The attack from the south will come from several other Middle Eastern nations, which is later followed by another attack, this time by the kings of the east and the north.

The kings of the east lead 200,000,000 mounted troops, led by the released demons who were previously bound at the great Euphrates River (Rev. 9:14). Led by demons, the 200,000,000 cross the, to be, dried-up Euphrates River (Rev. 16:12), assembling with kings of the whole world for the battle on the great day of God the Almighty (Rev. 16:14). They assembled at the place that in Hebrew is called Armageddon (Rev. 16:16). The prophet Joel adds to the prophecy referencing this powerful army. Never has there been anything like them before or will be again (Joel 2:2). Nothing escapes them (Joel 2:3), for they are God's warriors (Joel 2:11), designed and purposed to produce repentance (Joel 2:12-17).

The reference to a demonic led army being God's warriors simply means, they are under His sovereignty, in the same way, God raised up Pharaoh (Rom. 9:17) and referred to Nebuchadnezzar as His servant (Jer. 27:6), and to Cyrus as His anointed instrument (Isa. 45:1). All were under God's sovereign rule.

Interestingly, in context with Joel's prediction of the demon-led, supernatural/superhuman (transhuman) army, there is also a reference to the tribulation locust (Joel 2:25), preceding the mighty 200,000,000 strong warriors (cf. Rev. 9). And, again within the same context (Joel 2), there is the reference calling for repentance during the tribulation (Joel 2:12-17). For those who do, their years will be restored (Joel 2:25-26).

The purpose of the plagues is that Israel may know that God is in their midst, that He is their God, and that there is none else (Joel 2:27). In other words, God is God, and the antichrist is not! The plagues are designed to bring everyone to that conclusion. During the tribulation, anyone who calls upon His name shall be saved (Joel 2:32, cf. Rom. 10:9-13).

As mentioned, earlier, the kings of the east (Rev. 16:12) primarily point to China, and co., while the king of the north points to Russia and Turkey (cf. 11:44). Russia, and surrounding northern nations, have been of interest for centuries regarding the fulfilment of Ezekiel's prophesied invasion led by Gog and Magog (Ezek. 38-39, cf. Rev. 20:7-10). Ezekiel's prophecy is still yet to be fulfilled and will be fulfilled during the tribulation. The king of the 'furthest north,' referring primarily to Russia, is first mentioned in verse forty of Daniel, chapter eleven. This king of the north is not the same as the northern king mentioned in verses five – thirty-five, being Greek. The difference being, the latter king of the north will come in like a whirlwind (11:40), later following the king of the south (11:44), attacking Israel, which is the headquarters of the antichrist.

Again, when the king of the south comes into Israel, the antichrist will counter-attack, and tens of thousands shall fall (11:41a). Others will become apostate, turning against one another (Matt. 24:10) as in the days of Antiochus, and again, others will flee (11:41b.cf. Matt. 24:16). The antichrist will respond to the king of the south by sweeping his armies across Europe into the Middle East like a flood. Responding to the invasion, he will first destroy Egypt and her allies, reaping treasures, and rule over her southern lands (11:41-42). However, not all southern lands will fall into the hands of the antichrist, Edom, and Moab, the Ammonites' main part, are delivered from him (11:41).

Following the antichrist's victory over the king of the south, sometime later, towards the end of the tribulation, the kings of the east and north will attack. The antichrist will again respond, as he did with the king of the south, only this time he will not be victorious (11:45a). Where the antichrist previously had the support of ten nations, this time he will be left standing alone (11:45b), coming face to face with Jesus Christ (Rev. 19:20), which is discussed later.

From Ezekiel's prophesy (chapters 38-39), we learn God is against O Gog, chief prince of Meshech and Tubal (Ezek. 38:3, 39:1), drawing them out for battle (Ezek. 38:4, 39:2). They are joined by Persia (Iran), Cush (Sudan, and south of Egypt), and Put (Libya) (Ezek. 38:5), and Gomer and all his hordes; Beth-Togarmah from the uttermost parts of the north with all his hordes (Ezek. 38:6).

God draws this mighty army out for battle, to be destroyed (Ezek. 38:18-23, 39:3-6), for the purpose that everyone will know that God is God (Ezek. 38:23, 39:6, 7, 22, 28). In the latter years of the tribulation (Ezek. 38:8, cf. 39:8), the listed nations of the north will march against Israel for a battle that will end all battles.

The latter years refer to a time when Israel is dwelling securely (Ezek. 38:14, 39:9-10), being established, having built themselves up, independent of God. When the northern nations attack Israel, the north will be so severely slaughtered; taking seven months to bury the dead (Ezek. 39:11, 14). God will assist in cleansing the land by sending beasts to feast on the flesh of the dead (Ezek. 39:17-20, cf. Rev. 19:17-18). The linked references from Ezekiel and the book of Revelation provide an obvious timeframe of the future event, being the battle of Armageddon.

While the timing of Ezekiel's prophecy is debated, most agree it is yet to be fulfilled and will be sometime within the tribulation. As mentioned above, going by the conclusion of the prophecy, where God destroys the army from the north, and the correlation with John's revelation (Rev. 19:17-18), it stands to reason the event is set for the end of the tribulation and, therefore it is also the same unfulfilled event revealed to Daniel (11:44).

Again, unlike with the king of the south, the antichrist is unsuccessful when attacked by the king of the north, who is joined by the kings of the east in a joint attack against Israel. An explanation for the antichrist's defeat, having none to stand with him, is that God deals with him (7:11, 26, Rev. 19:20), in the same way, He dealt with the northern armies. Thus, the antichrist, who claimed to be God, now comes face to face with the One True Living God, Jesus Christ.

Through God's intervention by delivering Israel from the invading armies and the antichrist, everyone will know that He (alone) is God (Ezek. 38:23, 39:6, 7, 22, 28, Joel 2:27), and that the antichrist is not. Again, at the midpoint of the tribulation, the antichrist will claim to be God (7:8b, 2 Thess. 2:4) and demand that the global population worship him (Rev. 13). Revelation, chapters thirteen and fourteen reveal ongoing spiritual warfare over the souls of humanity. Those who take the mark of the beast are eternally dammed (Rev. 14:9-11). Those who resist the beast are slain (Rev. 13:10, 15).

In conclusion, the latter half of the tribulation is a time like never before (12:1, Joel 2:2b), marked by war. The battle of Armageddon, or 'campaign' of Armageddon, is the conclusion of the tribulation, ushering in the return of Jesus Christ. In the latter days, the antichrist will attempt to rule the world; yet will be resisted by many. Nations from the south, east, and the north will attack him, resulting in a final battle, World War III, set to take place in Megiddo.

In fulfilment of prophecy, the antichrist will gather his armies at the place called Armageddon (Rev. 16:14, 19:19) to not only war against the invading nations but also war against Jesus Christ Himself (Rev. 19:19). At the conclusion of the tribulation, all hell will break out; again, it will be a time unlike anything previously seen (Jer. 30:7, Matt. 24:21). If Jesus did not shorten those days by returning, no flesh would be left

(Matt. 24:22). Through His return and the events leading towards His return, everyone will know that Jesus is God (Ezek. 38:23, 39:6, 7, 22, 28, Joel 2:27), and the antichrist is not.

At the end of the seven years (12:7b), Jesus will return to deal with the antichrist, delivering the elect (12:1, Matt. 24:22) and resurrecting the just. The resurrected just (tribulation martyrs) will then join the resurrected dead in Christ, and the raptured saints for the marriage supper of the Lamb, which takes place on earth (Rev. 19:6-10). The marriage supper will occur during the seventy-five-day interval (12:11-12), before the Millennial dispensation, or the Messianic Kingdom. Daniel, chapter twelve will address the seventy-five-day intervention.

Chapter Twelve

Part One
'A Time of Trouble'
(vv. 1-4)

Unlike the false prophets who deceived and led Judah astray, evidently through the book of Daniel, Daniel, like Jeremiah, is greatly concerned about his people. Daniel chapter nine is most notable for Daniel's concern and desperate plea to God, wrapped in repentance. Daniel's desperate prayerful plea in chapter nine (vv. 1-19) prompted God to respond by sending the angel Gabriel (vv. 24-27). Chapters ten to twelve are one-piece, continuing from chapter nine, following a three-year gap. A messenger angel brings detailed understanding to Daniel regarding the last days, briefly addressed in chapter nine (vv. 24-27).

Throughout these chapters, notable is the reference "your people" seen four times in chapter nine (vv. 15, 16, 19, 24), once each in chapter ten (v. 14), and chapter eleven (v. 14), and again in chapter twelve (v. 1). The importance of identifying these references brings an understanding of to whom the prophecy primarily refers. The prophecy refers to God's people being Israel. The nation of Israel is the principal focus of the book. The purpose of the prophesied event is to bring the rebellious nation back to God, causing them to, again, remember Him and their covenant with Him.

Despite many claiming God has done away with Israel and that the church has replaced her, promoted through the false teaching of replacement theology, the church and Israel are separate entities. Paul could not have made that any clearer through his writings in Romans (chapters 9-11). Many today claim the blessings of Israel, for themselves, through the false teaching of replacement theology, subscribed by dominionism, also known as reconstructionism. Dominionists promote the senseless seven-mountain mandate. As mentioned previously, dominionism is rooted in the prosperity 'gospel,' noticeable for its false teaching that runs opposite to the Bible.

The seven-mountain mandate recklessly states believers are called to dominate the seven key areas of worldly influence in preparation for Jesus' return. Again, the Bible teaches the opposite; instead of dominating this world, this side of Jesus returning, faithful followers of Christ will be persecuted (Jn. 16:33, Rev. 2:9-10, 3:9-8). Conversely, compromised (Rev. 2:14), corrupt (Rev. 2:20-21), dead (Rev. 3:1-2), and lukewarm (Rev. 3:15-16) churches, having a reputation of being alive and wealthy, that appear to be dominating this world, are in danger of judgement.

Increasing persecution is particularly true for Israel, confirmed through Daniel, chapters seven, nine, eleven, and twelve. While dominionists love to claim the blessings of Israel for themselves, they conveniently overlook prophecy predicting Israel's severe and increasing persecution through the coming tribulation. The worst, not best, is still yet to come. During the coming tribulation, Israel will suffer persecution unlike any time before, or any time again (12:1, Jer. 30:7, Matt. 24:21); for this reason, Daniel was greatly concerned.

Although the prophecy predicts unprecedented persecution for the nation of Israel, it also promised deliverance to those trusting in Jesus, executed through Michael, the chief prince archangel appointed over Israel (12:1, cf. 10:13, 21). Michael is Israel's protector, and as their guardian, he will preserve them during the tribulation. Satan will seek to wipe the chosen nation off the map (Rev. 12); however, Michael will come to their aid, 'flying' them into the wilderness (Rev. 12:6, 14). Jesus warned of the same unprecedented event (Matt. 24:21), where, during the tribulation, Israel will flee (Matt. 24:16-21), confirming the reference of being flown on eagles' wings (Rev. 12:6, 14), probably to Petra (Ps. 60:9-12).

As mentioned in previous chapters, Satan will seek to destroy the Jews to prevent Jesus from returning. Unless and until the Jews say, "Blessed is He who comes in the name of the Lord" (Matt. 23:39, cf. Ps. 118:26), Jesus will not return. The Jews, therefore, are the key to Jesus' return, and it will not be until the church is removed and the tribulation commences that the hearts of the Jews are softened (Rom. 11:25), enabling them to see, hear and call on the name of Jesus (cf. Rom. 10:8-13, 11:26, 29). When Jesus returns in response to the Jews calling on His name, Israel will be delivered from their sin and of Gentile rulers, following great persecution (Lu. 21:24). The worst Gentile (with Jewish lineage) ruler to come, and be delivered of, is the antichrist (7:7-8, 23-26, 11:36-45).

Through intense persecution during the tribulation, a remnant of faithful Jews will be delivered, some preserved in this life, albeit most will be slain in preparation for the next (11:33). During the tribulation, most will be killed; however, those trusting in Jesus (Rev. 12:11, 14:4), thereby having their names written in the book (12:1), will be resurrected (12:2). The resurrection of the just occurs when Jesus returns ("they came to life and reigned with Christ one-thousand years" Rev. 20:4). The resurrection of the unjust takes place at the end of the millennial dispensation (Rev. 20:5). Alongside Daniel, both John (Jn. 5:28-29) and Luke (Acts 24:15) touch on the resurrection of the just and the unjust.

The terms 'just' and 'unjust' refer to those who are saved and those who are dammed. The resurrection of the just refers to those who believe in Jesus, and due to being just, they, and they alone, will be given new and eternal life (1 Cor. 15:52). At the time of the rapture (Rev. 3:10), the faithful remnant will be transformed, trading earthly bodies for heavenly ones (1 Cor. 15:52-53, Phil. 3:21a), like that of Jesus' resurrected body (1 Jn. 3:2). At that time, believers are rewarded (Lu. 14:14) and crowned according to what they were called to do.

Following the rapture, the next resurrection occurs when Jesus returns. (Rev. 20:4). Those slain in the tribulation are then resurrected. Like the raptured church, the tribulation slain saints (Rev. 6:9, 7:13-14, 12:11, 13:10, 15, 14:13, 16:6, 17:6, 19:2, 20:4) will receive their glorified bodies after the seven-year ordeal.

As for those rejecting Jesus, being the unjust (cf. Jn. 3:18, 20, 36), who do not have their names written in the Lamb's Book of Life (12:1, Rev. 3:5, 20:12, 21:27), they will receive their resurrected and eternal body after the millennium (Rev. 20:5), for the purpose of everlasting destruction (cf. Matt. 10:28, Mk. 9:43-48, Rev. 20:11-15). The 'reward' of the unjust is eternal, unending suffering (Rom. 2:6), where the whole body will burn in hell (Matt. 5:29-30).

To cater for the numbers who rejected Jesus, hell has enlarged its mouth to receive the multitudes who go that way (Isa. 5:14). The lake of fire is their eternal destination. Any that end up in the eternal lake of fire remain there forever and ever in a continual conscious state of torment (Rev. 14:11, 20:10). They can be there (cf. Rev. 19:20) for one thousand years (cf. Rev. 20:10) and not have one less day to stay. Hell is a literal place, with literal time, of day and night (Rev. 14:11, 20:10).

During the tribulation, only the wise (11:33-35, 12:2, 10) purify themselves through repentance by calling on the name of Jesus, and therefore, they alone will be saved, escaping the second death. While some escape physical death during the tribulation (cf. Joel 2:32), all who call upon Jesus will escape spiritual (the second) death (cf. Rev. 20:4-5). The wise are those who have ears to hear (Matt. 11:15, Rev. 2:7, 11, 29, 3:6, 13, 22), and they alone shall shine like the brightness of the sky above (12:2, Matt. 13:43). The wise are defined as wise due to having tuned into Jesus, trusting Him alone, which means the wise have tuned their ears out and away from worldly, antichrist, narrative, rejecting it altogether. As a result of trusting in Jesus, and not the world, the ruler of this world will hate and persecute the wise (11:33-35, 12:1, Rev. 12, 13:10, 15), as Jesus prewarned (Jn. 15:18-25, 16:33).

During the tribulation, through intense persecution, the wise will not only remember their covenant with God, but they will also cause others to remember God, turning many to righteousness (11:33, 12:3, Rev. 7). Leading up to and during the tribulation, only the wise will stand firm to the covenant, taking action by proclaiming Jesus (11:32). During the tribulation, through the proclamation of the sealed Jews, many Israelites will be purified (cleansed from their sin, cf. Rom 11:26-32).

Through the testimony of the tribulation's sealed Jewish evangelists (Rev. 7:1-8), countless millions from every nation will also come to faith in Jesus and be slain (Rev. 7:9-17, 13:10, 15). Through the ministry of the 144,000 Jewish evangelists (Rev. 7, 14), and those coming to faith through their testimony, Jew, and Gentile (Rev. 7), and the two witnesses (Rev. 11), and the ministering angels (Rev. 14), the gospel will be preached to the whole world. Then Jesus will return (Matt. 24:14). When Jesus returns, He will reward the wise, being the ones who put their trust in Him, enduring to the end (Matt. 24:13, cf. Rev. 13:10b, 14:12), proclaiming His name (12:3).

In sum, in a time reserved for the last days, there shall be great trouble on the earth, as never seen before, or again (Dan. 12:1a, Matt. 24:21). In that time, only the enduring, faithful remnant (Rom. 9:27, 11:26) of God shall be delivered (Dan. 12:1b). The faithful will be hidden (Zep. 2:3) and locked away (Isa. 26:20). Only those having their names written in the book of life shall be rescued from eternal death (Dan. 12:1c).

Through the time of trouble, God will save Israel and destroy their worthless shepherds who say trouble will not come (Jer. 23:1-40). Although Jeremiah's prophecy was fulfilled through the Babylonians, it was only fulfilled in part. The worthless shepherds are still around today, peddling their false promises of prosperity (Your Best Life Now); therefore, they are still yet to be dealt with. When Jesus does deal with them, He also replaces them.

Despite the difficulty in understanding the prophecy, Daniel drew this hope from its conclusion: While the Messiah is coming to judge the nations, God is still seeking to save those seeking Him; those striving to enter in (Lu. 13:24). Again, this was the reason the messenger angel came (10:20) to comfort Daniel regarding his concern for God's people.

Logically, when Daniel received this vision, he had no way of understanding it; only the wise in these last days can (12:9). In these last days, the wise can comprehend the prophecy due to increasing prophetic knowledge (12:4), resulting in an understanding (12:10). Due to the understanding of the mystery being unavailable to Daniel, he was told to shut up the words (12:8), which is to 'seal,' preserve and reserve them until the end (Dan. 12:4, 10). Although Daniel could not understand the mystery then (12:8), he will when standing before God in his allotted place at the end of days.

From above, Daniel will watch the prophecy being fulfilled (12:13) alongside the raptured saints and the resurrected dead in Christ (Rev. 3:10, chapters 4 & 5). However, those left behind will recognise the end of the time through a first-hand experience of the prophesied events and a previous (not acted on) knowledge of scripture. When the events unfold, the awakened left behind will then connect the dots regarding the signs of the times. In the context of chapter twelve, the end of time specifically refers to when the king of the south attacks Israel (11:40).

In conclusion, as mentioned earlier, despite Daniel's lack of understanding, the prophecy still produced hope that God would not forget or forsake His chosen people during the tribulation. In the time of Jacob's trouble (Jer. 30:7), God will remember them, and through His judgements, He will cause them to, once again, remember Him. In the time of the end, God will deliver those who call on His name (Joel 2:32). For this reason, alone, the messenger angel came to tell Daniel (cf. 10:20); despite the terrifying things to come, God can and will rescue His people, Israel (12:1).

God rescuing Israel was all Daniel could gain from the detailed prophecy; therefore, he was told to shut it up until the end. Conversely, when John received the same revelation of the future, he was advised to instruct the church to keep the book open due to the nearness of Jesus' return (Rev. 22:10). Only part of what John saw would remain closed until the time of its fulfilment (Rev. 10:4a).

John's revelation, and therefore, Daniel's mystery, is to stay open so it's wise and blessed readers and hearers (Rev. 1:3) are not only aware of the things to come. They can also tell others, in recognition of the timeframe (shortness of time) through the signs of the times.

A significant sign of the times is an increase in knowledge (Dan. 12:4b). Increased knowledge/awareness can refer to science and technological advancements and Bible prophecy. Both are very relevant and apparent today. The advances in technology have given humanity the means to travel at speed, 'running to and fro.' Today, we also have available to us greater revelation of Bible prophecy, through increased understanding. God has increased the knowledge of the wise regarding Bible prophecy for this time - which is a fulfilment of prophecy (12:4).

While the wise are predicted to increase in understanding, the reference to 'running to and fro' (12:4), could also be applied to the unwise, who pursue every other voice, but God's. Even professing Christians run to and fro across continents to hear the latest talk and to see and experience the latest 'revival.' While the wise are increasing in knowledge and understanding, the unwise are decreasing in the ability to know, think and discern for themselves. Many have been blinded by the god of this world (2 Cor. 4:4), who operates in the church, through his sown weeds/ministers (Matt. 13:25, 2 Cor. 11:4, 13-15).

Proportionate to the blind unwise, the wise increase in understanding of Bible prophecy, discerning the signs of the times. Another significant sign of the times is signing the Middle East Peace Treaty (Dan 9:25-27, Isa. 28:15, 18). Remember, the church is raptured at the time of signing, triggering the tribulation, which lasts for seven years (Dan. 9:27, 12:7).

As written, Daniel, chapter twelve is set midway through the tribulation. The wonders (12:6) Daniel asked about will occur forty-two months into the seven-year ordeal, confirming chapter twelve to be at the halfway mark (Daniel 9:25-27, 11:31, 12:7, 11, cf. Matt. 24:15, 2 Thess. 2:3-4, Rev. 13:14-15). Midway through the tribulation, the antichrist proclaims to be God, having rebuilt the tribulation (third) temple, and having set up his new world order (Dan. 11:36-45, 12:11). When the antichrist announces that he is God, ordering everyone to worship him and receive his mark (666), many will remember what they had been previously told, that this event is the fulfilment of prophecy (Jn. 14:29, Rev. 13:18). On realisation, the wised up shall then flee, purifying themselves, making themselves white and refined (Dan. 12:10). At the midway point, many Jews will, then, realise they have been left behind, granted one last opportunity to repent, having missed their Messiah, not once, by twice.

Part Two

'Blessed is He Who Waits and Arrives at the 1,335 Days' (vv. 5-13)

In the last section (12:1-4), the closing words to Daniel were to "Shut up the words and seal the book until the end" (12:4). Daniel was told to seal the book due to the words being reserved and preserved until the time of the end (12:9). Due to Daniel having, and admittedly to (12:8), no way of understanding the prophecy referring to the end, he was told twice, "Go your way" (12:9, 13).

As mentioned in the previous section, the messenger angel came (9:22, 10:20) to inform Daniel that Israel would be saved, albeit through severe persecution in the tribulation. As much as Daniel wanted to understand the prophecies (8:15, 27, 12:8), he had no way of doing so, so far out. Thus, the mystery was sealed until the latter days. He would, however, understand from heaven (12:13). At the appointed time (8:19, 11:27, 29, 35), Daniel will stand in his allotted place and watch the mystery unfold, just as it was prophesied.

While Daniel, or his immediate readers, could not understand, the wise today can (12:10), and should (cf. 1 Thess. 5:1). Arguably, the mystery was unlocked with Jesus' reference to Daniel when addressing the end times of the signs, saying, "Let the reader understand" (Matt. 24:15). Specifically, Jesus is referring to the abomination of desolation, where the antichrist set himself up in the tribulation temple, proclaiming to be God. Jesus' reference unlocked the sealed mystery commencing the period of increased knowledge (12:4).

Further support for that statement is told again where Paul wrote about the coming antichrist and signs leading to his appearance (2 Thess. 2). The first sign is the great falling away, or apostasy, where whole denominations and movements fall away from sound biblical doctrine (2 Thess. 2:3). The second sign is the removal of the church (2 Thess. 2:7). The antichrist cannot be revealed until the church is first taken out of the way (2 Thess. 2:8). When the antichrist is revealed, he will be through the signing of the Middle East peace treaty (9:27) and by taking his seat in the temple, announcing himself to be God, which is the abomination of desolation (2 Thess. 2:4). He will also be revealed when resurrected from the dead after receiving a mortal wound (Rev. 13:3, 12, 17). Due to being killed in the tribulation, the beast who was, and is not, will again be (Rev. 17:8).

Following his resurrection, the son of perdition (2 Thess. 2:3), the antichrist, will then be able to operate by the activity of Satan, with power and false signs and wonders (2 Thess. 2:9). Then the antichrist will take his seat in the temple, demanding to be worshipped, and he will enforce his mark (666). Only then will most, acquiring belated wisdom, understand (Rev. 13:18).

Only a remnant understands now, but more again will understand during the tribulation. The closer we get to the end, more and more will come into an understanding of the prophecy, confirmed by Jesus, "Many prophets and kings longed to see what you see, but they didn't see it. And they longed to hear what you hear, but they didn't hear it" (Lu. 10:24). Peter said something similar (1 Pet. 1:10-12), those who wrote about the things to come could not understand them, yet they longed to. Those who do understand now, are privileged, and blessed beyond measure.

In these last days, the wise can understand the sealed mystery and should be bringing others to an understanding (11:33). For this purpose, Daniel was given a detailed account of the things to come, not for himself, but for us. The sealed words of the book have been reserved for us in these last days, yet many unwise (from the church) scoff at the prophecy today. Instead of longing for, living for, and looking for Jesus, they follow their sinful desires (cf. 2 Pet. 3:1-13), of sensuality and greed (2 Pet. 2:2, 7, 13, 14, 18, cf. Rev. 3:17-).

For this reason, Jesus said to each of the seven churches addressed in the book of Revelation, "He who has an ear to hear, hear what the Spirit is saying to the churches" (Rev. 2-3). The words imply, either conquer this world by rejecting it, through repentance and pure, uncompromised worship, and by setting your eyes on Jesus and His return (cf. Lu. 21:24-36), or else you will be captured/trapped and conquered by it. If conquered by it, you will be left behind (cf. Rev. 2:22, 3:3).

As stated, the initial request for Daniel was for God to forgive His people of their sins (9:1-20). Now, there are two more requests, another by Daniel and the other by an angel. The first request is made by an angel, asking how long shall it be till the end of the wonders (12:6). The second comes from Daniel, asking what will the outcome be (12:8)? The first request is answered in verse seven, and the second is answered in verses nine to thirteen. Other angels answered both questions.

The first request of, "How long shall it be till the end of these wonders," refers to the events of chapter eleven (vv. 36-45). The closing portion of chapter eleven predicts the coming antichrist, who will mirror Antiochus. The events of chapter eleven will be achieved in a "time, times and half a time" (12:7, cf. 7:25), being over of period of seven years. John confirms that same period in the book of Revelation, splitting the seven years into two parts (Rev. 11:2, 12:6, 14, 13:5). Daniel, chapter eleven does likewise (11:36-39 & 40-45). Some refer to the two parts as the 'tribulation' (first part) and the 'great tribulation' (second part). Support for the latter part being the great tribulation is found in Matthew's account, where Jesus said, "For then there will be great tribulation, such as has not been from the beginning of the world until now, no, and never will be" (Matt. 24:21). The great tribulation is marked by the abomination of desolation (Matt. 24:15, Dan. 9:27. 11:31, 12:11).

In addition to Jesus, John provides two more references to the great tribulation (Rev. 2:22, 7:14). The first is a warning to the church of Thyatira that unless they repent, they will be cast into the great tribulation. Suppose the Thyatira's church members heed the warning. In that case, they will partake in the promise given to the church of Philadelphia, "Because you have kept My word about patient endurance, I will keep you from the hour of trial that is coming on the whole world, to try those who dwell on the earth" (Rev. 3:10).

The next time John refers to the great tribulation (Rev. 7:14) he speaks of those who did not repent this side of the coming event, who instead were tried and tested, resulting in repentance in the time of trouble. As a result, most lost their natural lives but secured their eternal life with Christ (Rev. 7:14-17). During the tribulation, most who come to faith in Christ will be slain by the antichrist (Rev. 13:10, 15). During that time of trouble, dwarfing anything before or after it (Jer. 30:7, Dan. 12:1, Matt. 24:21), the blessed ones die early (Rev. 14:13). The blessed, moreover, avoid it altogether (Rev. 3:10).

Further support for the seven-year tribulation being split into two parts, with the greater time of trouble being reserved for the latter forty-two months, is seen in chapter nine (v. 27). Again, and supported through additional letters, triggering the tribulation is the signing of the Middle East Peace Treaty. Paul confirmed, "When people are saying, there is peace and security, then sudden destruction will come upon them as labour pains come upon a pregnant woman, and they will not escape" (1 Thess. 5:3).

At the midway point of the tribulation, the antichrist will break the covenant (9:27, cf. Isa. 28:15, 18)), which is also when the king of the south and the king of the north will attack Israel (11:40). After defeating the king of the south, the antichrist will establish himself in the land of

Israel, slaughtering tens of thousands of Jews refusing to worship him (11:31). The antichrist will attempt to rule the world from Jerusalem, claiming to be God in the latter half of the tribulation (Rev. 13:5-7). In the last period, he will be the one world leader until the end, wherein he shall come to an end, and none will help him (11:40-45).

Following the first request, the second request was made by Daniel, asking, "What shall be the outcome of these things?" (12:8). Still concerned for his people, Daniel requested to know what the outcome for Israel would be, after the tribulation,. Although Daniel did not understand the tribulation (12:8), as we can now (12:10), however, he did know something about the millennial dispensation.

In the millennium, the Messiah will rule and reign on the earth, and the saints will also reign under Him (2:44, 7:14, 22, 27). THEN (not before), the saints will have restored dominion (cf. Rev. 1:6, 5:10, 11:15) possessing the earthly kingdom (7:27), which was lost in the garden of Eden, due to treason against God (Gen. 3). The same promise is given to the church of Thyatira, providing they repent and hold fast until the end (Rev. 2:25-27). Due to considerable scriptural support, there is simply no excuse for confusing the dominion of the saints in the millennium for the kingdom now 'theology.' Much more is said about the saints having dominion over the earth in the millennium through the prophets Isaiah, Haggai, Zechariah, and Malachi.

The sealed words of the book have been opened for the wise to read, hear (Rev. 1:3) and understand (12:10), and they are to remain open until the end (Rev. 22:10). Although knowledge of the end times has increased (12:4) and will continue to increase, many will not understand until midway through the tribulation, which is precisely what the time of the end refers to (11:40, 12:9). Then, many Jews will recognise and turn to Jesus, thereby shining like the brightness of the sky above (12:3), purifying and making themselves white and refined (12:10a). The wise, having understanding, will also recognise the antichrist by calculating his number, the number of a man (a man, not a system). His number is 666 (Rev. 13:18).

Despite the mystery being made known, the unwise and wicked will continue to remain ignorant and act wickedly (12:10b). The wicked, scoffing at prophecy, reject Jesus and will continue to do so during the tribulation. During the tribulation, instead of repenting, the wicked curse God, (Rev. 9:20-21, 16:8-11), worshipping the antichrist by taking his mark (Rev. 13:1-18, 14:9-11). The wicked worship the antichrist following the abomination of desolation, which is where he announces himself to be God from the rebuilt (tribulation) temple.

Again, the abomination of desolation (12:11, cf. Matt. 24:15) occurs at the midway point of the seven-year tribulation (7:25, Rev. 12:14), which is forty-two months in (Rev. 11:2), or 1,260 days (Rev. 11:3). The abomination that causes desolation is set up for 1,290 days (12:11), thereby remaining in place for the duration of the tribulation. When the antichrist commits the abomination of desolation, he will put an end to all other scarifies (9:27).

Interestingly, with the reference of 1,290 days, there is a difference of thirty days from the great tribulation time of 1,260 days. A possible explanation for the additional thirty days is that the antichrist introduces his religious system (Rev. 13:14-15) thirty days before the midway mark, enforcing it thirty days later. Some suggest, however, that the additional thirty days follows the conclusion of 1,260 days, which is rejected due to Jesus, then ruling and reigning on the earth.

When Jesus returns, everything and everyone will be subject to Him. No idol, including the desecrated temple (1211), or unclean vessel, or any kind of false worship will remain (Zech. 14:21, Rev. 2:27). Nothing of the Babylonian (beast) system will remain, just before Jesus returns, as it will be no more, repeated five times (Rev. 18:21-23). The antichrist will also be no more (7:11, 26, Rev. 19:20), likewise the false prophet (Rev. 19:20). Satan will be removed for one thousand years (20:1-3), and the nations will be judged (Joel 3:1-2, Rev. 19:15-18).

Coinciding with the judgement of the nations, the judged, tribulation saints will be resurrected (12:2, Rev. 20:4), and invited to the marriage supper of the Lamb (Matt. 22:1-14, Rev. 19:90). When Jesus returns, the whole world will be filled with the knowledge of Him (Hab. 2:14), every knee will bow, and every tongue will confess that He is Lord (Rom. 14:10b-12, Phil. 2:9-11). The above-mentioned leaves no allowance for a thirty-day residual beast system.

Adding to the additional thirty days is another forty-five days (12:12), which some refer to as the seventy-five-day interval. However, arguably, the extra thirty days and the forty-five days come at opposite ends of the remaining 1,260 days of the tribulation. The additional thirty days is best positioned just before the midway mark, and therefore the other forty-five days are added to 1,290 days, following the tribulation period. The one that waits and arrives at the 1,335 days is blessed (12:12). They will be blessed due to having endured the tribulation (Rev. 13:10b, 14:12), conquering the devil by the blood of the Lamb and the word of their testimonies (Rev. 12:11). They will be blessed due to staying awake, keeping their garments on (Rev. 16:15), and blessed because they are invited to the marriage supper of the Lamb (Rev. 19:9), avoiding the second death (Rev. 20:6). Again, they are blessed because they kept the words of the prophecy (Rev. 22:7, cf. 1:3), and finally, they are blessed because they washed their robes, so that they may have the right to the tree of life and that they may enter the city by the gates (Rev. 22:14).

Note the blessings extended to the blessed; each one was also promised to the seven churches on the provision they repent and or remain. For example, providing Ephesus repented, they would eat of the tree of life which is in the paradise of God (Rev. 2:7, cf. 22:14). Smyrna would receive the crown of life, providing they remain faithful (2:10, cf. 22:7). Pergamum would be given a white stone (innocence) providing they repent (Rev. 2:17, cf. 20:6). Thyatira will have authority over nations, providing they repent and hold fast until the end (Rev. 3:25-27, cf. 22:6). Sardis would be clothed in white garments, if they repent, and thereby would not have their names blotted out of the book of life (Rev. 3:5, cf. 16:15, 20:6). Philadelphia will be a pillar in the temple, providing they hold fast (Rev. 3:12, 22:7, 14). And, Laodicea, they will sit with Jesus on His throne, on the condition that they repent (Rev. 3:21, cf. 22:14).

Evidently, the blessings are reserved, alone, for the blessed who repent, and or remain. The reverse is also true; instead of being blessed, the unrepentant are cursed. Alongside the blessings, note the threat to each of the five failing churches (Ephesus, Pergamum, Thyatira, Sardis, and Laodicea). When considering the threats collectively, they can only refer to one thing - salvation is at risk, or under threat, of being lost.

Picking up again on Daniel's concluding verse (12:13), at the end of the days, now the blessed enter, rule, and reign with Jesus Christ in the long-awaited millennial kingdom. When Jesus returns to the earth to set up His kingdom, there will be forty-five days between ending one dominion and starting the next.

As mentioned earlier, during the gap, the marriage supper of the Lamb will take place on the earth. The wedding ceremony occurred in heaven, lasting seven years, following Jesus and the bride (church) returning at the end of the tribulation to judge the nations (Rev. 19:11-16). The Messiah coming to set up His kingdom on the earth and to judge the nations is what Daniel was so concerned about, resulting in Daniel, chapters nine to twelve being written.

Although Daniel did not live to see any prophesied events fulfilled from chapter seven onwards, he will see them unfold from heaven (12:13), alongside the heavenly saints and those raptured (Rev. 3:10). Chapter five of the book of Revelation reveals the scene in heaven where the saints, who are standing around the throne, with Jesus, witness the prophesied judgements being fulfilled on the earth. The wise, this side of the tribulation, avoid the prophesied trials. The wised-up, during the tribulation, then recognise, and receive Jesus Christ, waiting and arriving at the end to be received by Him.

While the mystery has been revealed, and the information has been made available to all, only those seeking to understand will (12:10), making others, who are wise, understand also (11:33).

APPENDIX

The Middle East Peace Treaty

With so much media coverage of the Middle East today, many might ask: Why? Moreover, what does it have to do with us? And, similarly, what is so crucial about peace in the Middle East, and why the strong push towards the Middle East Peace Plan?

These are questions that need careful consideration. To answer them, one need only look at 9/11, wherein the whole world changed forever in a single day and in a single hour,. When a handful of Islamic extremists got together and successfully executed an attack against the most powerful nation in history, the whole world stopped and watched in horror and was bewildered by how such a powerful nation could be brought to its knees so quickly! The crippling effect of the United States economy alone, according to the 9/11 Commission Report, has suffered an estimated loss of $100 billion in direct damages, with a further $2 trillion wiped off the stock market. What took place on September 11th, 2000, was nothing less than a spectacular win for Islam in a conflict dating back thousands of years.

The conflict, according to the Bible, dates back well before the Balfour Declaration (1917), in fact, some 4000 years back. The conflict, which was primarily between the Arabs and the Jews, now also includes Christians. The Christian Crusaders entered the conflict, with eight major crusades taking place between 1098 and 1187 A.D. (Folda, 1995). The purpose of the crusades was to liberate, protect, and secure the Holy Land against Muslims. The three mentioned religions are known as the Abrahamic, monotheist faiths.

To properly understand the Middle East, it is essential to recognise the significance of these Abrahamic faiths (Middle East Prophecy, 2016) of which, Israel is the cradle, with two of them recognising and regarding Jerusalem as the most valuable piece of real estate on the planet, the third, Islam regarding Jerusalem second only to Mecca. Thus, it is argued that the situation of the Middle East is profoundly religious and deeply political. Based on the above, religion and politics cannot be separated.

History

According to the Bible, the Middle East conflict is not new but instead dates back some 4000 years to when Abraham was born in Ur, Mesopotamia. Later, Abraham departed Ur making Canaan his new home (Genesis 12:1). Canaan, also referred to as the Promised Land, is today known as Israel, and surrounding areas (Genesis 13:14-15).

The importance of referencing the Hebrew Bible or Old Testament is that the three faiths are pertinent to peace in the Middle East, holding to the same historical story and fundamental belief regarding Abraham and the Land, albeit favouring their interpretation.

The facts mentioned above are essential and are the basis for the claims both the Jews and Palestinians have over the Holy Land, claiming to be descendants of Abraham (Genesis 12:7), as do Christians as Abraham's offspring (Romans 4:11-17).

When in the land (Genesis 16:1-3), Abraham had two sons, Ishmael and Isaac. The Ishmaelites are descendants of Ishmael from where Islam derives. On the other hand, Isaac, who fathered Jacob, later renamed Israel, is where the Jews have derived. Ishmael was prophesised to be at war with the nations (Genesis 16:12), which is evident today regarding Islam, the Jews, and now the West (Christians).

The story of two brothers was repeated through Abraham's sons, Jacob and Esau, who were struggling against each other, even in the womb (Genesis 25:22). As with Ishmael and Isaac, likewise, Jacob and Esau would represent two nations (Genesis 25:23).

Esau sold his birth right to Jacob for a bowl of soup (Genesis 25:29-34), then later Jacob deceived Isaac, his father, into giving him the blessing of the firstborn, which was reserved for Esau (Genesis 27). The blessing refers to the land. This story is said to be the root cause of the ongoing feud between the two nations (Genesis 27:41).

While many in secular societies dismiss the Bible and its tale of two brothers, the monotheistic faiths regard the story as fact and history. Again, the above-mentioned is the reason for the ongoing conflict in the Middle East between the Arabs and the Jews, dating back 4000 years.

Since the original squabble, there have been numerous other conflicts, in particular since the Nation of Israel was re-established in 1948. The most recent of serious conflicts was in 1967, in the Six-Day war between Israel and surrounding Arab States which served towards a semi-successful attempt in establishing a Middle East Peace Plan, known as the Oslo Accords (1993). The Oslo Accords worked towards recognising the Palestinian Authority, allowing self-governance of the Gaza Strip and the West Bank. Although the intentions were to work towards a peaceful co-inhabitation in the land shared by both the Israelis and the Palestinians, the Oslo Accord was not the two-state solution the Palestinians are wanting. Therefore, the Oslo Accord failed to recognise Palestine as an independent State, albeit perhaps it is a step forward in the general direction.

Past and Current Peace Treaty Attempts?

Since Israel's reestablishment in 1948, there have been many attempts to establish lasting peace in the Middle East led by many players, located throughout the region, Europe, and the West. In part, some attempts have been successful, with agreements between Egypt and Israel and Jordon and Israel, yet fragile, nonetheless. Peace between Palestine and Israel has not yet been established, mainly due to land disputes. Albeit, the U.N. Security Council Resolution 242 of 1968 is one of the more successful attempts at peace, brokering a deal in exchange of land for peace. Since then, this resolution has had significant influence over succeeding attempts, exchanging Land for peace, including peace talk efforts from the United States.

Fawcett (2016) provides an extensive account of the United States' attempts to establish peace in the Middle East, which include the Rogers Plan (1969), the Camp David Accord (1978, 1979, 2000), the Taba proposal (2001). These were followed by Barrack Obama's attempt in 2010. The most recent, ongoing, proposal through the Trump Administration was led by Jarod Kushner, which was tabled in June 2019.

Again, until now, the most successful attempt was in 1978, motivated by the Six-Day war, otherwise known as the Yom Kippur War. Peace talks took place at Camp David, focusing on 1. Peace between Israel and the Palestinians, and 2. Peace between Israel and Egypt. The latter of the two was successful, however, and again, establishing peace between Israel and the Palestinians has not been established.

Other attempts have been less successful. For example, Said (1992), notes that one journal called the 1978 peace process: "The new world (dis)order," referring to the difficulties, mainly when dealing with the Palestinians. Peace, however, was still established between Egypt and Israel due to Israel agreeing to withdraw from Sinai. Albeit, peace talks failed between Palestine and Israel due to the Palestinians not reaching 'final status' in the land as the State of Palestine (Beauchamp, 2013), but rather a recognition only of self-governance within Gaza and the West Bank.

Following 1978, there was a second accord in 1979 that focused on strengthening the agreement between Egypt and Israel. After Israel withdraw from Sinai, it was recognised by the Arabs as the State of Israel. The 1978 treaty was again followed up in 1991 under a joint initiative involving the United States and the Soviet Union. This is known as the Madrid Conference, which resulted in establishing peace with Jordon (1994), alongside Egypt (1978). Still, the Palestinians did not agree. It was not until 1993 under the Oslo Accords that the Middle East peace process drew in the Palestinians where an agreement was signed in September 1993 at the White House under the watchful eye of Bill Clinton, President of the United States. The agreement involved Israel withdrawing from the Gaza Strip and the West Bank, and with a view of recognising each other's legitimate and political rights per U.N. Resolution 242 and 338. The Oslo agreement was not, however, welcomed by all. Palestinian extremists responded with acts of terror against Israel, therefore the Oslo Accord, albeit the most successful to date, was not fully achieved.

In the year 2000, at Camp David, further attempts were made to achieve the objectives set out in the Oslo Accords, however falling short of reaching an agreement between the PLO and Israel (Helmick, 2004). The issues, once again, revolved around land. The failure saw an increase of terrorism from Palestinian actors, stimulating continued talks in Washington, Cairo, and Taba, Egypt, 2001, where President Clinton made one last, albeit unsuccessful, attempt to establish peace in the

Middle East. Helmick (2004), concludes: Camp David and Taba failed because Arafat would not make the painful compromise.

Following Bill Clinton's departure from Office, the next attempt was initiated by the Arabs in 2002, tabled in Beirut, known as the Arab Peace initiative. The objective worked towards a two-state solution, which involved Israel withdrawing to the lines of 1967. Due to the same failures of the past, this also shared the fate of previous attempts.

In 2003 further efforts were made to get peace talks 'back on track' (Lis and Nir, 2003), known as Roadmap 2003. These talks involved four representatives, including Russia, the United States, the United Nations, and the European Union. The agenda was to establish a two-state solution, following newly elected President George W Bush's push towards the establishment of a Palestinian state in 2002. In the same year, 2003, the Geneva Accord took the opposite approach to the Roadmap (2003), focusing more so, and again, on the 1967 lines.

After some recess from the last attempt in 2003, 2007 was the next under George W. Bush in Annapolis, which worked towards achieving a full peace solution by 2008. This initiative was a return to the Roadmap of 2003. No agreement, however, was reached.

Succeeding George W. Bush was Barrack Obama. He also attempted to establish peace in the Middle East recommencing talks known as Washington 2010. Although starting well, discussions quickly came to an end, leaving the conflict unresolved.

The above provided an historical list of Mid-East peace talks, and was gleaned from BBC News (2013). As mentioned earlier, initiated under the Trump administration, yet another attempt to establish peace in the Middle East is ongoing, tabled in June 2019, in Bahrain, taking a very different approach from the past. The new approach focuses on peace through prosperity, doing away with the 'peace for land' formula of the past. This proposal has been heralded: The Deal of the Century. A 'deal' predicted to backfire on all concerned, according to Telhami (2019).

Despite the best intentions, Palestinian Authority President Mahmoud Abbas', spokesman, Nabil Abu Rudeineh, told CNN (2019), that the proposed plan is futile. According to Middle East media sources, the West has failed to recognise what matters to the Palestinians - a Palestinian State with East Jerusalem as its capital. Perhaps contributing to the failure is Said's (2003) findings: Identifying the West's inability to understand Eastern Culture, believing this is an ongoing issue, going further to say: Western attitudes go as far as ignoring and dismissing Eastern culture, perceived by some as being guilty of imperialism and racism. Trump's 2019 peace plan arguably falls into Said's (2003) conclusion, where Western ideologies dominate those of the East. Elgindy (2019) expands further on the issue, calling it the 'American blind spot' by not understanding Palestinian politics. Politics plays a big part in understanding and resolving conflict.

Again, as identified in previous peace talks, the two key factors to be met in establishing lasting peace narrow down to Land and Recognition/People, which is both religious and political to the core. Again, these crucial elements are missing from the current proposal. For this reason, and perhaps this reason alone, the Israel Times (2019) concludes: The proposal would be rejected before it is even presented.

2019 Peace for Prosperity

The previous section of this paper covered what the current peace plan does not include the following section will now expand on what it does include.

Establishing peace in the Middle East has been an ongoing objective, particularly for the United States, and President Trump is no exception. Trump's son-in-law, Jarod Kushner has led current efforts. He was the senior advisor to the former Trump administration, and he is a practicing Jew and a long-time friend of the former Israeli Prime Minister, Benjamin Netanyahu. Kushner is also well connected and respected within the Arab community. He is educated in law and is a successful businessman, making his mark in real estate through the family business. Kushner is said to be the mastermind of the 2019 Peace for Prosperity proposal, which was tabled on June 25th, in Bahrain, albeit, in part. The part presented only focused on economics, promising a better, more prosperous future for all, according to the Jerusalem News (2019). Representatives from the United States, the European Union, the Arab world, and Palestinian businesspeople attended the forum. According to Amr and Anderson (2019). The peace plan is made up of four principles:.

1. Freedom
2. Respect
3. Security, and
4. Opportunity

The promise of prosperity is said to be an attractive proposition for the majority of the two million Palestinians currently living in the Gaza Strip, most of which are experiencing the highest rate of unemployment on the planet today, according to Amr et al., (2018) in their article: Order from Chaos. CNN (2019) reports, Kushner is set to resolve this humanitarian crisis by modelling details of the economic proposal on what has worked in Poland, Japan, Singapore, and South Korea. Recognising the immediate objection, regarding peace for land, he insisted the 2019 solution is superior to previous attempts. Thereby, Kushner is reported to be appealing to Palestinians: "Do not let your grandfathers' conflict destroy your children's future" (CNN, 2019). Kushner believes his proposal will present a pathway to peace and prosperity, which is not currently existing or otherwise obtained.

The peace proposal is aimed at breaking down barriers by presenting promises of peace and prosperity. It takes careful aim at the current situation of poverty and presents solutions to overcome this. The theme is: You cannot have peace without economic opportunity and stability, thereby putting prosperity at the forefront of the agenda. To achieve this, the United States is willing to put some 'skin in the game,' according to CNN (2019), which will comprise a combination of grant money, low-interest loans, and private capital. However, they are also looking for Arab partners to foot most of the bill. A bill said to be in the tens of billions (Amr, Anderson, 2019).

Why is the United States Involved in the Middle East Peace Process?

The United States has been strong supporters of Israel since the early 1900s - following the Balfour declaration (1917), in favour of the State of Israel having its home in Palestine (Moore, 1974). In 1950, the United States became allies with Israel, signing the Tripartite Declaration alongside Britain and France. Since then, Israel has received a great deal of support, in particular, financial aid. The United States alone has given Israel nearly three billion dollars since 1985 (Sharp, 2010). Sharp (2010) further states: The United States has been donating more than three million annually to Israel since 2014. These funds are for military purposes, which supports the opening statement in the introduction, narrowing in on 9/11 as a reason why peace in the Middle East concerns the United States and everyone else.

At the heart of 9/11 was a mix of political and religious ideologies, as it is in the Middle East. But, mainly if war breaks out between Israel and its Arab neighbours it will involve the United States, and its allies, the West. This supports, the opening argument: What happens in the Middle East affects the whole world. Hence the reason the United States has been involved in nearly every peace talk process between the Israeli's and the Arabs.

Up until 1979, The United States and Iran were close allies until Iran changed its government to a Republic Islamic State. Since then, The United States has sided with Israel, as its only ally within the Middle East (Fisher, 2003), bringing stability to the region. While stability is said to be the goal, others believe the United States has another agenda.

According to Louise Fawcett (2016), oil is the reason and the key attraction, dedicating an entire chapter (chapter 5) of her book 'International Relations of the Middle East' supporting her argument. Fawcett is far from being alone in her statement, for many academics, alongside conspiracists, have come to the same conclusion. Some have gone as far as to declare that 9/11 was an inside job to invade Iraq and gain control of the oil. In support of this view, an interview conducted by Knight (2008) found that one in five Germans also believe 9/11 was an inside job.

Furthermore, half of New Yorkers surveyed in 2004 believed the government knew about the 9/11 attack beforehand and did nothing to stop it. Again, a Scripps-Howard poll, conducted in 2006, found that a third of all Americans believed the government was involved in 9/11, or at least 'looked the other way,' so they could go to war against Iraq and Iran. Zwicker (2006) argues the same in his book: 'The Towers of Deception', stating the ultimate goal is Iran and its oil.

The '9/11 conspiracy theory' is now gaining greater traction as the conflict between Iran and the United States is at boiling point with the prediction of a war on the horizon. While these accusations seem far-stretched, support is growing, not just from conspiracy theorists, but well-respected academics and journalists with strong arguments, combined with supporting polls, surveys, and interviews. Moreover, these allegations are not going away, with further investigation and research being conducted. Maris (2006), for example, has revised his original work, stating: There are a vast number of challenging and unanswered questions to which the United States government has failed to provide satisfactory answers.

In Conclusion

As stated in the introduction, the Middle East conflict dates back some 4000 years and is one deeply rooted in both religion and politics. The religious elements comprise Judaism and Islam, and more recently, Christianity. Christians entered the conflict around 1098 A.D. through the crusaders who sort to liberate, secure, and protect the Holy Land from Muslims and are still very much involved both politically and religiously to this day.

At the heart of the dispute throughout the centuries, and on every occasion through past peace talks from 1917, and 1948 onwards, is the land, what it offers to whom, and who has a legitimate right to it.

Throughout this paper, it has been maintained the critical elements to bring about peace in the Middle East are 1). Recognition/People, and 2). Land. These findings are identified throughout previous peace talks, albeit the latter (land) is absent in the current. For this reason, the current proposal has been predicted to be rejected by the Palestinians based on the missing and critical element.

How the Middle East conflict started is essentially how it remains to this day, with escalating conflict between Israel and the Arabs, and or the Jews and the Muslims, included now in the mix, are Christians. The United States, which is a key contributor in the peace talks, is the most significant representation of Christianity today, as a predominantly Christian nation.

Despite the Abrahamic Accord being predicted to fail, even before it was tabled, and again after Trump lost the election (2020), recent reports confirm that it has 'Grown its own legs.' The Abrahamic Accord is gaining traction, now attracting more interest and signatures than when tabled in 2019. Albeit the Palestinians are still the point of resistant, but that is expected to change sooner rather than later.

In sum, the Abrahamic Accord is one to watch, potentially being the Middle East Peace Treaty predicted by the prophet Daniel (9:27).

About the Author

Marc R. Wheway, Ph.D., is the founder and director of Kingdom Seekers. Kingdom Seekers is an eschatological ministry focused on preparing the bride of Christ for the return of Christ. Dr. Wheway has earned a Ph.D., majoring in eschatology, through Louisiana Baptist University and Theological Seminary, complemented by post-graduate studies in International Relations through Griffith University. Dr. Wheway also has an MBA through the Australian Institute of Business, which is further complemented with post-graduate studies in Employment Relations through Griffith University, utilized to run a medium-sized enterprise.

www.ingramcontent.com/pod-product-compliance
Lightning Source LLC
Chambersburg PA
CBHW071311110426
42743CB00042B/1271